THE UFO PHENOMENON

Robert Davis, Ph.D

SHOULD I BELIEVE?

4880 Lower Valley Road • Atglen, PA 19310

Copyright © 2014 by Robert Davis, Ph.D

Library of Congress Control Number: 2014954433

Cover Image: Near Space photography—20km above ground/real photo. © by dellm60.

Alien UFO Invasion Nearing Earth © 3000ad. Courtesy www.bigstockphoto.com.

All rights reserved. No part of this work may be reproduced or used in any form or by any means—graphic, electronic, or mechanical, including photocopying or information storage and retrieval systems—without written permission from the publisher.

The scanning, uploading, and distribution of this book or any part thereof via the Internet or via any other means without the permission of the publisher is illegal and punishable by law. Please purchase only authorized editions and do not participate in or encourage the electronic piracy of copyrighted materials.

"Schiffer," "Schiffer Publishing, Ltd. & Design," and the "Design of pen and inkwell" are registered trademarks of Schiffer Publishing, Ltd.

Designed by Matt Goodman

Type set in Georgia & Trebuchet

ISBN: 978-0-7643-4764-1

Printed in The United States of America

Published by Schiffer Publishing, Ltd.
4880 Lower Valley Road
Atglen, PA 19310
Phone: (610) 593-1777; Fax: (610) 593-2002
E-mail: Info@schifferbooks.com

For our complete selection of fine books on this and related subjects, please visit our website at www.schifferbooks.com. You may also write for a free catalog.

This book may be purchased from the publisher. Please try your bookstore first.

We are always looking for people to write books on new and related subjects. If you have an idea for a book, please contact us at proposals@schifferbooks.com.

Schiffer Publishing's titles are available at special discounts for bulk purchases for sales promotions or premiums. Special editions, including personalized covers, corporate imprints, and excerpts can be created in large quantities for special needs. For more information, contact the publisher.

Dedication

To my wife, Randy:
It is a pleasure to share my life, and love, with you.
To my children Michelle and Scott:
You provide a constant source of joy and pride.

Acknowledgments

My sincere appreciation to all who have made meaningful contributions to better understanding the UFO phenomena.

WITHDRAWN

Contents

CHAPTER ONE

Introduction

Overview

As a scientist, I find the unexplained intriguing and, for some unknown reason, the unidentified flying object (UFO) phenomenon, which has stimulated my interest since childhood, as intriguing as it gets. Maybe this affinity evolved from the "flying saucer" hype and *Star Trek* episodes over frozen TV dinners during the 1960s. And while a *Star Trek* rerun fifty years later would still be engaging, I also find *this* phenomenon to be so as well. It presents unique topics of debate and research challenges that, once adequately addressed, may have potential important implications for science and society.

This book is intended to evoke critical thought of the extraordinary phenomena that encompasses the field of "ufology" (*i.e.*, the study of issues and activities associated with UFOs, an anomaly not identifiable as a known object in the sky). The term UAP (Unidentified Aerial Phenomenon) is sometimes used as a more neutral alternative to UFO. My preference is Unexplained Aerial Event but, given its historical precedent, the acronym "UFO" is used throughout this book.

This book is not intended to convince the UFO skeptics and believers that some unexplained UFOs are governed by alien beings [referred to as non-human intelligence (NHI) from another solar system or space-time], or that all UFOs can be explained as natural and/or man-made phenomena. The primary goal is to present evidence, theories, topics for debates, and associated scientific analysis and perspectives to better understand the UFO phenomenon and the possible force that governs and regulates its behavior. An associated objective is to address the many longstanding issues and related questions regarding the phenomenon, which include, but are not limited to:

1. The possible nature or origin of the UFO phenomenon. Is it extraterrestrial, extra-dimensional, paranormal, an atmospheric, geological, and/or meteorological phenomenon, a man-made phenomenon, or psycho-cultural, among others?

2. Have pilots and astronauts encountered UFOs?
3. Does the UFO evidence provide irrefutable proof that NHI has visited Earth?
4. Are UFO occupants abducting humans?
5. How should we address future research of the UFO phenomenon?
6. Do declassified government/military UFO documents acknowledge that UFOs are under intelligent control?

It is also hoped that discussion of these topics will help readers, at every level of knowledge and belief in UFOs, to develop an objective and informed perspective of the many controversial and intriguing issues associated with this phenomenon. One question that can be answered with an unequivocal "yes" is: Do UFOs exist? The existence of UFOs, however, does not necessarily mean physical craft from another solar system has visited Earth. It simply indicates it is an unexplained moving object in the sky, typically a weather balloon, satellite, meteorological/atmospheric event, or advanced aircraft, among others. The more elusive, fundamental question is: Does the collective evidence provide undeniable confirmation that non-human intelligent beings are operating UFOs and interacting with humans? This question serves as the primary foundation of discussion in this book.

My position on the UFO phenomenon is that of an agnostic. That is, based on a thorough and objective analysis of the UFO evidence, I am unable to firmly commit to a belief in either the existence or nonexistence of intelligently controlled UFOs of non-earthly origin. I simply do not know. I am certain, however, that highly unusual aerial events have occurred that defy logical explanation. Despite the extraordinary steadfast convictions by many UFO researchers that UFOs are extraterrestrial, extra-dimensional, and/or from our future, no empirical evidence exists that provides undeniable proof to support such claims. This position does not exclude the remote possibility that some unexplained UFOs are operated by a form of intelligence from somewhere other than Earth. It simply means that my scientific-based education and professional background has trained me to form conclusions based on studies using established scientific protocol and verified by different independent research investigations. And since this approach has not been routinely applied in UFO research, if at all, my agnostic perspective will remain until the nature and origin of the phenomenon is defined using traditional and newly adopted scientific protocol (if possible), or until "they" land on the White House lawn.

Ufology

The term "ufology," which sounds like a true science, but which is generally perceived as a "pseudoscience" or as having no scientific basis by the scientific community, is an umbrella term for a range of topics that pertain to the UFO phenomenon that incorporate evidence, theories, exopolitics, and the alien abduction phenomenon, etc. Each topic has served as a foundation for both sensible and unfounded views by both writers and researchers within and external to the ufology community. Despite this context, belief in UFOs as extraterrestrial craft has remained high over the past several decades, regardless of the tenuous evidence which has served to support the extraordinary and controversial claims proposed by several UFO researchers:

1. NHI in physical craft has visited our planet.
2. NHI has abducted humans.
3. The military has retrieved crashed UFOs.
4. The government/military continue to withhold information of UFOs from the public, among others.

Evolution

Over time, the focus of ufology has changed in numerous ways since its birth on June 24th, 1947, when private pilot Kenneth Arnold observed nine shiny "saucers" flying near Mount Ranier in Washington. From that day forward, sightings of "saucers" dramatically increased in frequency with mass sightings occurring on several occasions around the world. Ufology evolved through:

- New Age movements, official scientific investigations (*e.g.*, Condon Report, Robertson Panel, Project Blue Book, The Sturrock Panel, etc).
- Analysis and debate of major UFO incidents (*e.g.*, Roswell, NM, 1947; Lonnie Zamora, 1964; Shag Harbor, Nova Scotia, 1967, Tehran, Iran 1976; Rendlesham Forest, Woodbridge, England, 1980, Japan Air Lines Flight, 1986; etc).
- Mass UFO sightings (Washington, D.C., 1952; Phoenix, Arizona, 1997; Hudson Valley, New York, 1980s, Stephenville, Texas, 2008; United Kingdom, 1996; Belgium, 1989-90, Varginha, Brazil, 1996, etc).
- Claims of UFO conspiracy theories such as government and military cover-up and disinformation campaigns.
- The alien abduction phenomenon sparked by the Betty and Barney Hill incident in 1966.

In more recent years, a significant focus within ufology has involved exopolitics and related initiatives such as, The Disclosure Project and The Citizen's Hearing on Disclosure, to facilitate government revelation of their knowledge and involvement with UFOs to the public.

The Debate

Several UFO investigations have concluded that approximately ninety to ninety-five percent of all reported UFOs are explainable, with the remaining of unknown origin.[1,2] Since a very small percentage cannot be reliably identified as "known" objects or events, we must accept the fact that UFOs do exist. The key question is whether or not any of the five to ten percent unexplained UFOs represent a physical craft governed by a form of NHI. While controversial, those who contend that UFOs are intelligently controlled believe sufficient evidence exists in many forms to support their position. This includes:

• The similarity of anecdotal testimony by credible witnesses.
• Simultaneous radar and visual sightings.
• Multiple witness experiences.
• Declassified government/military UFO documents.
• Witness testimony of alleged crashed UFOs and recovered alien bodies.
• Inexplicable UFO maneuvers, among others.

An all-encompassing theory, however, has yet been proposed to describe this small percentage of unexplained UFOs.

The "smoking gun" evidence that proves NHI has visited Earth has served as a major source of debate between the UFO believers and skeptics. There are those, in fact, who consider the debated UFO crash in Roswell, New Mexico, in 1947, as the "smoking gun." This incident, in combination with the inexplicable kinematic behavior of UFOs, that appear inconsistent with known physical laws, (*i.e.,* neutralize effects of inertia and gravity), lend support to the UFO proponents steadfast position that NHI has visited Earth.

In contrast, the UFO skeptics contend there is no compelling evidence to support the notion that NHI has visited Earth. According to the skeptic, the likelihood of natural or man-made phenomenon serves as the basis for "unexplained" aerial events such as hoaxes, poor memory recall, atmospheric phenomenon, weather balloons, advanced "black box" military projects, and psycho-cultural, among others. Surely an answer exists to all phenomena and, in time, the nature and origin of unexplained UFOs will also be defined.

Discussion

Thousands of individuals worldwide have and will continue to experience UFO encounters of varying kinds. The UFO evidence presented in the following chapters clearly indicates that unusual aerial events defy logical explanation, are a source of considerable concern and controversy, and present potential aviation safety problems. For these reasons, among others, scientific and political communities worldwide should consider the phenomenon more seriously, and commit needed resources that can be best applied to better understand the force that governs and regulates its behavior.

Many people desire to know whether or not some unexplained UFOs are real physical craft under intelligent control from another solar system or space-time and, if so, its potential implications for science, society, and our understanding of the universe. Unfortunately, impeding our progress to better understand the phenomenon is the absence of on-going, rigorous investigations by teams of scientists from several disciplines, such as biology, psychology, sociology, physics, astronomy, and epidemiology, etc. Compounding this problem is the difficulty trying to understand and explain, with sufficient confidence, the nature and origin of the phenomenon using evidence primarily anecdotal in nature. In other words, the lack of tangible, objective evidence compromise the methodological considerations that are required as part of the scientific method to test several hypotheses to help determine if the UFO phenomenon is associated with:

1. NHI from another planet, space-time, etc.,
2. Psycho-cultural influences, and/or
3. Atmospheric, geological, and/or meteorological phenomena, among other possibilities.

In light of the current state of affairs in ufology, there exists a need to dramatically alter the way in which to study the UFO phenomenon (See Chapter Nine: The UFO Phenomenon: A New Approach). Greater attention towards the development and application of uniformly applied scientific-based, multidisciplinary research models that offer greater potential to better define this phenomenon must be considered a major goal. Unless a new research approach is initiated, under the leadership of an organized governance structure, little, if any, additional progress will be made to better understand an extraordinary phenomenon that remains as perplexing today as it did decades ago. Until then, if ever, the many controversies and unresolved questions will remain as a source of debate and entertainment through various media forms. And if you happen to be a steadfast UFO advocate or skeptic, consider a more neutral perspective of the phenomenon until that so-called "smoking gun," or at least some highly potent gun powder, reveal the true nature of one of the most significant issues of our time.

CHAPTER TWO

The UFO Phenomenon, Ufology, and Science

The Legitimacy of Ufology

Science is "legitimate" since standard research protocol incorporates procedures to ensure the reliability and validity of well-controlled experiments to prove, or refute, a hypothesis. For a discipline to be considered a science, there must be identifiable natural phenomena for study using accepted scientific procedures. Consequently, ufology is not considered a "legitimate" science by the general scientific community. Thus, ufology holds a paradoxical relationship with science. That is, despite the fact that this poorly understood phenomenon appears inconsistent with known natural phenomena and physical laws like inertia and gravity, it is through the methods of science that the phenomena must be studied.

A major goal for UFO researchers should be to establish agreed upon methodological protocols and theories to be tested by recognized scholars from different scientific disciplines, and supported by independent studies to verify research outcomes. This research mission, however, is impeded by the following:

1. Intangible personal accounts serve as the primary source of UFO evidence for study. There is a lack of tangible, objective UFO evidence available for study.
2. UFO investigations have been generally conducted by those with relatively little or no educational background or advanced degree in a scientific discipline.
3. Comparatively few investigations involve the analysis of physical evidence such as ground traces from UFO landings, UFO photos and videos, visual-radar confirmation, and physiological effects by appropriate scientists.

4. The absence of a widely approved theory of the phenomenon.
5. Research cannot be performed and replicated upon demand or be well-controlled in a laboratory setting.
6. According to the general scientific community, extraordinary claims made by many leading ufologists and UFO researchers have not been sufficiently supported by empirical evidence.
7. The U.S. government and NASA contend that UFOs are either aeronautical or weather events, and/or man-made structures.
8. Limited progress has been made to understand the nature and origin of the phenomenon despite many decades of UFO investigations.

Collectively, for the reasons provided prior, the scientific/academic community will likely continue to not embrace the phenomenon with sufficient credibility to engage in UFO related research. As a result:

- Public and private sponsored support in the form of human and fiscal resources to facilitate UFO research is highly unlikely in the foreseeable future.
- The general scientific community will likely continue to be critical of colleagues pursuing UFO research, and remain reluctant to study the phenomenon.
- The field of ufology will continue to lack credibility as a legitimate area of scientific inquiry and investigation.

Ufology and Science

The lack of acceptable research protocol applied in the study of the UFO phenomenon has contributed to our inability to adequately define, with sufficient confidence, the nature and origin of this unsolved mystery. Part of the difficulty is in applying the scientific method to the study of the phenomenon itself, which seems too intangible for controlled experiments. Accordingly, ufologists have generally evaluated the evidence by whatever means necessary. The problem is that the approaches used have not consistently conformed to the expected standards routinely applied by research scientists. This limitation is further compounded by the problem incurred by the lack of qualified scientists interested in studying the phenomenon and sponsored public/private funds to support UFO research. For these reasons, among others addressed in this and later chapters, research science foundations do not consider UFOs a subject for scientific study. Despite these obstacles, UFO research should be considered an important scientific endeavor since several different scientific investigations have concluded that five to ten percent of UFO sightings remain "unexplained." With a focus on more so-called "fringe topics" (*e.g.*, abductions, conspiracies, and exopolitics/disclosure), the current primary foundation of ufology is, unfortunately, not about investigating and identifying what people are reporting to have seen in the sky. Ufology must undergo a transformation if significant advances towards understanding this phenomenon have a chance to be realized. (See Chapter Three: UFO Behavior and Effects and Chapter Four: UFO Evidence, Chapter Five: Theories and Cases of High Strangeness).

All the theories that attempt to explain the UFO phenomenon can't be correct and maybe they are all incorrect. But how do we know who and what to believe when the preponderance of evidence is hearsay, anecdotal, and lacking in hard, verifiable, indisputable facts? In other words, evidence-based conclusions must be subjected to verification and authenticity to sufficiently prove a hypothesis. All too often, this is not the case in UFO research as evidenced by the extraordinary conclusions by many leading researchers, unsubstantiated by compelling factual evidence. Compounding this issue are the many unsubstantiated conclusions by well-known anonymous ufologists:

1. UFOs are manifesting in our time-space as physical spacecraft with biological life forms.
2. The Earth has been visited by advanced Inter-Stellar Civilizations that can travel through other dimensions faster than the speed of light.
3. We don't have to invent a new fanciful theory regarding interdimensionality and paranormal occurrences to explain the existence of UFOs. They are manifesting in our time-space as physical spacecraft with biological life forms, and also manifest utilizing non-linear, non-local technologies that involve interfacing with what we would call the mind stuff of reality. Not only mind in terms of individual thought, but the transcendent substrate of consciousness that is the universe.
4. The interesting thing is trying to understand the attitude of the UFO operators themselves, the aliens, or the extraterrestrials. On the one hand, they engage in various provocative ways with the militaries of the world, often playing cat and mouse games, almost seeming like they are having fun with, toying with us.... There are reasons to be very suspicious, deeply suspicious of what they are.
5. They have several dozen extraterrestrial vehicles and dozens of deceased [ET] life-forms of various races. Some are stored in an underground facility near Fort Huachuca in Arizona. We can prove, through the testimony of dozens of witnesses, that there have been covert programs that have studied and figured out the energy and propulsion systems behind UFOs. We're talking about a whole new type of physics that would enable humans to generate energy from what's called the "quantum vacuum."

6. There is more than enough documentation to establish military interest in UFO's. Attempted interceptions and military close encounters are a constant feature. The president/government doesn't really know much at all and is not really in charge to begin with. The [privatized] military industrial complex and private transnational corporations seem to be involved with alien technology, UFO-crash retrievals, back-engineering, and possible study of alien bodies, closed off from any government or official overview.
7. Over the past half-century we have had intermittent contact with extraterrestrial civilization. We do not know the motives and cannot predict the future behavior of the extraterrestrials who observe us and who occasionally catch and release some of us to satisfy their curiosity about the predominant species on this planet.

Such unconfirmed conclusions are counterproductive. They create disillusion in the minds of scientists and politicians that impede cooperative efforts to help promote and enhance the quality of UFO based research initiatives.

The longstanding debate and related fundamental question associated with the UFO phenomenon is whether or not existing evidence provides irrefutable proof to support the belief by many UFO researchers that alien beings from another solar system or space-time have visited Earth. This question is difficult, if not impossible, to answer using traditional scientific methods, especially since the primary evidence to support this claim include anecdotal descriptions of:

1. Luminous objects maneuvering strangely in the sky.
2. Unusual-shaped craft that suddenly appear, hover, and accelerate at tremendous speeds.
3. Close-encounters of varying kinds with UFOs and/or their occupants.

Skepticism is incorporated in the scientific method, which integrates the observation of a phenomenon, the development of a hypothesis about the phenomenon, experimentation designed to demonstrate the truth (or not) of the hypothesis, and a conclusion that supports or amends the hypothesis. That is, a hypothesis becomes a fact when confirmed by strict scientific standards, which is of course, subject to challenge. So, when we hear an extraordinary claim that the strange light in the sky that made a right-angle turn, split in half, and then disappeared, is under intelligent control from another solar system, I say: "Great, prove it." In other words, skeptical analysis of UFO claims can be very constructive. It serves as a necessary component to the scientific process and in refining theories and initiating the continuation of related investigations to seek verification, or not, of experimental results and conclusions.

Astronomer Seth Shostak of the SETI Institute depicts this concern:

> If aliens have been visiting the Earth for 50 years, you would think that it would not be so hard to convince a lot of people that that was true. It's convinced 50 percent of the American public, but it's convinced very few academics. As an astronomer friend said to me, if I thought there was a one percent chance any of that was true, I'd spend 100 percent of my time on it. In other words, if the evidence were the least bit compelling, you'd have lots of academics working on it because it's very interesting. To me that says that the evidence is weak from the scientist's perspective. Whereas if we pick up a signal—it's not anecdotal; you may or may not believe it, but immediately what will happen is that anybody with a big antenna will try and prove us wrong. And either they will prove us wrong, or they will prove us right. But there will be very little doubt about it.[1]

Leading UFO researcher Robert Hastings, who for about forty years interviewed former and retired U.S. Air Force personnel regarding their involvement in UFO-nuclear weapons incidents, provided a counter argument directed at the scientific community who, according to Hastings, "considers the legitimacy of the UFO phenomenon as unthinkable."[2] He wrote:

> It is still not too late to refrain from claiming insight into a subject you have not studied, and about which you know little or nothing. I do not expect the vast majority of the UFO skeptics in academia to embrace the revelations and proposals presented in this book. I know that most will haughtily dismiss my material as unadulterated nonsense, unworthy of their superior sensibilities and intellectual acumen. However, perhaps a few of those self-appointed experts will pause a moment and honestly reflect on the limited extent of their knowledge about UFOs, and ask themselves whether it justifies their negatively-biased assumptions about the phenomenon.[2a]

Astrophysicist and UFO researcher Dr. Massimo Teodorani believes the media and the Internet enhance the "escalation of fakes and/or ephemeral information" of the UFO phenomenon and has emphasized the limitations of evidence to study the UFO phenomenon:

> The witness of a given UFO event doesn't furnish a real map of what happened due to the many contradictions, subjective manipulations and constructions of the witness: here some visual testimony is continuously mixed with unconscious or subconscious factors: objectivity is always melted with subjectivity. This constant uncertainty renders the scientific treatment of the UFO phenomenon very difficult,

> unless such phenomenon can be effectively monitored and measured in areas of recurrence using the appropriate instrumentation, which due to its intrinsic nature cannot be misled by any form of subjective thinking.[3]

Teodorani's perspective is consistent with the position held by Director of the Hayden Planetarium, Dr. Neil deGrasse Tyson:

> ...even if in a court of law, eyewitness testimony is a high form of evidence, in the court of science, it is the lowest form of evidence you could possibly put forth (UFOs). Ufology's principle evidence of eyewitness testimony might be considered acceptable to start some form of investigation if a specific scientist feels it worth the effort but not something upon which to base any conclusion.[4]

An additional cautionary tone pertaining to witness testimony was presented by Tim Printy, who wrote:

> Multiple and independent eyewitness reports can be considered the best UFO cases for scientific evidence, especially when good scientific data is obtained from these reports. However, these cases can also be full of misidentifications.[5]

Consistent with the statements above, Dr. J. Deardorff, a professor of atmospheric sciences, wrote:

> Although individual, localized and usually brief sightings may have provided sufficient evidence to be convincing to the observers and sighting analysts, the fact is that, since the widely-reported sightings began in 1947, no event has persisted in a prominent place a sufficient number of hours at a time, or demonstrated its abilities to enough witnesses at a time, for the news media to congregate and publicize it to the world. Nor have they left quite enough evidence behind to be totally convincing to very many scientists.[6]

Since evidence within ufology is largely based on such anecdotal claims, it is very difficult to build testable hypotheses to either reject or confirm through a validation process, such as, testing predictions against observations to confirm a hypothesis. Despite decades of UFO investigations, the phenomenon has not been verified through rigorous scientific study. For this reason, ufology would greatly benefit from collaborative research efforts with the scientific community, but instead, have often alienated (no pun intended) them. This presents a unique paradox for the field of ufology, which has been criticized by many scientists and skeptics, such as James Oberg, who share the viewpoint that UFOs are an "appallingly weak basis for the foundation of the would-be science of ufology." Similarly, Nick Pope, who worked for over twenty years at the British Government's Ministry of Defense (MoD), where his duties included investigating reports of UFO sightings, among others, wrote:

> Sadly, much ufology is not scientific, either because investigators (skeptics and believers alike) are conclusion-led, or because they lack the appropriate expertise and resources, or both. Ufologists and scientists are generally wary of each other, though some bridges have been built. Good ufology (official or private) should be science-based, but it often isn't.[7]

Richard Hall, former assistant director for the National Investigations Committee on Aerial Phenomena (NICAP) and C.A. Maney also emphasized the limitations of ufology as a scientific discipline:

> Although the ranks of ufology contain the seeds of a science, it should not now pretend to be a science, but a popular movement advocating scientific investigation. It should (and could) clarify and present the factual evidence in a manner designed to encourage a true scientific investigation, which would make use of all the techniques and facilities available to science today.[8]

British astrophysicist Dr. P. Sturrock stated that "scientists are interested in UFOs, but unwilling to become involved publicly. Scientists say "show me the evidence, but do not study the available evidence."[9] Michael Shermer, science writer, and founder of The Skeptics Society, and Editor in Chief of its magazine *Skeptic*, wrote:

> In all fields of science there is a residue of anomalies unexplained by the dominant theory. That does not mean the prevailing theory is wrong or that alternative theories are right. It just means that more work needs to be done to bring those anomalies into the accepted paradigm. In the meantime, it is okay to live with the uncertainty that not everything has an explanation.[10]

Shermer's pragmatic perspective has not been pursued by the general scientific community, who continue to explain the UFO phenomenon as natural and man-made phenomenon. The foundation for this position is largely based on the absence of an accepted theory to explain the nature and origin of the UFO phenomenon and related experimental evidence to support that theory.

One prominent exception to the general lack of interest in UFO research by the scientific community was Dr. James McDonald, a senior physicist at the Institute for Atmospheric Physics and professor of meteorology. A proponent of the extraterrestrial hypothesis, he was considered a leading scientific expert on UFOs, and openly argued for more UFO research during the 1960s. He interviewed hundreds of UFO witnesses and revealed government/military UFO documents. McDonald wrote:

> ...There are hundreds of good cases in the Air Force files that should have led to top-level scientific scrutiny of [UFOs] years ago, yet these cases have been swept under the rug in a most disturbing way by Project Blue Book investigators and their consultants.[11]

McDonald's statement on UFOs to the House Committee on Science and Astronautics in 1967 is as follows:

> The scope of the present statement precludes anything approaching an exhaustive listing of categories of UFO phenomena: much of what might be made clear at great length will have to be compressed into my remark that the scientific world at large is in for a shock when it becomes aware of the astonishing nature of the UFO phenomenon and its bewildering complexity. I make that terse comment well aware that it invites easy ridicule; but intellectual honesty demands that I make clear that my two years' study convinces me that in the UFO problem lie scientific and technological questions that will challenge the ability of the world's outstanding scientists to explain—as soon as they start examining the facts.[11a]

In the same statement, McDonald said he had "become convinced that the scientific community...has been casually ignoring as nonsense a matter of extraordinary scientific importance."

The UFO Debate: Skeptics, Debunkers, and Believers

The decades of debate between the UFO skeptics and believers has detracted from the serious nature of the phenomenon and has left the public confused about who and what to believe. The difficulty incurred from the diversity of opinions proposed is in trying to filter fact from fiction, especially since skeptics often adopt the position that those who believe UFOs are extraterrestrial in origin consider that because their claims have not been disproved. In contrast, the UFO advocate often contends that because skeptics have not explained every UFO sighting; some UFOs must not be from Earth. While theoretically possible, the skeptic is forced to prove the claim to be unlikely. However, since we cannot prove UFOs are extraterrestrial, the lack of evidence does not prove, or disprove, they are from our planet. Confused?

According to Robert Hastings:

> Skeptical scientists currently view the existence of extraterrestrial UFOs as a far-fetched idea that is mildly amusing but certainly not worth pursuing. Debunkers, on the other hand, react to this proposal with righteous indignation and a crusader's zeal. For them, the suggestion that aliens might be visiting Earth is an utterly foolish notion, which must be stamped out before it infects rational, properly-thinking individuals.[11b]

The way the evidence actually points, supporting or not supporting the existence of intelligently controlled UFOs, is not conclusive in this debate as "experts" vie against each other to support their position. The skeptics, who question the validity of a UFO claim by calling for evidence to prove or disprove it, debunk ufology since existing evidence has failed to support the conviction held by many ufologists that extraterrestrials have visited Earth. In other words, reports of UFOs are usually dismissed by skeptics as another planet, hoaxes, atmospheric phenomenon, space junk, or of other earthly origin. Furthermore, skeptics consider the alleged famous "Roswell UFO crash" as anything but a "flying saucer," such as a secret aircraft or weather balloon, and that reports of alien abductions are caused by isolated sleep paralysis and/or hypnotic-led confabulation. In contrast, UFO believers advocate that sufficient compelling evidence corroborates the UFO phenomena as a manifestation of a form of NHI visiting Earth and that government/military conspiracy and disinformation campaigns serve to suppress this information from the public. Evidence to support their position includes:

1. Anecdotal testimony in the form of mass sightings, multiple witness observations, simultaneous radar-visual sightings, and close encounters with UFOs and alien beings.
2. Electromagnetic effects from UFOs.
3. Psychological effects experienced from UFO encounters.
4. Physical evidence, such as, photo/video, radar, and analysis of trace elements from reported landing sites.
5. Scientific studies and related government/military investigations.
6. Witness testimony to members of the U.S. Congress through The Disclosure Project, and The Citizens Hearing on Disclosure.
7. Official declassified government/military UFO documents obtained under the Freedom of Information Act.
8. Investigations of specific UFO incidents.
9. Activation and deactivation of nuclear missiles at bases in the U.S. and Russia.
10. Astronauts/cosmonauts have reported UFOs.

11. The Earth cannot be the only planet in the universe with intelligent life. The Drake equation, which is controversial since several of its factors are currently unknown, estimates a wide range between 1,000 and 100,000,000 civilizations in the galaxy.
12. Those who claim being abducted by aliens from UFOs share very similar reports of their encounters.
13. Many people reported seeing dead alien bodies in the alleged UFO crash in Roswell, New Mexico, in 1947.
14. Military pilots claim to have been pursued by UFOs.
15. Air traffic controllers report UFOs on radar moving at speeds of up to 10,000 mph.
16. Major UFO incidents have been reported by multiple witnesses in Washington, D.C. (1952), Phoenix, Arizona (1997), Hudson Valley, New York (1980s), and O'Hare International Airport (2006), among others.

In contrast, skeptics staunchly discredit such evidence and the associated claims of "space aliens" contending they are the result of mass hysteria, hoaxes, conclusions made without sufficient evidence or study, confabulations, and/or a wishful desire to believe. While UFO skeptics can manifest an impenetrable bias of their position on UFOs, we need their perspective to help keep those who claim to have convincing UFO evidence honest and objective. Opposing viewpoints are essential to maintain an open debate of the phenomenon and to encourage UFO researchers to provide more scientific-based corroborative evidence to support their conclusions. Author of the "UFO Trail Blog" (http://ufotrail.blogspot.com/), Jack Brewer, for instance, has been critical of the methods used in UFO investigations, which he considers a "sham inquiry."

Given the prior context, assume that two people report a bright light suddenly appearing in the sky. Photos confirm their claims and record this as a light of unknown origin. One person explains the light as a meteor, while the other attributes it to an emitted luminous beam from a "flying saucer." Follow up investigation will be needed to determine if a meteor was present in that location at that time to confirm the origin of the light as space debris. If an investigation is not conducted, the UFO can have several interpretations, subject to possible study, and if no conclusion is made, the incident will persist as a controversy and considered as an "unknown" in a UFO database. The absence of data validated through careful scientific analysis, such as this "unknown" creates a fine line between the UFO "skeptic" and "believer" and thus between objects in the sky interpreted as "identifiable" or "unidentifiable." Both sides, however, must be careful to not base firm conclusions of UFO cases using evidence not subjected to appropriate study. A fundamental question concerns the issue of what type of evidence represents "proof" that UFOs are under intelligent control from somewhere other than earth? The answer will likely depend if you are a "skeptic" or "believer." This issue is discussed in Chapter Ten: The UFO phenomenon: Should I Believe?

The UFO skeptic assumes an important role within ufology by asking appropriate questions to help ensure the objectivity of research analysis and associated conclusions. The skeptic will question the basis of the evidence, how it was obtained and analyzed, and the reliability and validity of the evidence. This line of questioning is inherent in the scientific method and must be maintained as a routine approach in all UFO research. In contrast, a UFO debunker's approach to the UFO phenomenon is generally counterproductive and impedes UFO research, which they regard as "nonsense." Despite their general lack of knowledge of the UFO evidence, the debunker will still discredit any statement or position that promotes the possibility that UFOs are under intelligent control from a non-earthly origin.

Robert Hastings captured the distinction between the "skeptic" and "debunker" in this statement:

> While it is absolutely valid to insist that rational skepticism be utilized in the analysis of any unexplained phenomenon, it is essential that one carefully and honestly differentiate between genuine, justifiable skepticism, and one's own biases. For example, refusing to undertake an objective, in-depth examination of something, simply because one believes it to be impossible, is not skepticism. Furthermore, such premeditated ignorance is not, and never will be, rational. Additionally, there is a fundamental difference between rational thought and rationalization. The former is essential to any scientific investigation; the latter is merely a refuge for those who have not done their homework.[12]

In his discussion of the UFO debunker, Hastings added, "a more accurate description of their actions would be to say that they merely explain away the phenomenon, with no real evidence to support their position." This position is represented in the views expressed by NASA scientist James Oberg who contends that purported confirmation of extraterrestrial visitations by NHI in physical craft made by ufologists is based on:

> ...lack of data, lack of repeatability, false reporting, wishful thinking, deluded observers, rumors, lies, and fraud. A residue of unexplained cases is not a justification for continuing an investigation after overwhelming evidence has disposed of hypotheses of super normality, such as beings from outer space.[13]

According to UFO researcher Stanton Friedman, debunkers employ four major rules:[14]

1. What the public doesn't know, we certainly won't tell them. The largest official USAF UFO study isn't even mentioned in twelve anti-UFO books, though every one of those books' authors was aware of it.
2. Don't bother me with the facts, my mind is made up.
3. If one can't attack the data, attack the people. It is easier.
4. Do one's research by proclamation rather than investigation. It is much easier, and nobody will know the difference anyway.

Astrophysicist and prominent UFO skeptic, Donald Menzel, one of the first scientists to offer an opinion on the UFO phenomenon, influenced the scientific communities position on the subject by concluding that UFOs have "natural explanations."[15] This longstanding contentious debate between the skeptics and believers comes down to the skeptics who are asked to disprove the evidence and the believers who are asked to prove the evidence. Astrophysicist Dr. Carl Sagan's statement pertaining to one's belief in UFOs provides a unique perspective of the validity of the extraterrestrial hypothesis that suggests NHI has visited Earth from another solar system:

> The idea of benign or hostile space aliens from other planets visiting the earth is an emotional idea. There are two sorts of self-deception here: either accepting the idea of extraterrestrial visitation by space aliens in the face of very meager evidence because we want it to be true; or rejecting such an idea out of hand, in the absence of sufficient evidence, because we don't want it to be true. Each of these extremes is a serious impediment to the study of UFOs.

Further, Dr. Sagan wrote:

> With insufficient data it is easy to go wrong. Human beings have a demonstrated talent for self-deception when their emotions are stirred. What counts is not what sounds plausible, not what we would like to believe, not what one or two witnesses claim, but only what is supported by hard evidence rigorously and skeptically examined. Extraordinary claims require extraordinary evidence.[16]

Sagan, who considered the claims of those who accept the reality of UFOs to be extraordinary, and not supported by sufficient objective evidence, was rebuked by noted alien abduction researcher Budd Hopkins:

> Extraordinary phenomena require an extraordinary investigation. In other words, the scientific community does not have the proof it needs because the scientific community is not undertaking a serious

> investigation of the UFO phenomenon. Why? Because the prevailing opinion among scientists is that UFOs do not exist. Since UFOs do not exist, there is nothing to investigate.[17]

Maybe Dr. Arroway, a character in Carl Sagan's story and movie, *Contact,* captured the general ideology of the skeptics position of the phenomena in the statement, "you can't convince a believer of anything for their belief is not based on evidence; it's based on a deep-seated need to believe."[18] Leading UFO skeptic P. Klass provided a statement of the skeptic's position on UFO sightings by citing "Occam's Razor," which states that the simplest explanation for an unexplained phenomenon is probably the correct one. That is, conventional explanations—natural or man-made phenomena—account for all UFO sightings. Klass, who offered "prosaic explanations"[19] to all UFO reports, was denounced by optical physicist and UFO researcher Dr. Bruce Maccabee:

> The problem faced by the skeptics is that there are sightings for which the generally accepted (by skeptics!) prosaic explanations are wrong or at least unconvincing. The failure of UFO skepticism, from the scientific point of view, has been to allow such explanations to be accepted by the scientific community. If UFOs were "ordinary science," the proposed explanations would have been rigorously analyzed, and probably rejected, rather than simply accepted. Scientific ufology needs skeptics, but skeptics who are capable of recognizing when a sighting simply cannot be explained by any prosaic explanation.[20]

Another counter argument of Klass' position was provided by UFO researcher Robert Hastings:

> Frequently, UFO skeptics—scientists and laypersons alike—invoke Occam's Razor to support their position that there are far more likely, prosaic explanations for the UFO phenomenon than the extraterrestrial spaceship theory. These persons have never studied UFOs and are, therefore, offering uninformed opinions—whether they choose to recognize this fact or not.[20a]

Dr. J. Allen Hynek, an astronomer who served as a scientific adviser to several UFO studies undertaken by the U.S. Air Force, directed UFO investigations like Project Sign (1947–1949), Project Grudge (1949–1952), and Project Blue Book (1952 to 1969), and who founded the Center for UFO Studies (CUFOS) in 1973, altered his position of UFOs after years investigating the phenomenon. According to Hynek, it was the "all available physical evidence" that caused him to transition from a UFO skeptic to a believer. What he considers to be "all available evidence" may be much less than what a skeptic would require. For example, he considered the evidence appealed to by ufologists as:

1. The testimony of people who claim to have seen aliens and/or alien spacecraft.
2. Facts about the type of people who give the testimony.
3. The lack of contrary testimony or physical evidence that would either explain the sighting by conventional means like a weather balloon, prank, meteor shower, or reflection of light to discredit the reliability of the eyewitness.
4. Alleged weaknesses in the arguments of skeptics against the ufologists.

Given his academic and professional background and experiences, Hynek was in a unique position to offer insight on theories of the phenomenon as a manifestation of an extraterrestrial or extra-dimensional intelligence. He expressed his position on the UFO phenomenon in a speech at the UFO Hearing held at the United Nations Special Political Committee meeting on November 28, 1978, and concluded to the UN members that there is "sufficient evidence to defend both the extraterrestrial and extra-dimensional hypothesis."[21] He further stated:

> There is a global phenomenon the scope and extent of which is not generally recognized. It is a phenomenon so strange and foreign to our daily terrestrial mode of thought that it is frequently met by ridicule and derision by persons and organizations unacquainted with the facts.

In support of Hynek's position, and of the existing evidence which supports the belief that NHI has visited Earth, Stanton Friedman published a paper titled, "The UFO Challenge," where he presented four conclusions based on his investigations of the UFO phenomena:[22]

1. The evidence is overwhelming that Planet Earth is being visited by intelligently controlled extraterrestrial spacecraft. In other words, some UFOs are alien spacecraft. Most are not.
2. The subject of flying saucers represents a kind of Cosmic Watergate, meaning that some few people in major governments have known since July, 1947, when two crashed saucers and several alien bodies were recovered in New Mexico, that indeed some UFOs are extraterrestrial. As noted in 1950, it's the most classified U.S. topic.
3. None of the arguments made against conclusions one and two by a small group of debunkers, such as Carl Sagan, can stand up to careful scrutiny.
4. The Flying Saucer story is the biggest story of the millennium. Visits to Planet Earth by aliens and the U.S. government's cover-up of the best data (the bodies and wreckage) have occurred for over fifty years.

Based on investigation of documents and report archives on UFOs under Majestic-12, a supposed code name of an alleged secret committee of scientists, military leaders, and government officials, formed in 1947 by an executive order by U.S. President Harry S. Truman, Friedman contends that at every lecture he proves that the "National Security Agency and Central Intelligence Agency are withholding UFO data," and "the problem is not that there is not enough evidence to justify my conclusions; but that most people, especially the noisy negativists, are unaware of the real, non-tabloid evidence." In his book, *Flying Saucers and Science: A Scientist Investigates the Mysteries of UFOs: Interstellar Travel, Crashes, and Government Cover-Ups,* Friedman emphasized his case for UFOs as being under intelligent control with:

1. 10-40 foot disc objects without visible wings or engine.
2. "High maneuverability," like sharp angle movements and vertical trajectory.
3. "Mother ships" up to 0.5 to 1 mile long.[23]

John Podesta, who served as President Clinton's former chief of staff, as co-chair of President Obama's transition team, and as the current president of the Liberal Center for American Progress has also been one of the more recent public proponents of the UFO agenda he termed "a new way forward":

> It is definitely time for government, scientists, and aviation experts to work together in unraveling the questions about UFOs that have so far remained in the dark ... it's time to find out what the truth really is that's out there. The American people and people around the world want to know, and they can handle the truth.[24]

Rationale to Support the UFO Phenomenon

Several scientists and military officials who have conducted investigations of UFO evidence have stated their support of the UFO phenomenon:

A. Present evidence surely does not amount to incontrovertible proof of the extraterrestrial hypothesis. What I find scientifically dismaying is that, while a large body of UFO evidence now seems to point in no other direction than the extraterrestrial hypothesis, the profoundly important implications of that possibility are going unconsidered by the scientific community because this entire problem has been imputed to be little more than a nonsense matter unworthy of serious scientific attention.
–Bernhard Haisch, Ph.D.
Physicist[25]

B. Fourteen percent of the 5,800 cases studied by SEPRA [a unit involved in the Rare Aerospace Phenomena Study Department based in Toulouse, France (1988-2004)] were utterly inexplicable and extraterrestrial in origin.
–Jean-Jacques Velasco
Head of official French UFO investigation for SEPRA[26]

C. The problem is not that there is not enough evidence to justify my conclusions; but that most people, especially the noisy negativists, are unaware of the real, non-tabloid evidence.
–Stanton Friedman
Nuclear Physicist[27]

D. The hassle over the word "proof" boils down to one question: What constitutes proof? Does a UFO have to land at the River Entrance to the Pentagon, near the Joint Chiefs of Staff offices? Or is it proof when a ground radar station detects a UFO, sends a jet to intercept it, the jet pilot sees it, and locks on with his radar, only to have the UFO streak away at a phenomenal speed? Is it proof when a jet pilot fires at a UFO and sticks to his story even under the threat of court-martial? Does this constitute proof?
–U.S. Air Force Officer Edward J. Ruppelt
Director of Project Grudge
(U.S. Air Force's secret investigation of UFOs in the early 1950s)[28]

E. 1) All UFO sightings cannot be attributed to conventional causes, 2) the existence of alien intelligence must be considered, but 3) extreme caution must be used in developing this latter hypothesis, with due respect for the complexity of the phenomenon.
–Jacques F. Vallee
Computer scientist, author, ufologist, and former astronomer[29]

F. It is my thesis that flying saucers are real and that they are space ships from another solar system. I think that they possibly are manned by intelligent observers who are members of a race that may have been investigating our earth for centuries...
–Hermann Oberth
German rocketry pioneer[30]

G. The reports of incidents convince us that there is something going on that must have immediate attention. Sightings of unexplained objects at great altitudes and traveling at high speeds in the vicinity of U.S. defense installations are of such nature that they are not attributable to natural phenomena or known types of aerial vehicles.
–December 1952 memo
from the Assistant CIA Director of Scientific Intelligence[31]

H. The UFO phenomenon, as studied by my colleagues and myself, bespeaks the action of some form of intelligence... but whence this intelligence springs, whether it is truly extra-terrestrial, or bespeaks a higher reality not yet recognized by science, or even if it be in some way or another a strange psychic manifestation of our own intelligence, is much the question.
–Dr. J. Allen Hynek
Astrophysicist[32]

I. The number of thoughtful, intelligent, educated people in full possession of their faculties who have "seen something" and described it grows every day...We can...say categorically that mysterious objects have indeed appeared and continue to appear in the sky that surrounds us... (they) unmistakably suggest a systematic aerial exploration and cannot be the result of chance. It indicates purpose and intelligent action.
–General Lionel M. Chassin
Commanding General of the French Air Forces, and General Air Defense Coordinator, Allied Air Forces, Central Europe (NATO)[33]

J. My three years of official research and investigation into the UFO phenomenon changed my life forever. I'd come into the job as a skeptic, but on the basis of the cases I'd looked at, and what I'd discovered in the files, I came to believe that some UFOs might well be extraterrestrial. If these files are now to be made public, I think people are in for a big surprise, and I believe that, like me, people will come to see that this is a serious subject that raises very important defense and national security issues. As far as these files are concerned...the truth is in there!
–Nick Pope
Desk Officer, UFO investigations for the MoD
United Kingdom[34]

K. Many of the reports that cannot be explained have come from intelligent and technically well-qualified individuals whose integrity cannot be doubted."
–Major General E.B. LeBaily
USAF Director of Information.[35]

L. We have, indeed, been contacted—perhaps even visited—by extraterrestrial beings, and the U.S. government, in collusion with the other national powers of the earth, is determined to keep this information from the general public.
–Victor Marchetti
Former CIA official.[36]

M. The day will come undoubtedly when the phenomenon will be observed with technological means of detection and collection that won't leave a single doubt about its origin. This should lift a part of the veil that has covered the UFO mystery for a long time: a mystery that continues to the present. But it exists, it is real, and that in itself is an important conclusion.
–Major-General Wilfred De Brouwer
Deputy Chief, Royal Belgian Air Force.[37]

N. The evidence that there are objects which have been seen in our atmosphere, and even on terra firma, that cannot be accounted for either as man-made objects or as any physical force or effect known to our scientists seems to me to be overwhelming...There have been thousands, perhaps tens of thousands, of sightings and encounters, physical results and of the latter, by people all over the world whose evidence on any other subject would be accepted without question.
–Lord Hill-Norton
Admiral of the Fleet, former Chief of the Defense Staff, former Chairman of the NATO Military Committee United Kingdom, 1988[38]

Rationale Against the UFO Phenomenon

Skeptics and debunkers of the UFO phenomenon often adopt Carl Sagan's opinion that "extraordinary claims require extraordinary evidence" to defend their reluctance to support the position held by many ufologists that extraterrestrials are visiting earth. For example:

A. The reliable cases are uninteresting and the interesting cases are unreliable. Unfortunately there are no cases that are both reliable and interesting. To the best of my knowledge there are no instances...of an alien aircraft.
–Dr. Carl Sagan
Astronomer[39]

B. On the basis of this study we believe that no objects such as those popularly described as flying saucers have overflown the United States. I feel certain that even the unknown three percent could have been explained as conventional phenomena or illusions if more complete observational data had been obtained.
–Donald A. Quarles
Served as both Secretary of the Air Force and Deputy Secretary of Defense.[40]

C. All non-explained sightings are from poor observers.
–Dr. Donald Menzel
Astronomer[41]

D. Almost every sighting is either a mistake or a hoax. These reports are riddled with hoaxes, and the flying saucer enthusiasts have so many cranks, freaks, and nuts among them that Hynek is constantly running the risk of innocently damaging his reputation by being confused with them.
–Dr. Isaac Asimov
Author[42]

E. From hundreds and hundreds of such stories and videos that I've studied, they all look to me to be "ordinary" visual effects of human space missions, understandable public misunderstandings of normal space conversations, and predictable exaggerations, confabulations, and even fabrications of people who enjoy—or profit from—telling wild tales. I've seen no compelling indication of anything beyond the realm of modern science—nothing.
–James Oberg
Former spaceflight operations specialist for NASA
and space analyst for NBC[43]

F. As far as I know, no claims of UFOs as being alien craft have any validity. The claims are without substance, and certainly not proved. The idea of benign or hostile space aliens from other planets visiting the earth is clearly an emotional idea.
– Dr. David Morrison
Senior Scientist at the NASA Astrobiology Institute[44]

G. ...nothing has come from the study of UFOs in the past 21 years that has added to scientific knowledge...further extensive study of UFOs probably cannot be justified in the expectation that science will be advanced thereby.
–Edward U. Condon
Nuclear Physicist[45]

H. Choose the nearest star; decide how long you're willing to travel, how fast you will need to go to get there in that time, what you will have to take with you, and how many should be in the crew. Make it a one-way suicide mission if you wish. As a final step, calculate the kinetic energy that must be imparted to the spaceship to get you there in that time (one half the mass times the velocity squared). I suggest you stay away from the relativistic limit; it complicates the calculation and won't help you anyway. The good news is that you will then sleep secure in the knowledge that UFOs from elsewhere in the galaxy are not subjecting humans to hideous experiments.
–Bob Park
Emeritus professor of physics
University of Maryland[46]

I. Ufology is the mythology of the space age. Rather than angels... we now have...extraterrestrials. It is the product of the creative imagination. So far, however, nothing has been positively identified as an alien spacecraft in a way required by commonsense and science. That is, there has been no recurring identical UFO experience and there is no physical evidence in support of either a UFO flyby or landing.
–Paul Kurtz
Professor Emeritus of Philosophy at University of New York at Buffalo[46a]

J. The truth is UFO news has been running on life support for years and years. I was out of the field for ten years, and when I came back no one—not a single person or organization—was any further to proving a single thing. There haven't been any huge cases, not really, no smoking guns, no disclosures.
–Ian Rogers
Ufologist[46b]

K. The main source of UFO evidence is the report made by eyewitnesses. What Ufology wants everyone to believe is that the testimony of the eyewitnesses is enough to establish the fact that structured craft of unknown origin that operate under intelligent control are producing these UFO reports. They have been somewhat successful in that the general public usually equates the word UFO (Unidentified Flying Object) with "flying saucers" or "little green men" from space. Unfortunately, this fact cannot be established from the eyewitness testimony alone.
–Tim Printy
UFO skeptic[47]

L. Many pro-ufologists, blame the lack of progress in "solving the UFO mystery" on disinterest of the "scientific community," This "neglect" could be overcome quickly if the past 50 years had yielded any scientifically credible evidence that even one UFO might be an extraterrestrial craft. Roughly ninety-eight percent of sightings are simply misidentifications of prosaic, if sometimes unfamiliar, objects by honest persons (and) the balance, roughly two percent, are self-delusions or hoaxes by persons who like to spin tall tales and become instant celebrities. That is, UFO reports are the results of misidentifications, delusions, and hoaxes, period!
–P. Klass
Former Editor, Aviation Week[48]

Discussion

Given the broad continuum of unproven UFO claims and associated theories (See Chapter Six: UFO Theories), combined with controversial evidence and the lack of acceptable, well-controlled scientific investigations of the phenomena, it should not be surprising that ufology lacks the credibility required to be perceived as a legitimate scientific discipline among the general scientific community. Regardless, UFOs are real. Credible witness testimony by military pilots, astronauts, air traffic controllers, scientists, and police officers, of inexplicable aerial events involving unidentifiable physical craft are too numerous to dismiss and ignore.

The essence of the UFO debate among the skeptics, debunkers, and believers comes down to defining how to "prove" that UFOs are intelligently controlled by alien beings from somewhere other than Earth. Scientists will accept this conclusion only after applied research, using the scientific method, verifies this to be true, or not, or until a UFO lands at the White House. Is it proof if a pilot observes a spherical silver object paralleling the plane for several minutes, and confirmed by ground radar, until it then suddenly accelerates at thousands of miles per hour out of sight? Yes, this has happened many times. But, no, this incident does not provide irrefutable proof that alien beings are visiting Earth. Just because it defies logical explanation, introducing the "space alien" card for justification is a bold leap without additional supporting evidence. However, as an admitted UFO agnostic, this statement does not conclusively rule out the possibility that some unexplained UFOs may be physical craft from another solar system or space-time. That is, I acknowledge that a physical phenomenon exists in our skies which cannot be easily explained. Consequently, the "space alien" conclusion may or may not be valid. I simply don't know.

The UFO phenomenon is analogous to the mystery behind the question of how the pyramids and other ancient great structures were built. Since we cannot determine, with confidence, how they were built, many believe it must have been built by "space aliens," often referred to as "ancient astronauts." Using similar logic, many ufologists contend that some of the unexplained UFOs must be governed by "space aliens," too. The argument that if you cannot disprove a claim it must be true must also be applied towards defining the nature of the phenomenon. For instance, since you can't prove that the devil does not exist or that UFOs are not governed by alien beings, does it mean the devil exists and aliens have visited earth?

The field of ufology and related UFO research is in a state of disarray since it has not consistently demonstrated the required scientific standards of investigation, on par with more established research oriented disciplines, to corroborate many extraordinary claims by leading UFO researchers. Given this context, it is not surprising that many UFO advocates have been subjected to ridicule by skeptics and the general scientific community. For example, leading UFO researcher Stanton Friedman believes that "the evidence is overwhelming that Planet Earth is being visited by intelligently controlled extraterrestrial spacecraft."[49] Similarly, psychologist Dr. D. Donderi wrote:

> over the past half-century we have had intermittent contact with extraterrestrial civilization. We do not know the motives and cannot predict the future behavior of the extraterrestrials who observe us and who occasionally catch and release some of us to satisfy their curiosity about the predominant species on this planet.[50]

While Friedman and Donderi conclusions may be valid, the general scientific community requires verification of the empirical evidence before reaching the same conclusions. Common reactions by scientists, when confronted with such extraordinary claims, are either an outright rejection of the topic or that UFOs are a psychological-sociological type of phenomenon, and/or natural and man-made phenomena. Those who denounce the subject and deem it unworthy of study, however, should critically analyze the large body of UFO evidence before forming this widely held opinion of the phenomenon. I have had conversations with many scientists who firmly reject the possibility that

NHI may be visiting earth in the absence of even a slight familiarity of the evidence. Could there be a subconscious reason for rejecting the phenomenon without sufficient study? A comprehensive and critical study of all the UFO evidence may convince even some of most skeptical scientists that some UFOs cannot be easily explained. Following this evidence-based review, some may possibly consider adopting a more objective approach towards the phenomenon. In contrast, many UFO advocates contend that the skeptical scientists and debunkers who believe there is no hard evidence to support the UFO-alien connection are incorrect. They contend that "hard evidence" exists in a variety of forms as mentioned previously. Could it be that a certain segment of those who either debunk or are apathetic towards the phenomena may also be driven by an unconscious emotion, a fear of UFOs? It is not far-fetched to understand that many people are concerned that if some UFOs are governed by NHI, our society and personal lives would be adversely disrupted. For such people, it would be a tremendous disadvantage that another life-form is visiting Earth, so its existence simply must not be conceded.

Our society, which is more receptive to new ideas and very interested in the possibility of other intelligent life in the universe, should serve as a public mandate for an organized effort to facilitate the required leadership and research support to effectively address the UFO phenomenon. After all, the decades of research and debates about whether or not:

1. A "flying saucer" crashed in Roswell, New Mexico, in 1947.
2. The government/military has recovered crashed UFOs and their occupants, and is withholding this information from the public.
3. We have reverse-engineered advanced UFO technology.
4. Aliens are abducting humans, among others, have provided little in the way of advancing our understanding of the phenomenon.

Consequently, we must shift away from "past practice" towards the discussion and application of ways to improve techniques to better study and understand the phenomenon. The primary objective, which is to determine the underlying processes that govern and regulate the UFO phenomenon, requires newly developed scientific investigations. This must be facilitated by an over-arching committee, such as a subcommittee of the United Nations, Senate, Congress, or a public/private institution, governed by leaders from diverse professions to provide the necessary direction, support, and related resources required for a multidisciplinary team of leading scholars to study the phenomenon. (The governance and research process associated with this endeavor is discussed in Chapter Nine: The UFO Phenomenon: A New Approach.)

CHAPTER THREE

UFO Behavior and Effects

Overview

Several reported common characteristics of unexplained UFOs may best be described by astronomer, and leading UFO researcher Dr. J. Allen Hynek:

> UFOs maneuver with ease in our atmosphere, and appear largely unaffected by gravity and the inertial properties of matter as exhibited by the ability of hovering a few feet above the ground or high in the air with seeming little effort, and the ability to accelerate, often noiselessly, at incredible rates by ordinary standards.[1]

Hynek's description evolved from his personal investigations as scientific adviser to several studies undertaken by the U.S. Air Force to analyze the UFO phenomenon. This evidence depicts the general appearance and behavior of a typical unexplained UFO:

1. Luminous and surrounded by a haze.
2. Can become invisible and then a few seconds later may appear a short distance away.
3. Physical dimensions can change or "shape-shift."
4. Wobbles, remains stationary, and is noiseless with no indication of a propulsion system, such as propellers or jets.
5. Appears to defy gravity and inertia.
6. Sudden motion from a stationary position, immediate stops, and angular maneuvers at extreme velocities.
7. Produces electromagnetic effects (EM), and physical ground traces in the form of landing marks, radiation, and disturbed vegetation and soil.
8. Induces physiological effects in humans such as sensation of heat, temporary paralysis, nausea, etc.

The National Aviation Reporting Center on Anomalous Phenomena (NARCAP), founded in 1999 by NASA aeronautical research scientist Dr. Richard Haines and Ted Roe, was developed because of concerns presented by UFOs for the aviation industry. According to the NARCAP:

> The aviation industry is operating under a bias that is causing an under-reporting of safety-related encounters with UFOs. Without this data, effective procedures have not been implemented and there is a real threat to aviation safety.[2]

In a study by Haines, an analysis of over 100 UFO reports generated several general characteristics with shape being one (*e.g.*, spheres, elliptical, triangles, cones, and diamonds, are the most commonly reported forms), and unique lighting patterns and their effects in the form of individual surface lights, glowing surface, color changes upon acceleration, and lights flashing at different frequencies and intensities. Based on evidence analyzed among several researchers, Haines concluded that UFOs "are associated with a very high degree of intelligence, deliberate flight control, and advanced energy management."[3] Further, he contends that UFOs are capable of producing physical effects in the form of "landing marks," disturbed plant life near landing sites, and physiological effects on humans, such as temporary paralysis, unusual sensations, eye irritation, headaches, and nausea.[3]

In an article by Ted Roe,[4] the author presented evidence analyzed by physicist Dr. Peter Sturrock and his colleagues of over 3,000 UFO cases reported by aircraft pilots studied by Dr. Haines. About four percent of the cases studied involved "transient EM effects" and/or malfunctioned navigational equipment and radios from UFO encounters. Gravitational and/or inertial effects in the form of rapid acceleration or change in direction, inconsistent with our understanding of physical laws, were also reported in many sightings. In a comprehensive report by Ted R. Phillips, director of the Center for Physical Trace Research (CPTR), and former research associate of Dr. Hynek, a statistical analysis of data from 3,059 UFO reports from 91 countries between 1940 and 2004 was conducted from "observations of anomalous phenomena or objects on or near the ground resulting in physical residues generated by the observed phenomena or objects."[5] Of the cases studied, forty percent involved multiple witness events, twenty-four percent included occupants/beings reported, sixty-three percent of the time, more than one being was seen, and fifty-seven percent of the beings were described as small.[5a]

In an investigation directed by P. Sturrock, known as the Sturrock Panel, the "strongest UFO evidence" presented by UFO investigators was analyzed by nine scientists. The main conclusions indicated:

1. Effects on witnesses: burns, sensations of heat, and eye problems are the most frequently reported forms. The evidence suggested possible sources, such as microwave, infrared, visible and ultraviolet radiation, although "a few cases seem to point toward high doses of ionizing radiation, such as X-rays or gamma rays."[6]
2. Radar detections of UFOs: the panel cited an unexplained case in January 1994 over Paris when the crew of an airplane reported "a gigantic disk" more than 3,000 feet in diameter. The disk was detected on military radar for 50 seconds, slowed abruptly from 110 knots to zero, and then disappeared.[6a]
3. Magnetic Disturbances: frequent sightings of strange lights sometimes associated with documented EM energy.[6b]
4. Disturbance to vegetation and ground traces: in Trans-en-Provence, France (1981) a witness reported an object landing, which upon investigation by Police and UFO researchers, found two concentric circles and other traces. Laboratory analysis showed the soil had been compressed, and the plants aged. A toxicologist concluded that some, though not all, of the effects could have been caused by powerful microwave radiation.[7]

UFO Sighting Databases

The reported physical features, behavior, and effects of UFOs have been recorded in several databases for documentation and analysis.

The National Investigations Committee on Aerial Phenomena (NICAP), a civilian UFO research group from the 1950s to the 1980s, provides a database (www.nicap.org/chrono.htm) of incidents before 1900 to 2009 of sightings, major government reports and activities, and other important events, arranged by year and chronological order. This database also contains information of UFO encounters, trace evidence, psychological/physiological effects, and simultaneous radar-visual sightings, among others.

The National UFO Reporting Center (NUFORC: www.nuforc.org) also maintains a UFO sighting database beginning before 1900 to the present catalogued by event date, state, and shape.

Another comprehensive database developed by Ted Phillips is composed of cases from 1969-1999.

The Mutual UFO Network (MUFON) also maintains an extensive record of sightings in their UFO Type catalogue (www.ufostalker.com/?mufon=true) of a variety of statistics and trends.

Additionally, *The UFO Evidence* website (www.ufoevidence.org) includes a catalogue of recent and featured sightings and photos.

Other databases include:

- Daniel Guenther's, Just the Cases (www.jtc-ufo.com/database).
- The Magonia Database: A Century of UFO Landings (www.ufoinfo.com/magonia).
- The Project Blue Book Archive (www.bluebookarchive.org), which provides access to over 50,000 official U.S. Government UFO documents.

Other key resources that address the behavior and effects of UFOs may be found in several articles and books by:

1. Theoretical physicist James M. McCampbell (*A Major Breakthrough in the Scientific Understanding of Unidentified Flying Objects, and Effects of UFOs Upon People*), which may be found on the NICAP website (www.nicap.org).
2. Astrophysicist Dr. Massimo Teodorani ("A Comparative Analytical and Observational Study of North American Databases on Unidentified Aerial Phenomena").
3. Dr. Richard Haines (*Aviation Safety in America: A Previously Neglected Factor*).
4. Plant physiologist Dr. Frank Salisbury (*The Utah UFO Display*).
5. Researcher and field investigator for the Center for UFO Studies Francis L. Ridge (*Regional Encounters: The FC Files A Century of UFO Sightings and Close Encounters in the Midwest*).
6. Leading research and development engineer and manager for NASA, Dr. Paul Hill (*Unconventional Flying Objects: A Scientific Analysis*).

Based on eyewitness reports and evidence collected and analyzed from the UFO resources mentioned prior, several features of UFOs and their effects on witnesses are presented in the remainder of this chapter. Additional resource information is also represented in Chapter Four: UFO Evidence and Chapter Five: Cases of High Strangeness.

UFO Kinematic Behavior and Effects

The maneuverability of UFOs is characterized by rapid acceleration from a stationary position, hovering for long periods of time, descending like a leaf falling as if wobbling, decelerating quickly to a stop and then accelerating in a different direction, making acute-angle turns, "tilts leading edge down to go forward, leading-edge up to stop or reverse, and banks to turn,"[8] etc. The invisibility attribute of the phenomenon has also been a major source of debate. One thought is that the UFOs' rapid acceleration from a motionless state creates the appearance of vanishing. Changes in diameter have also been described as "winking out, from the outer edges inward," and that it "seemed to implode and shrank, and at a higher level it reappeared again."[8a] Such ability may reflect an unknown type of interrelationship among propulsion, gravitational fields, and momentum.

Dr. P. Hill, who provides a comprehensive evaluation of UFO maneuverability in his book, *Unconventional Flying Objects: A Scientific Analysis*, contends that UFOs are able to travel up to 9,000 mph through the use of an "airflow-control force field" that results in a "constant-pressure and density flow" around the craft to reduce friction and heating.[8b] Hill believes, based on his experience with missile dynamics, familiarity with UFO maneuvers, and "advanced knowledge of UFO technology," that UFOs "adhere to the laws of physics."[8c] In support of Hill's analysis of UFO behavior, Dr. H.E. Puthoff, from the Institute for Advanced Studies at Austin stated:

> In the final analysis, one must conclude that Hill has assembled as good a case as can be made on the basis of presently available data that the observation of some "unconventional flying objects" is compatible with the presence of engineered platforms weighing in at something around 30 tons, which are capable of 100-g accelerations and 9,000-mph speeds in the atmosphere. Perhaps more important for the technical reader, however, is Hill's supporting argumentation, based on solid analysis, that these platforms, although exhibiting the application of physics and engineering principles clearly beyond our present-day capabilities, do not appear to defy these principles in any fundamental way.[9]

Based on reported pilot testimony, Ted Roe, from the NARCAP, concluded that spherical UFOs engage in complex maneuvers that include circular passes around aircraft and instantaneous changes in direction at extraordinary velocities. Fifteen of the UFO pilot and air crew cases he reviewed were described as near "mid-air collisions or separation of less than 1,000 feet." Further, witness's report that the UAP seems to "wobble like jelly," "split into smaller objects," and "explode with bright light."[10] Additionally, Roe wrote:

> ...the "UFO can appear very suddenly and a situation can escalate quite quickly leaving split second decisions in the hands of aircrew that have not even been advised of the existence of such phenomena."[10a]

Brightness

When a stationary UFO starts to accelerate and increase power, a corresponding increase in the objects brightness is often reported. According to P. Hill, this effect is related to an increase in the "activation power" of the UFO and the brightness and associated power change suggest that radiation is an important component of the UFOs control system.

Shape

An analysis of UFO shapes reported in the NICAP, NUFORC, and the CPTR databases are presented in Table 1 that follows.

Table 1.

INCIDENCE OF REPORTED UFO SHAPE FROM THE NICAP, NUFORC, AND CPTR DATABASES.

Database	**NICAP**	**NUFORC**	**CPTR**
Shape	N (percent)	N (percent)	N (percent)
Disc	149 (26)*	5638 (16.5)	
Round	96 (17)	7187 (21)	(57.2)*
Oval/Elliptical	77 (13)	3721 (11)	(21.2)
Cylindrical	48 (8.3)	1129 (3)	(6.0)
Triangular	11 (2)	7665 (22.5)*	
Sphere		4950 (14.5)	
Cigar		2102 (6)	
Teardrop		755 (2)	
Egg		780 (2)	
Diamond		1167 (3)	
Various Other			1.0
Total	575	33,965	3,059

*Denotes largest percentage in each database

The difference in the number of reported sightings and terminology used to describe the shape of the UFO among the three databases in Table 1, suggest that conclusions of shape incidence should be made with caution. With this in mind, over the past several decades there has been an increase (20 percent) in dark/black triangles and a decrease (~10 percent) in reported "disc" shape UFOs. One possible explanation for the increase in triangular shaped crafts may be due to the introduction of advanced military aircraft like the B2 stealth bomber with its triangular design. The CPTR also reports a much larger percentage of "round" objects (57.2 percent) than that reported by NICAP (17 percent) and NUFORC (21 percent). Surprisingly, no "disc" shape was categorized by the CPTR, which is likely related to the differences in terminology used to describe the UFO, especially since "disc" shape was frequently reported in the NICAP (26 percent) and NUFORC (16.5 percent) databases. That is, the CPTR database may have catalogued "disc" objects under the "round" (57.2 percent) or oval/elliptical (21.2 percent) reported shapes. The different shapes in each database may also be related to the possibility that we are dealing with several different phenomena, and/or to the variability in description of witness reports. According to NASA research, scientist Dr. Richard Stothers, at close range, UFOs appear as "discs or other extended objects," including "vertical cylinders enveloped in clouds."[11] The NICAP document, The UFO Evidence, also contains a summary of patterns in appearance and behavior determined from UFO cases studied through 1963.[12]

Size

The GEIPAN, formerly known as GEPAN (1977-1988) and SEPRA (1988-2004), is a unit of the French Space Agency whose objective is to investigate UFOs and make its findings available to the public. Their report[13] of 600 cases of pilot encounters with one or more UFOs during flight concluded:

1. In 443 cases (74 percent), the UFOs were described as "objects" and 42 percent as circular-shaped.
2. The size of UFOs ranged from as small as 1 foot to over 0.5 miles.
3. The more common disk- and sphere-shaped craft ranged in diameter from 20-30 feet and the triangular shaped objects were reported up to and over 0.5 mile.

A general review of the literature and UFO databases indicate that UFOs reported near the ground are generally up to 15 feet in diameter and shaped as a sphere, egg, or triangle. Interestingly, however, no reports in the NICAP database (Table 1) included "sphere" or "egg"-shaped objects.

Color

The UFO appearance in daylight is usually described as white or "metallic" ranging from dull gray "aluminum" to silver, which varies based on the brightness of the surrounding environment. In a comprehensive report by T. Phillips, the highest percentage of UFO color was reported as metallic (59.6 percent) followed by red (11.0 percent), white (10.1 percent), orange-red (5.5 percent), orange (3.7 percent), yellow (3.7 percent), and blue-white (2.8 percent).[13a] A similar result was reported by NICAP in 253 cases of daytime observations with the color silver or metallic (34.8 percent; 88 cases) constituting the highest percentage of reported color followed closely by the color white (32.0 percent; 81 cases). Based on the NICAP database of 162 cases, the reported colors of UFOs seen at night are: red (38.3 percent, 62 cases); orange (15.4 percent, 25 cases); yellow (17.3 percent, 28 cases); green (13.0 percent, 21 cases); and blue (16.0 percent, 26 cases). Of 82 cases in the NICAP database, which contained reports of brightness and color change, 23 out of 25 cases showed a change in brightness and color upon a maneuver or velocity change.

An explanation of UFO color by P. Hill involves the effect from "ionizing radiation," generated by the UFO. In other words, the UFO ionizes the air which causes its self-illuminating character and fuzzy, indiscernible outline. According to Hill, the colors red and orange correspond to the least energy, which are most commonly seen when hovering or operating at low-power, while blue and white colors are observed frequently when traveling fast or operating at high-power.[13b] At night, UFOs are generally described having a "phosphorescence" or "aura," while during the day, UFOs appear as if "shimmering," like a mirror or shiny metal, or as having a "glowing haze."[13c] This appearance may be due to plasma reflecting off the UFO.[13d] The changes in color associated with acceleration, and the time of day or night of the sighting, may contribute to the large variability in UFO color both within and between the NICAP and CPTR databases.

Sound

In a report by T. Phillips, sound was reported in only 9.3 percent of the 3,059 cases analyzed. When present, a whistling sound was reported most often (31.1 percent), followed in order by humming (22.6 percent), hissing (11.3 percent), buzzing (11.1 percent), beeping (10.0 percent), electronic (10.0 percent) and roaring (4.9 percent).[13e] P. Hill theorized that the UFOs' force field neutralizes gravity resulting in a vibratory effect that manifests as a "hum" sound. In contrast, McCampbell contends that the UFO "hum" is related to the effect of EM energy on the auditory system. Further, no shock wave or "sonic boom" has been reported, even when the UFOs are traveling several times the speed of sound. When sound is present, it tends to increase in pitch and intensity level just before and during acceleration from a motionless state.[14]

Habits

The UFOs appear to frequently visit defense installations and nuclear sites, hydroelectric installations and dams, and lakes. They seem to prefer encountering lone individuals, or small groups and isolated cars, and are most often observed at dusk or early evening. At times, the UFO also returns to a recently visited area within hours or a day.

Electrical Interference and Radiation

Frequent visits by UFOs of electrical power facilities, along with incidents involving vehicle engine interference or failure during close encounters, have been recognized for many years.

According to P. Hill, UFOs emit EM energy with ionizing capability that is synchronized with the UFO's "gravity-like" force fields that may cause electrical interference.[14a] He estimated UFO radiation in the range between the bottom of the X-ray band and the lower end of the Gamma-ray band which he suspects may be responsible for the "ion sheath around UFOs."[14b]

According to UFO researcher James McCampbell, magnetic fields produced by UFOs have induced "magnetism in ferrous objects such as signs and flagpoles," and wristwatches that stopped during a UFO sighting also became magnetized.[14c]

UFO researcher Richard Hall, editor of *The UFO Evidence* from the NICAP, reported more than sixty cases of EM interference by UFOs resulting in engine disturbance.[15] During a typical UFO-car encounter, a bright light suddenly appears and hovers over the car as the lights fail and the engine dies. However, after a few minutes when the UFO leaves, the car functions normally.

France's project for the study of UFOs (GEPAN/SEPRA) also reported 81 (14 percent of the 600 cases) aircraft incidents where pilots reported EM effects on one or more aircraft systems, such as, communications, compass, and weapons.

Aeronautical scientist Dr. Richard F. Haines and Technical Specialist Dominique F. Weinstein, who conducted a study of aviation-related UFO encounters concluded:

1. Private airplane are more likely to be affected by EM effects than military or commercial aircraft.
2. Communication systems and compasses are the most affected systems.
3. Most of the EM effects involve encounters with circular-shaped UFOs, and occur more frequently when near the UFO.[16]

Physiological Effects

The most common physiological effects reported by witnesses close to a UFO include burns, temporary paralysis, prickling sensation, and irritated eyes. A considerable variety of other physiological effects have also been noted in isolated instances, such as skin irritation, nausea, general weakness, amnesia, headache, and loss of vision, among others.[17] These effects have been attributed to the complex EM field that may induce the sensation of heat in most instances of close UFO encounters. In a study by James M. McCampbell, he summarized witness reports collected from other studies, which included the common complaint of the sensation of body heating during a close encounter, occasional temporary paralysis, and/or loss of consciousness.[17a] Further, approximately fifty percent of those temporarily paralyzed, or who had lost consciousness, also described feeling a prickling sensation. According to P. Sturrock, cases that involve physiological effects are "not well documented," since the accuracy of reports is compromised by the individual's reluctance to discuss the UFO encounter.[17b]

Propulsion

Several research scientists, such as H. Oberth, L. Cramp, J. Harder, J. McCampbell, P. Hill, and C. Poher, who have studied the kinematic behavior of UFOs, believe an anti-gravity-like "force field" acts as its propulsion. Witness description of the effects of this "force field" includes bending tree branches, cars spinning out of control, and stopping or knocking people down. During these incidents, no jet propulsion or downdraft is reported when they hover and no air-disturbance or sound occurs when they move. Terms such as "floated" or "glided" are often used to describe UFO motion.

In the General Theory of Relativity, Dr. Albert Einstein theorized that matter (*i.e.,* mass) is the same in response to gravity or to accelerations. For those with a math background, that means that the small "m" (*i.e.,* mass) is the same in both the gravitational (Force = GmM/r2) and inertial (Force = ma) equations. This implies that if a method should be developed to cancel out gravity, it would also abolish inertia. Accordingly, a hovering UFO that neutralizes gravity would be able to accelerate without the restraint of inertia. According to P. Hill, UFOs may employ "acceleration-type (*i.e.* gravity-like) force fields for propulsion and airflow-control (*i.e.,* shockwave suppression and drag reduction)" which neutralize inertia. Without inertia the occupants can tolerate the tremendous acceleration from a motionless position.[17c]

Velocity

The UFOs have been tracked on radar traveling at speeds that substantially out-perform current, experimental aircraft. An analysis by R. Hall of over 80 radar cases, from 1941 to 1962, included an incident in 1952 of a UFO tracked by Air Defense Command radar at 4,000 mph.[17d] In a separate incident that year, radars operated by the Air Force tracked UFOs "on the order of 7,500 mph." Other documented cases noted by Hall include objects tracked on radar aboard military planes of up to 9,000 mph at altitudes over 15,000 feet.[17e]

Beams and Running Lights

Many reports of light beams from UFOs have been described as "searchlights" that sweep over an area. At night, a light or series of lights have also been reported to move in various directions and between UFOs. According to P. Hill, many disc-shaped UFOs have light emitted from windows or vents, which are often located around their circumference. The sphere-shaped UFO generally has an "equatorial ring," whereas the cigar-shaped objects may have "brightly lit windows along their length."[17f] Witnesses have also described intermittent flashes like "mirror reflecting sunlight," which may be due to the bright reflection off the UFO from luminous plasma.[17g]

Landing Traces

Many reported UFO landing cases involve an extended landing gear with legs and footpads. Generally, the disc-shaped objects of up to 30 feet in diameter have 3 legs, and the 20 feet egg-shaped UFOs have 4 to 6 legs. Based on a review of P. Hill's research, J. McCampbell concluded that UFOs observed near or on the ground consistently fell into the following categories, sorted by size:[18]

A. The "smaller hemispherical" objects (4-12 feet in diameter) leave behind circular areas which are "depressed, burnt or dehydrated."
B. The "oval/egg-shaped" objects (6-8 feet in diameter) usually land and cause burnt areas, and tree damage.

C. The "typical" UFO (range 10-40 feet) leaves burnt or depressed areas with an "irregular configuration on the ground." The larger discs typically have landing gear composed of "three legs in a triangular pattern."

Structural Details

Most UFOs are described as symmetrical with smooth and featureless surfaces, but sometimes with light emitted through windows. The surface of UFOs, by those who have reportedly touched them, is solid and very smooth. Protrusions like fins and antenna are also occasionally reported. In a few cases, a door has been seen to open in the side where the witness could not detect an outline before it started to move. In a study of fifty cases by R. Hall, the shape of window openings have been reported as "round or rectangular," and the number and location of openings vary considerably among different types of UFOs.[19] Reported features include landing gear, stairways, and antennas, and people who have looked through windows of landed craft described seeing chairs, benches, tables, lights, and control consoles.

UFO Occupants

Two databases contain over 10,000 reported encounters with humanoids, entities, beings, little men, giants, and Men in Black, among others:

1. A catalogue of UFO occupant reports (http://ufologie.patrickgross.org/indexe.htm).
2. The Humanoid Sighting Reports & Journal of Humanoid Studies (www.ufoinfo.com/humanoid/).

An article titled, "Physiological Effects,"[20] by J. McCampbell, also include reported sightings of humanoid beings in and near UFOs, and incidents involving communication with the beings, interpreted as messages of peace, and warnings about nuclear weapons.

There are many variations of humanoid-like descriptions with the general characteristics being wide, slanting eyes, peculiar-shaped ears, long or absent nose, and a horizontal, small opening for a mouth. If such descriptions are valid, it would be difficult to believe these beings are from Earth, unless from Earth in our future.

Based on anecdotal evidence, there appears to be two distinct races inhabiting UFOs: the dwarves (over 100 cases: average estimated height = 3.5 feet) and normal humans that are sometimes up to 8 feet tall. The majority are about 3.5 feet, followed by those 5-6 feet, with a few up to 8-9 feet tall. In McCampbell's article,[20a] the physical features in 23 reported cases describe a being of very short stature, with abnormally large, bald heads, having two large, round, bulging eyes that are wide apart. The eyes are usually solid black, with no pupils. Other features include a protruding forehead, wrinkled skin, absent nose except for nostrils, a horizontal slit for a mouth, large pointed ears, and long arms and fingernails. McCampbell also mentioned reports of over 85 cases of "human"-appearing beings described as a white, Caucasian race having variable skin tone, with heights similar to humans and shoulder-length blonde hair, oriental-shaped eyes and human-like noses and ears.[20b] Much less frequently, witnesses report the appearance of hairy animals with claws and large yellow eyes. Some witness reports include beings with long fingers and arms extending below their knees and, in a few cases, claws or strange tool-like instruments have been observed instead of hands. Their skin has been described in varying ways. For example, "Grays" have smooth, pale, hairless, skin, while some have wrinkled, scaly, reptilian, or hairy skin. When the speech of the beings was heard, it was impossible to understand their language. The "dwarves" seem to carry on normal conversations among themselves and sometimes talk to the witnesses in an unintelligible language perceived as high-pitch guttural sounds. The normal human types are believed to manifest greater language ability than the dwarves.[20c]

The UFO occupants, as described by witnesses over the past fifty years, display a great diversity of shape, size, skin color, and other features. Patrick Huyghe, editor of *The Anomalist* (www.anomalist.com), wrote:

> Through the years there have been aliens of all colors: black, white, red, orange, yellow, blue, violet, and of course, gray and green. They can be minuscule, just a few inches tall, or tower above the witnesses, standing 10 feet tall or more. They range from small hairy dwarfs to bald giants. Some look nearly human, others comically alien. A few are living manifestations of a nightmare. While they often look like flesh-and-blood or metallic beings, many can perform ghostlike feats such as walking through walls. They display various eccentricities in their dress, behavior, and speech content. Some act like saints, others like demons. And when it comes to telling fibs, it has been noted, no politician on Earth could do better.[21]

In 1968, NICAP investigated several reports of UFO occupant encounters. All reports involved observations of small humanoid like beings (3-4 feet tall), with two arms and legs, dressed with an outer suit and gear. Many reports also described "two-occupant" craft, addressed in a book by Richard Hall, *The UFO Evidence, Volume II: A Thirty-Year Report*, (2001).[22] Interestingly, before 1987, when Whitley Strieber's book *Communion*, and Budd Hopkins's book *Intruders*, were published in England, a relative small percentage of UFO occupants reported in Britain's abduction cases were of the non-"Gray" type. Following the publication of these books, over half of the cases reported included descriptions of the "Gray" humanoid type.

A 6-Layer Model for Anomalous Phenomena

One approach to understanding the behavior of UFOs is to analyze the patterns of case reports that characterize UFO experiences. In a classic paper by Jacques F. Vallée and Eric W. Davis titled "Incommensurability, Orthodoxy and the Physics of High Strangeness: A 6-layer Model for Anomalous Phenomena," the authors attempted to explain the UFO phenomenon using six lines of evidence incurred from anomalous events. This model implies that if the NHI behind incidents of "high strangeness" has a different evolutionary path and living environment than us, they may have a technology and biology consistent with their unique physical laws, and an understanding of science that is fundamentally different from ours. According to the authors, "current hypotheses are not strange enough to explain the facts of the phenomenon, and the debate suffers from a lack of scientific information."[23]

A highlighted summary of the Vallée and Davis categorization scheme is presented below:

1. **Layer 1:** "occupies a position in space; moves as time passes; interacts with the environment through thermal effects; exhibits light absorption and emission from which power output estimates can be derived; produces turbulence; when landed, leaves indentations and burns from which mass and energy figures can be derived, leaves material residue consistent with Earth chemistry; and gives rise to electric, magnetic, and gravitational disturbances."
2. **Layer II:** "Anti-physical." Similar to Layer 1, but they "conflict" with physical laws (*e.g.,* "sink into the ground, shrink in size, grow larger, or change shape; become fuzzy and transparent, and divide into two or more objects," etc.).
3. **Layer III:** Psychology—Witnesses "tend to see UFOs while in their normal environment and in normal social groupings," but "they try to explain them away as common occurrences until faced with the inescapable conclusion that the object is truly unknown."
4. **Layer IV:** Physiological reactions—The phenomenon is reported to cause effects perceived by humans as a variety of "sounds, vibrations, burns, partial paralysis (inability to move muscles), extreme heat or cold sensation, and odors," etc.
5. **Layer V:** Psychic Effects—"Impressions of communication without a direct sensory channel, poltergeist phenomena: motions and sounds without a specific cause, outside the observed presence of a UFO, etc."
6. **Layer VI:** Cultural—"Society's reactions to the reports, the way in which secondary effects (hoaxes, fiction, and science-fiction imagery, scientific theories, cover-up or exposure, media censorship or publicity, sensationalism, etc.) become generated, and the attitude of members of a given culture towards the concepts that UFO observations appear to challenge."

CHAPTER FOUR

UFO Evidence

Overview

Collectively, the evidence presented in this chapter clearly indicates that unidentified anomalies in the skies exist, with several investigations consistent in showing a small percentage to be "unexplainable" UFOs.[1] The UFO phenomenon seems analogous to our understanding of our own physiological marvel, the brain, in which considerably more is unknown, than known, of its complex patterns of behavior. And what little we do know of the phenomenon is still difficult to comprehend and explain. The UFOs have been seen by multiple witnesses to appear and then disappear instantaneously, move at thousands of miles per hour on radar, change shape, induce physiological effects, activate and deactivate nuclear missiles, and leave a depression in the ground. Based on such reports, the extraterrestrial hypothesis (ETH) has been the most popular theory advanced by ufologists to explain the phenomenon.

The UFO phenomenon has sparked tremendous curiosity and confusion among the general public who yearn for an explanation. One major obstacle contributing to our inability to adequately understand the phenomenon is that the vast majority of UFO evidence to analyze is anecdotal in nature and usually unconfirmed by supporting scientific analysis and verification of physical evidence such as, radar, photo/video, physiological effects, electromagnetic (EM) effects, and landing traces. For example, one is challenged, as well as disillusioned, by explaining a multiple witness UFO experience similar to the report that follows:

> One observes a very large round physical craft approaching and rotating slowly with white lights along its center. Suddenly, the object stops overhead, divides into several smaller craft, and then instantaneously flies off in different directions at tremendous speeds, without generating a sound.

The UFO Phenomenon: Should I Believe?

For decades, we have debated the meaning of extraordinary anecdotal evidence such as this. That is, is this an illusion, advanced military technology, or a craft governed by non-human intelligence (NHI) from another star system or space-time? Does compelling witness testimony and other forms of UFO evidence, as bizarre as it seems, suggest that the phenomenon is an important concern serious enough to warrant greater consideration by the scientific and political community? I believe so! Rationale to justify heightened concern and an organized effort to rigorously study the UFO phenomenon includes:

1. The similarity of UFO experiences by credible witnesses worldwide.
2. Simultaneous radar and visual sightings.
3. Multiple witness sightings.
4. Declassified government/military UFO documents.
5. Inexplicable aerial maneuvers.
6. Compelling commercial and military pilot testimony of UFO encounters.
7. Reported activation and deactivation of nuclear missiles at missile sites in the U.S. and Russia.

UFOs have been reported for decades and possibly even centuries by thousands of people around the world. The phenomenon has been observed frequently above and beneath lakes and oceans, on land, and in space. But despite the evidence obtained to date, the so-called "smoking gun," which undeniably verifies that some unexplained UFOs are under intelligent control from somewhere other than Earth, remains elusive. The UFO phenomenon also remains vague and confusing since the evidence, in general, has been characterized by:

1. Hoaxes and confabulation.
2. The lack of scientific analysis of evidence by too few qualified scientists.
3. Unsubstantiated extraordinary claims, *e.g.,* UFOs are from another solar system, the government has knowledge of crashed UFOs, and aliens are abducting humans, etc.

Given the context above, this chapter presents UFO evidence compiled and analyzed from several sources, which include:

1. Anecdotal testimony from reported observations and close encounters with UFOs and their occupants.
2. Psychological and physiological effects.
3. Physical evidence.
4. Scientific studies and related government/military investigations and hearings.
5. Testimony from The Disclosure Project, and The Citizens Hearing on Disclosure.
6. UFO incidents and mass sightings.
7. Pilot and astronaut/cosmonaut experiences, among others.

Additional evidence obtained from declassified government and military UFO documents made public in the United States and other countries are addressed in Chapter Eight: Exopolitics.

Supplementary to the study of the UFO phenomena are other unexplained topics and associated evidence that have been linked to UFOs, such as crop circles, alien abductions, star children, and alien implants. These areas are studied as a phenomenon in their own rights, but also serve as supporting evidence for many ufologists who believe they help validate the ETH, extra-dimensional, and/or other hypotheses to explain UFOs. They form an important sector of ufology and are regarded as an alternative, albeit controversial, domain of the discipline. For example, reports of bizarre close encounters with UFO occupants include descriptions of humanoid and non-humanoid alien beings termed the Grays, Nordics, Reptilian, and Giants, which add another layer of mystery to the phenomenon. A rather radical alternative hypothesis further proposes that our planet may be an "extension" of an ET civilization that was "here before humanity" and that humans were genetically engineered by them (Sitchin 1976, et.al., Bramley 1989).If true, it would address several arguments against the ETH:

1. The high frequency of UFO encounters.
2. The long-standing existence of the UFO phenomenon over possibly hundreds or thousands of years.
3. The biological similarities between humans and extraterrestrial beings who are reported to appear humanoid.[2,3]

Many ufologists also claim that some government and/or military officials know the answer to the UFO phenomenon and are purposefully withholding this information from the public. According to Dr. Steven Greer, physician, and founder of the Disclosure Project, a research initiative to fully disclose the facts about UFOs, "the government has several dozen extraterrestrial vehicles and dozens of deceased extraterrestrial life-forms of various races."[4]

It is important to note that the authenticity of the UFO evidence reported in this book is not guaranteed to be valid and should be carefully interpreted within the context of the collective evidence and information sources before reaching a conclusion of the UFO phenomenon. With that in mind...

UFO Investigations

Skeptics tend to argue that all UFO evidence is anecdotal and can be explained as "prosaic natural phenomena," while proponents of the phenomenon counter that evidence exists to support the ETH, and that very little UFO evidence is known by the scientific community. Despite this on-going debate, some declassified government UFO documents have acknowledged the possibility of the physical reality of UFOs, but have not supported the ETH. These same conclusions are consistent with classified studies conducted by Project Condign, and the CIA-sponsored Robertson Panel (discussed in the following section).

The Robertson Panel (1952)

Composed of military personnel and scientists, the Robertson Panel was developed in response to a recommendation from a Central Intelligence Agency (CIA) review of the U.S. Air Force investigation into UFOs. The Panel, who did not believe that the UFO evidence (up until 1953) involved ET intelligence, nor was a threat to national security, recommended UFO cases be classified and kept secret, and influenced government policy of UFOs for many years. The members were especially concerned that the misinterpretation of UFOs for Soviet aircraft might delay an appropriate response in the event of a Soviet attack—a major political and military consideration at that time. The Panel's major conclusions were:

1. That the national security agencies take immediate steps to strip the Unidentified Flying Objects of the special status they have been given and the aura of mystery they have unfortunately acquired.
2. The Air Force should begin a "debunking" effort to reduce "public gullibility" and demystify UFO reports.
3. Ninety percent of UFO sightings could be identified as meteorological, astronomical, or natural phenomena, and that the remaining ten percent of UFO reports could eventually be explained given further study.[5]

Dr. Allen Hynek, astronomer and scientific advisor to several U.S. Air Force UFO investigations, such as Project Blue Book, Grudge, and Sign, and who participated as a member of the Robertson Panel, criticized the Panel report by stating, "the implication in the Panel report was that UFOs were a nonsense matter, to be debunked at all costs. It made the subject of UFOs scientifically unrespectable."[6]

The Condon Report (1968)

This controversial report, which presented findings of the Colorado Project on a scientific study of UFOs, remains the most influential public document regarding the UFO phenomenon. The 1968 University of Colorado report to the Air Force examined the evidence obtained since 1947 and concluded, "no UFO reported, investigated and evaluated by the Air Force was ever an indication of threat to our national security." Physicist, Dr. Peter Sturrock, an emeritus professor of applied physics at Stanford University, disagreed with Condon's conclusion that there was nothing significant about UFOs stating that, "the evidence presented in the report suggested that something was going on that needed study."[7] Several scientists and UFO researchers, such as Dr. James McDonald and Stanton Friedman, among others, also refuted the report's conclusions since "thirty percent of the cases studied" in the report remained "unexplained."[8] In fact, many ufologists believed that the evidence in the report could have supported the opposite conclusion, that UFOs warranted much more scientific study rather than the official conclusion, which recommended no further study. Interestingly, major discrepancies of the report's press release and its actual contents have been revealed. For example, Sturrock stated:

> Condon's summary bears little relation to the work, analyses, and summaries of his own staff. Hence, a minimal criticism that one might make is that the efforts of many individuals found no satisfactory integration. Concerning these strange objects, we do not know where they are, we do not know what they are, and we can only speculate on how they function; but these limitations, severe as they are, by no means deter astronomers and astrophysicists from studying them as intensively as possible. We are not sure whether they are hoaxes, illusions, or real. If real, we do not know whether the reality is of a psychological and sociological nature or one that belongs in the realm of physics. If the phenomenon has physical reality, we do not know whether it can be understood in terms of present-day physics or whether it may present us with an example.[8a]

Astronomer, Dr. Hynek, also criticized the Condon Report for factual errors, noting that although the Condon Report claimed there was no evidence that UFOs represented anything other than "hoaxes and/or misidentifications of known aerial objects," the report could not find "normal" explanations for nearly one-third of the UFO incidents it examined, and had to list them as "unsolved."[9] The report conclusions, endorsed by the National Academy of Scientists, were also criticized by the scientific review of the UFO subcommittee of the American Institute of Aeronautics and Astronautics (AIAA).[9a] Similar to expressed opposition of the Report, the AIAA also disagreed with Condon's conclusion, noting that a large percentage of the cases studied remained unexplained and that scientific benefit might be gained by continued study. The UFO subcommittee generated several interesting conclusions:

1. We find it difficult to ignore the small residue of well-documented but unexplainable cases which form the hard core of the UFO controversy.
2. From a scientific and engineering standpoint, it is unacceptable to simply ignore substantial numbers of unexplained observations and to close the book about them on the basis of premature conclusions.[9b]

Incentive to conduct UFO research on the part of the scientific community may have been impeded for decades, in part, by the following recommendation in the Condon's Report:

> Careful consideration of the record as it is available to us leads us to conclude that further extensive study of UFOs probably cannot be justified in the expectation that science will be advanced thereby... If they (scientists) agree with our conclusions, they will turn their valuable attention and talents elsewhere.[10]

Consequently, the general scientific community considered the phenomenon to be of earthy origin explained by atmospheric phenomenon, hoaxes, psychological factors, and conventional aircraft, and not worthy of investigation.

U.S. House Committee on Science and Astronautics

In 1968, the U.S. Congress held hearings to obtain testimony from several noted scientists to better understand the nature of the UFO phenomenon. Of the six scientists who testified, five believed that UFOs presented a valid scientific anomaly that should be further investigated. The complete testimony may be found at: www.ufoevidence.org/topics/GovernmentStudies.html. Brief statements from several participants are presented below:[11]

> **Dr. J. Allen Hynek, Astronomer:** "The UFO reports which in my opinion have potential scientific value are those reports of aerial phenomena which continue to defy explanation in conventional scientific terms."

> **Dr. Carl Sagan, Astronomer:** "In the search for extraterrestrial life there is a high risk, high possibility, that is the one we are talking about today; namely, UFOs—there is a high risk that they are not of extraterrestrial origin, but if they are, we are sure going to learn a lot."

> **Dr. James Harder, Engineer:** "Over the past 20 years a vast amount of evidence has been accumulating that bears on the existence of UFOs. Most of this is little known to the general public or to most scientists. But on the basis of the data and ordinary rules of evidence, as would be applied in civil or criminal courts, the physical reality of UFOs has been proved beyond a reasonable doubt."

> **Dr. Robert L. Hall, Sociologist:** "My conclusion would be that hysteria and contagion of belief can account for some of the reports, but there is strong evidence that there is some physical phenomena underlying a portion of the reports."

> **Dr. James McDonald, Atmospheric Physicist:** "The possibility that the Earth might be under surveillance by some high civilization in command of a technology far beyond ours must not be overlooked

in weighing the UFO problem. I am one of those who lean strongly towards the extraterrestrial hypothesis. I arrived at that point by a process of elimination of other alternative hypotheses, not by arguments based on what I would call "irrefutable proof."

U.S. Air Force Investigations

Among the three U.S. Air Force projects dealing with UFO investigations (*e.g.*, Project Sign, Project Grudge, and Project Blue Book), 701 of 12,618 (5.5 percent) UFO reports investigated remained unexplained. The Air Force declared that no sighting "...could be considered an extra-terrestrial vehicle [and] throughout Project Blue Book there was never a shred of evidence to indicate a threat to our national security." An overview of the recommendations made by these investigations are discussed below:[12]

Project Blue Book (PBB): Conducted by the U.S. Air Force from 1947 to 1969, PBB compiled and analyzed over 12,000 UFO reports and concluded most were natural phenomena or aircraft with a small percentage (~5 percent) classified as "unexplained." More specifically, PBB concluded that UFOs were produced by:

1. A form of mass hysteria.
2. Individuals who fabricate reports as a hoax or for publicity.
3. "Psychopathological" individuals.
4. Misidentification of conventional objects.

These conclusions, however, were contradicted by the results and conclusions presented in Blue Book "Special Report #14."[13] This report, prepared from the analysis of UFO cases from 1947-1952 by a private scientific research organization (Battelle Institute), included 3,201 reported UFO sightings that were analyzed by several scientists who categorized the reports into "knowns," "unknowns," and "insufficient information." The "unknown" group was defined as: "Those reports of sightings wherein the description of the object and its maneuvers could not be fitted to the pattern of any known object or phenomenon." The results revealed that 69 percent were identified, 22 percent unidentified, and 9 percent had insufficient information to make a determination.

In a similar study of 1,307 UFO reports, Air Force astronomer Allan Hendry categorized 89 percent as "identified" with only 9 percent as "unknowns" or UFOs.[14] Both PBB and Hendry found that three types of objects, such as astronomical, aircraft, or balloons, accounted for the vast majority of identifiable UFO reports in the two studies. Interestingly, in the PBB study, the higher the quality of the case, the more likely it was classified as unknown. For example, 35 percent of the excellent cases were deemed "unknowns," as opposed to only 18 percent of the poorest cases.

The PBB concluded that the unidentified evidence did not represent "technological developments or principles beyond the range of modern scientific knowledge" or extraterrestrial vehicles. However, the report did not conclusively disprove that NHI is visiting earth, only that the evidence contributed nothing to science. Dr. Hynek, who served as a scientific advisor to PBB, expressed his disagreements with the conclusion and considered the research effort as a:

> cover-up to the extent that the assigned problem was glossed over for one reason or another. In my many years associated with Blue Book, I do not recall ever one serious discussion of methodology, of improving the process of data gathering or of techniques of comprehensive interrogation of witnesses.[15]

It is generally agreed that the Air Force used PBB as a cover to direct public attention, for reasons not clearly known, away from the sensitive UFO subject. In his book *The UFO Experience: A Scientific Inquiry*, Hynek wrote: "The entire Blue Book operation was a foul-up based on the categorical premise that the incredible things reported could not possibly have any basis in fact."[15a]

Project Sign: In 1947, when Air Intelligence demanded a report from Air Materiel Command regarding the "flying disks," Lieutenant General Nathan F. Twining, the Commander of the Air Materiel Command at Wright Field, sent a memorandum to Brig. General George Schulgen, Chief of the Air Intelligence Requirements Division. He wrote:

> The reported operating characteristics such as extreme rates of climb, maneuverability, and actions which must be considered evasive when sighted or contacted by friendly aircraft and radar, lend belief to the possibility that some of the objects are controlled either manually, automatically, or remotely.[16]

Based on this conclusion, among others, Twining requested that a directive be issued assigning a permanent project to study the UFO phenomenon that established Project Sign to, "... collect, collate, evaluate and distribute to interested government agencies and contractors all information concerning sightings and phenomena in the atmosphere which can be construed to be of concern to the national security."[16a]

In 1948, Project Sign studied UFO reports at Wright-Patterson AFB and concluded that there was a possibility that some UFOs were not from Earth. Following this conclusion, a Top Secret Estimate of the Situation prepared by the U.S. Air Force's Air Technical Intelligence Center concluded that UFOs were "interplanetary spacecraft." The potential implications of this conclusion concerned military officials, who decided to reject the conclusions of the report.

This campaign, led by Chief of Staff, General Hoyt Vandenberg, stated that this conclusion was "bereft of any firm evidence to support such beliefs."[17] Although rejected, it demonstrates that those who investigated numerous UFO sightings had reached a significant conclusion about their nature.

By the end of 1948, Project Sign reviewed several hundred UFO reports, of which almost 40 were considered to be "unknown." Project Sign, which supported the ETH, terminated in December 1948, which then led Brigadier General Donald Putt to initiate the UFO debunking Project Grudge in 1949.

Project Grudge: Declassified on July 23, 1997, Project Grudge was designed as a secret Technical Report by the Air Materiel Command at Wright Patterson AFB. It contained a large number of UFO sightings along with investigation analysis, conclusions, and supplementary reports, but served primarily as a foundation of UFO sightings by credible military witnesses. The Project concluded:

> Upon eliminating several additional incidents due to vagueness and duplication, there remain 228 incidents, which are considered in this report. Thirty of these could not be explained, because there was found to be insufficient evidence on which to base a conclusion.[18]

Sturrock Panel (1998): Dr. Peter Sturrock directed and authored a scientific study of UFOs that was published in the *Journal of Scientific Exploration* titled, "Physical Evidence Related to UFO Reports."[19] This report presented findings from the proceedings of a scientific review panel on their evaluation of UFO evidence, which included radar, photographic, vehicle interference, ground traces, physiological effects on witnesses, and analysis of debris. The panel, not convinced the evidence revealed unknown physical processes or indicated involvement of an ET intelligence, recommended that new data, "scientifically acquired and analyzed (especially of well-documented, recurrent events), could yield useful information." The panel also acknowledged that the UFO problem is, "not a simple one, and it is unlikely that there is any simple universal answer." One example cited involved an aircraft above Paris in 1994. The crew reported "a gigantic disk," more than 3,000 feet in diameter, confirmed on military radar, that slowed "abruptly from 110 knots to zero and disappeared." Other unexplained incidents included sightings of strange lights associated with measured magnetic disturbances, and damage to vegetation and other ground traces from reported UFO landing sites.

COMETA (Committee for in-depth studies): A French government agency composed of officials, scientists, and engineers developed a report in 1999 based on a three-year study of approximately 500 UFO sightings, radar/visual cases, and pilot reports. The report emphasized that the "accumulation of well-documented observations of UFOs compels us to consider all hypotheses as to the origin of UFOs, but especially the extraterrestrial hypothesis." In its conclusion, the COMETA Report titled, "UFOs and Defense: What Should

We Prepare For?" claimed that "numerous manifestations observed by reliable witnesses could be the work of craft of extraterrestrial origin," and although not proven, "strong presumptions exist in its favor." The report also concluded that about "five percent of sightings on which there is solid documentation seem "to be completely unknown flying machines with exceptional performances that are guided by a natural or artificial intelligence."[20] Retired Major General Denis Letty, who organized the investigation which led to the COMETA, wrote:

> All the testimony we retained for the COMTA Report is supported by tangible pieces of evidence: radar echoes, tracks on the ground, photographs, electromagnetic phenomena, and even the modification of the process of photosynthesis in plants. It became clear that five percent of sightings for which there is solid documentation cannot be attributed to man-made or natural sources... I was astonished to discover, and now know for certain, that silent and completely unknown objects sometimes penetrate our airspace with flying capabilities that are impossible to replicate on Earth. The COMETA Report shows, that the extraterrestrial hypothesis is the most rationale explanation, although of course it has not been proven.[20a]

General Letty said he voiced support for an international investigation of UFOs and vowed to continue his efforts, especially in light of the O'Hare Airport sighting in Chicago (2006) and Guernsey (2007), to "facilitate greater understanding leading to a unified international effort that will determine the true nature and origin of UFOs."[20b]

The Rare Aerospace Phenomena Study Department (SEPRA), based at France's national scientific research agency, developed a method to catalogue a database of over 2,000 UFO cases, which included 6,000 eyewitness accounts and approximately 100 sightings from aircraft. Based on the analysis of physical and biological evidence classified as cases in which "the witness testimony is consistent and accurate but cannot be interpreted in terms of conventional phenomena," the SERPA concluded:

> There generally can be said to be a material phenomenon behind the observations. In sixty percent of the cases reported here, the description of this phenomenon is apparently one of a flying machine whose origin, modes of lifting and/or propulsion are totally outside our knowledge. Thus the conclusion is that among the investigated UFO cases, enough cases have been found in which there is strong evidence that UFOs are governed by intelligence with performances far beyond anything conceivable in the current state of human aeronautic technologies.[20c]

Jean-Jacques Velasco, after many years of studying the phenomenon as head of the French government's UFO agency for over 20 years, is convinced that the phenomenon is related to an intelligence not of Earth. In a chapter titled, "France and the UFO Question," he wrote:

> We have reached a certain level of knowledge about UFOs. They seem to be artificial and controlled objects whose physical characteristics can be measured by our detection systems, radar in particular. They fall under a physics which is far superior and more evolved than the one we have in our most technologically advanced countries, highlighted by the stationary and silent flights, the accelerations and speeds defying the laws of inertia, the effects on the electronic navigation or transmission systems of aircraft, and the electrical blackouts.[20d]

The Condign Report (1996 to 2000): The British Ministry of Defense (MoD) completed a four-year study on Unidentified Aerial Phenomena (UAP) that analyzed data compiled from reports of UAPs received by the MoD.

The report concluded that "UAPs exist but they are not space ships. They are natural, atmospheric and other phenomena, some of which are not fully understood."[21a] Perceived as a "solid craft" by many witnesses, the report emphasized that plasma, created by burning meteors, was the likely explanation. The report stated: "The conditions and method of formation of the electrically-charged plasmas and the scientific rationale for sustaining them for significant periods is incomplete and not fully understood."[21b] Having reviewed over 100 UFO reports over a 30 year period, the author of the report wrote: "The possibility exists that a fatal accident might have occurred in the past as a result of aircrew taking sudden evasive action to avoid a UFO when flying fast and low."

The Condign report has been criticized for insufficient scientific methodology employed by its apparent lack of direct in-depth investigations of reported sightings and total reliance on the analysis of their UAP database.

Official Testimony

The more recent exopolitical movement within ufology, as evidenced by the Disclosure Project (www.disclosureproject.org), pioneered by Dr. Steven Greer, and the Citizen Hearing on Disclosure (www.citizenhearing.org), led by Stephen Bassett, has served to facilitate the end of alleged UFO secrecy through the disclosure of UFOs and ET intelligence visiting Earth by the government and military. To date, over 500 individuals from the government, military, and intelligence community have reported their "experience with UFOs, extraterrestrials (ET), ET technology, and the cover-up that keeps this information secret."[22] Testimony provided by those engaged in UFO research, those who had direct UFO encounters, and by those involved with government or military related UFO incidents, lend support to the possibility that UFOs are intelligently controlled physical objects. The continued attempts to uncover information believed to be classified in this fashion have helped both members of our political system and the general public to better understand the relative importance of the UFO phenomenon, but have not influenced those "in the know" to disclose "what they know" (if they know) about UFOs to the public.

Steven Greer's book titled *Disclosure: Military and Government Witnesses Reveal the Greatest Secrets in Modern History*[23] provides a comprehensive review of the testimony presented at the 2001 Project Disclosure meeting at the National Press Club in Washington, D.C. and may be viewed at: www.youtube.com/watch?v=BtmpaMoPqyI, and at: www.youtube.com/watch?v=lkswXVmG4xM. Some of the uniquely compelling testimony from pilots, and military and government officials provided at the National Press Club in 2010 and 2001 are presented as follows:

> **Steven Greer**, during his opening statements at the 2001 press club, stated that UFOs are "structured craft often traveling at thousands of miles per hour," that "suddenly stop, hover or move in a nonlinear fashion. These are solid objects. They are metallic and they give strong and unambiguous radar returns."[23a]

> **Dr. Claude Poher**, a retired astrophysicist and space research engineer from the National Center for Space Studies in France, who founded the Group for the Study of Unidentified Aerospace Phenomena (GEPAN) in France, added, "the official conclusion of GEPAN in 1979, was that about fifteen percent of cases remained unidentified after careful analysis by our experts. We concluded that the objects, in most of these cases, were compatible with flying machines whose flight physics were foreign to the expert's knowledge."[24]

In one of the most well-documented military encounters with anomalous phenomena in history, **Parviz Jafari**, a retired General of the Iranian Air Force provided the following account of a UFO encounter while piloting a F-4 jet to investigate a sighting in Tehran, Iran in 1976:

> I approached the object, which was flashing with intense red, green, orange and blue light so bright that I was not able to see its body, and four other objects with different shapes separated from the main one at different times during this close encounter. Whenever they were close to me, my weapons were jammed and my radio communications were garbled. One of the objects headed toward me. I thought it was a missile. I tried to launch a heat seeking missile to it, but my missile panel went out. Another followed me when I was descending on the way back. One of the separated objects landed in an open area radiating a high bright light, in which the sands on the ground were visible.[25]

According to Air Force Major Colonel Roland Evans, this case met several criteria to help validate the UFO encounter:

1. Observed by several witnesses from different locations and viewpoints (*i.e.,* airborne and from the ground) and confirmed by radar.
2. High witness credibility (*e.g.,* aircrew, air traffic controllers, and an Air Force General).
3. Electromagnetic effects were reported by several planes during the encounter.
4. Witnesses reported very similar accounts of extraordinary maneuverability by the UFOs.
5. Crew members experienced physiological effects (loss of night vision due to brightness of UFO).[25a]

It was obvious the government considered this case of high interest, since the Evans memo stated that Jafari's account was "confirmed by other sources." Jafari mentioned that the Shah of Iran invited him to discuss the incident and, when the shah asked him, "What do you think about it?" he replied, "in my opinion they cannot be from our planet." Jafari is convinced that what he experienced was not of this world. For example, while looking at it 70 miles out, he said it "jumped all of a sudden 10 degrees to my right. This 10 degrees represented about 6.7 miles per moment, and I don't say second because it was much less than a second. Also, it was able to shut down my missile and instruments somehow." Jafari's account of the incident can be found in a Chapter he wrote titled, "Dogfight over Tehran," in Leslie Kane's book, *UFOs: Generals, Pilots, and Government Officials Go on the Record.*[26a]

In 2000, **Captain Rodrigo Bravo Garrido**, who worked as a UFO researcher for the Aviation Branch of the Army of Chile wrote:

> The crew of a Chilean plane observed a long cigar-shaped brilliant gray object. It flew parallel to the right side of the aircraft for two minutes and then disappeared at a very high speed. This object was detected by the radar of the Control Center of Santiago which notified the crew minutes before the incident.[26b]

Additional details can be found in his book, *Ufología Aeronáutica,* and in the Chapter he co-authored titled, "Chile: Aeronautics Cases and the Official Response," in Kane's book.[26c]

Ray Bowyer, a civilian airline Captain, described several "multiple unidentified objects" over the English Channel in April 2009:

> On nearing the object a second identical shape appeared beyond the first. Both objects were of a flattened disk shape with a dark area to the right side. They were brilliant yellow with light emanating from

> them. I estimated them to be up to a mile across. I found myself astounded but curious. But at 12 miles distant these objects were becoming uncomfortably large, and I was glad to descend and land the aircraft. Many of my passengers saw the objects as did the pilot of another aircraft 25 miles further south.[27]

Mr. Enrique Kolbeck, a senior Air Traffic Controller at Mexico City International Airport discussed incidents about frequent UFO sightings seen at the airport visually and on radar and stated: "They are clocked at tremendous speeds and making almost instantaneous hairpin turns."[28] Of the 140 air traffic controllers at the airport, he estimated that over 50 have seen this phenomenon. During one sighting, "32 controllers visually saw the same red and white lights simultaneously moving around a conventional landing aircraft."

Mr. Franklin Carter, an electronic radar technician in the Navy in the 1950s and 1960s discussed an incident where he witnessed a "clear, unambiguous radar contact traveling at 3,400 mph." He added that, in one case, an Air Force operator "tracked one of these UFOs 300 to 400 miles out in space," and, "when these reports repeatedly kept coming into General Electric, who manufactured the radar, their technicians came in and modified the electronics so that the radar would limit its reporting to 12 to 15 miles out into space."[28a]

Nick Pope, formerly with the British MoD, emphasized that "since 1950 the British Government has received over 10,000 UFO reports," of which "around 5 percent of cases no explanation could be found." These cases included:

> incidents where reliable witnesses such as police officers and pilots reported structured craft performing speeds and maneuvers significantly in excess of anything they had seen military jet aircraft perform. Other cases included in this category involved UFOs tracked on radar and incidents where photos or videos were produced and where the MoD's technical experts found no evidence of fakery.[28b]

Pope also described an incident he investigated in March 1993, where a UFO was seen by about 60 witnesses, including military personnel at two air force bases. One witness described a triangular-shaped craft midway in size between a C-I 30 and a Boeing 747. He said it emitted a low-frequency humming sound and that it moved slowly at first, before accelerating away many times faster than a military jet.[28c]

Dr. R. Haines, a NASA research scientist who worked on the Gemini, Apollo, and Skylab programs, compiled over 3,000 cases of unusual visual and radar sightings of unexplained aerial phenomena over the past 30 years. One interesting incident involved a B-52 captain who stated: "a round sphere, probably four or five feet in diameter with no markings, no rivets, no seams, no insignias, and no USAF on the side,"[29] appeared on his wing tip. According to Haines, his co-pilot said: "Captain, we have an object off our right wing tip," which he described as being identical to this one on the left wing." As part of his interview with the Captain, Haines stated:

> So there are two objects now keeping up with the aircraft at cruise altitude and cruise speed. Well, to make a long story short, he told me that an object showed up behind the aircraft, above the aircraft, below the aircraft and off each wing tip, five total. And, I said, "well, what did you do?" He said, "well, I hit the autopilot button on the control column and went into evasive maneuvers, which is kind of standard operating procedure, to try to shake these things." "Well," he said, "no matter what he did with that aircraft, they stayed with the aircraft, perfectly aligned." So he said, "after a while of this, we are running out of fuel and I have a job to do." So he added power, got back up to cruise altitude, and put her back on autopilot. After 15 or so minutes more the objects departed from the aircraft in the exact opposite order they arrived. To me that's not random. That is intelligence. That is deliberate.[29a]

R. Haines also contends that in the 1960s:

> The Air Force was still heavily involved in this subject, where they stepped in and interrogated commercial pilots. Not just their own military pilots, but also commercial pilots. The Air Force ended the interview by saying you are not to tell anybody about what you saw.[29b]

In a remarkable account of a UFO incident on the USS *John F. Kennedy* in the summer of 1971, U.S. Navy, National Security Agency, **James Kopf** reported:

> We observed a large, glowing sphere over the ship. It looked huge. I would say it was anywhere from three or four hundred feet to a quarter of a mile depending on how high it was. A few days later, the Commanding Officer looked at the camera—and I will never forget this—and he said, "I would like to remind the crew that certain events that take place on board a major combat vessel are considered classified and should not be discussed with anyone without a need to know."[30]

Lord Hill-Norton, a five-star Admiral and the former Head of the British MoD, stated:

> ... There is a serious possibility that we are being visited — and have been visited for many years—by people from outer space, from other civilizations; that it behooves us to find out who they are, where they come from, and what they want. This should be the subject of rigorous scientific investigation, and not the subject of rubbishing by tabloid newspapers.[30a]

A former Air France captain, **Jean-Charles Duboc**, said that in 1994 he and his crew saw "a huge flying disc" near Paris that "became transparent and disappeared in about 10 to 20 seconds." Air traffic control recorded the object at the location and time of the sighting by the crew, which also disappeared from radar and view at the same time. He stated:

> We observed it over one minute on the left on our plane, surprisingly totally stationary in the sky, and it disappeared progressively. This large object was below us at the altitude of 35, 000 ft (we were at 39, 000 ft), at a distance of about 25 nautical miles. The apparent diameter of this object could be compared to the diameter of the moon, or the sun. That means that it was about 1000 feet wide. We had no idea of the structure of the UFO that seemed to be embedded in a kind of magnetic or gravitational field, with no lights or visual metallic structure, which gave it a really fuzzy appearance.[31]

On April 11, 1980, **Oscar Alfonso Santa Maria Huertas**, a retired pilot of the Peruvian Air Force, recounted his experience while piloting a jet with orders to shoot down a UFO. In brief, he wrote:

> I approached the object and strafed sixty-four 30mm shells at it. Some projectiles went towards the ground, and others hit the object fully, but they had no effect at all. The projectiles didn't bounce off; probably they were absorbed. The cone-shaped wall of fire that I sent out would normally obliterate anything in its path. The object then began to ascend, and move farther away from the base. When I was at about 36,000 feet, it made a sudden stop, forcing me to veer to the side since I was only 1500 feet away. I flew up higher to attack it from above, but just as I had locked on to the target and was ready to shoot, the object made a straight vertical climb evading the attack.[32]

When positioned a few hundred feet from the object, he further stated:

> I was startled to see an object 35 feet in diameter with a shiny dome on the top that was cream-colored. The bottom was a wider circular base, a silver color, and looked like some kind of metal. It lacked all typical components of aircraft. It had no wings, propulsion system,

> exhausts, windows, antennae, and so forth. It had no visible propulsion system.[32a]

Upon landing, a briefing was held, when he was informed the object did not register on radar, even though the operators observed the object, while stationary, in the sky. The pilot added that he was not interviewed by any U.S. official, but a document from the U.S. Department of Defense dated June 3, 1980 ("UFO Sighted in Peru") described the event, stating the "object is of unknown origin," since the object "performed maneuvers that defied the laws of aerodynamics."

Additional details of his experience can be found in a chapter, titled "Close Combat with a UFO," in Leslie Kean's book.[33]

Former **Air Force Lt. Col. Richard French**, an investigator of PBB, testified at the Citizen Hearing On Disclosure in Washington, D.C., in 2013, to six ex-Congress members regarding a UFO incident that he was ordered to investigate. His account described a large crowd looking down in the water observing two round craft approximately 20 feet in diameter and 3 feet in height, less than 20 feet from the shore off the coast of St. John. French said the "craft were a few feet apart floating below the surface of the water, with two alien beings (2-3 feet tall, very thin, light grey with long arms and two or three fingers) by the ships." He further recalled how the ships started to rise out of the water, accelerate at "approximately 2,500 to 3,000 miles per hour," and then disappear. However, the two craft returned after approximately 20 minutes, stopped before they submerged into the water again as the "two beings worked on the crafts," and then departed together at very high speed.[34]

At this same Hearing, an extraordinary line of testimony by **James Penniston**, a retired US Air Force pilot, described seeing and touching a UFO while stationed at an air base in Woodbridge, England in 1980.[34a] Penniston described an "inexplicable triangular craft" in a clearing in the woods with "blue and yellow lights swirling around the exterior" that was "warm to the touch and felt like metal." He said, one side of the craft had pictorial symbols and "the largest symbol was a triangle, which was centered in the middle of the others." Further, he explained that, "after 45 minutes the light from the object began to intensify and then shot off at an unbelievable speed before 80 Air Force personnel." Additional information of this incident is presented later in this chapter (Rendlesham Forest, Suffolk, England 1980) and Chapter Eight: Exopolitcs (The 1981 Halt Memo).

Commenting on two most influential witness testimonies at the Citizen Hearing On Disclosure in May 2013, Nick Pope, of the "UFO Desk" at the UK MoD, in an article titled, "Citizen Hearing on Disclosure Review," wrote:

> The most poignant moment was when Geoffrey Torres told the Committee about his father's terrifying encounter with a UFO. Milton Torres (now very ill and unable to attend in person) was a USAF

> fighter pilot on exchange with the UK's Royal Air Force back in the Fifties. One day he was scrambled in response to a UFO being tracked on military radar. To his amazement, he was ordered to shoot it down. He achieved a lock-on, but before he could fire his air-to-air rockets, the UFO moved from a virtual hover and accelerated away at Mach 10. His fighter jet's radar had indicated the UFO was the size of an aircraft carrier. Torres was debriefed and told that if he discussed the incident with anyone, he'd never fly again. He only spoke publicly about the incident decades later, in 2009. But to his eternal regret, Milton's father had died before this happened and he was never able to tell him. "My Dad's lost his voice now," Geoffrey said, his voice shaking with emotion, "but I've found mine." His heartfelt plea that secrecy on UFOs should end was a powerful reminder that whatever one believes about the true nature of the phenomenon, there's a human cost here.[35]

At this Hearing, video testimony by an anonymous alleged former CIA official, dying from kidney failure, who claims to have worked on the U.S. Air Force's PBB, disclosed "secret" information to UFO author **Richard Dolan**: "Anonymous" said he and his superior were:

1. Granted access to Area 51 to obtain information for President Eisenhower where he saw several alien spacecraft, including the craft that crashed in Roswell, New Mexico.
2. Taken to the another facility near Area 51 where they observed live extraterrestrials.[36] The video of this interview can be seen at: www.openminds.tv/deathbed-testimony-about-ufos-given-by-former-cia-official-video-1002/20644.

Other Testimony and Evidence

An excellent source for UFO reports and incidents may be found at the NUFORC "Case Briefs and Past Highlights" under the direction of Peter B. Davenport. Several especially interesting cases summarized from this database are presented as follows.[37]

Dr. Paul Czysz, a Professor of Aeronautical Engineering at Parks College in St. Louis, who worked at the Air Force at Wright-Patterson Air Force Base, and for McDonnell-Douglas in the field of exotic technologies recalled an incident while at Wright-Patterson:

> We had the flying saucers that covered the distance from Columbus to Detroit in something like the equivalent of about 20,000 miles an hour. Back then, I don't think anyone in the ordinary aerospace business would have had any knowledge of quantum physics or

wormholes or the types of things we know now. But, if you went to the European Organization for Nuclear Research known as CERN now and talked to the particle physicists, they would tell you certainly, some of this was possible, because they see it all the time.

Mr. Bentley, a nuclear engineer, who worked on classified projects with Government agencies, including NASA, witnessed a UFO crash at a Nike Ajax Missile Facility in Maryland and viewed UFOs on radar take off at 17,000 mph after hovering on the ground. His incredible account is as follows:

> In 1957 to 1959, I was outside of Olney, Maryland, just north of Washington, D.C. at a Nike Ajax Missile Facility. I was a radar operator. In May of 1958, at about 6:00 a.m. I first heard a sound that sounded like a pulsating transformer. I looked out the window and looked across the field and saw this [disc-shaped] object heading toward the ground and saw it crash. It broke apart and then it took off again in flight... The largest piece was actually glowing white hot and was probably the size of a washing machine...When the craft took off again after it crashed, it went through a grove of trees and actually sheered three, four or five inch limbs, in just one fell swoop, like a knife or a machete...The real exciting part happened the next evening while I was on duty. It was approximately 10:00 or 11:00 at night and I got a call from the Gaithersburg facility saying that they had twelve to fifteen UFOs, 50-100 feet off the ground. I had the radar on, the M-33 sweep radar, and right next to the ground clutter where Gaithersburg sits, we found the blip where these vehicles were. Then all of a sudden they all took off at the same time. From my radarscope, it went in one sweep. It is a thirty-three and a third RPM. To go that distance from the center out to where I got the next blip in the first sweep, at a constant velocity would have to be 17,000 miles an hour which we calculated from our analog computer...

Bentley also reported on a conversation he alleged to have overheard between Houston Control and astronauts in space about avoiding a collision with a UFO, and our astronauts communicating about seeing living beings moving about through portals on the UFO in 1968:

> On their trip to the moon itself I heard them say they had a bogey (term used for unknown target, and often specifically used to denote a UFO) coming in at 11:00. The astronauts asked for permission to do avoidance for a collision and Houston finally granted that permission to do that. Later the astronauts said, "It is not necessary. They are now paralleling our course" and there was a discussion as to what was paralleling that course. It was another type of ship. There were

> portals there that they could see in. They could see beings of some sort. They did not describe these beings. They just took photographs. And after a while, a few thousand miles, they [the bogey] took off from the capsule that they were flying in and went away. They just said it was a saucer-shaped craft. It was actually paralleling their craft. They saw movement. They saw something or somebody moving inside that ship. This happened before the lunar landing.... Then they said, "There they go." And they [the bogey] went out of sight almost immediately. This event was unedited because of where I was [a secret listening post]. It was an extremely restricted channel... There was only one gentleman there with me when this happened. He said something like, "You didn't hear anything."[38]

A must read paper by UFO researcher **J. Vallée** and astronomer and astrophysicist **Dr. Claude Poher** titled, "Basic Patterns in UFO Observations" concluded:

1. A significant proportion of the thousands of UFO reports analyzed by the authors come from witnesses who have really observed an object in the sky or at ground level.
2. The objects these witnesses have seen have characteristics very different from all identifiable objects and phenomena.[39]

More specifically, of the 878 incidents of close encounter reports in this article, in which the number of witnesses in the group is given, slightly less than half (44 percent) of the cases involved more than one witness at the time of the sighting. An analysis of the data revealed this proportion to be reasonably stable over different time periods:

Before 1947 (64 percent).
1947-1953 (40 percent).
1954 (45 percent).
1955-62 (53 percent).
1963-1968 (48 percent).[39a]

At an outdoor movie, an extraordinary multiple-witness UFO sighting was reported to have taken place in Fujian Province, China, in July 1977, in which about 3,000 people observed two bright orange objects pass low overhead as they descended towards them. The objects then ascended at a tremendous speed and quickly disappeared. Sadly, the people, who ran away in fear, caused the death of two children from the trampling. The incident was confirmed by a doctor at a local hospital who treated the injured.[40]

A chronological listing of UFO incidents involving physiological effects on human behavior has been compiled from several sources and studies by **John**

Schuessler.[41] An analysis of this database showed that injuries noted in at least eighty percent of the cases were classified by MUFON as Category 1 which represents, "injuries of a temporary nature, dealing with paralysis, dizziness, nausea, vomiting, headache, tingling sensations, electrical shocks, and feeling of heat, temporary blindness, mild burns, perception of odors, and perception of sounds."[41a] Schuessler also conducted an in-depth study of the famous Cash-Landrum case near Dayton, Texas, in December 1980, and wrote about the incident in his book, *The Cash-Landrum UFO Incident*.[42] This case involved three people who reported an encounter with a large, diamond-shaped object. The witnesses reported vomiting, headaches, hair loss, red skin, and blisters over the next few weeks, and one witness was hospitalized and treated for burns.

In Brazil, reports of rectangular UFOs firing beams at people at night caused serious and fatal injuries. In one reported case, a man was stunned and blinded after being hit by a beam of light and died that day. Many of the injuries were consistent with the effects of high-power pulsed microwaves. Military encounters with UFOs have also been reported to have led to fatalities. For instance, in November 1953, a military jet was scrambled from Kinross Air Force Base in Michigan to chase an unidentified object. The aircraft, which was tracked on radar, merged with the UFO over Lake Superior as both objects then disappeared from the screen. Despite an intensive search, no wreckage or bodies were found. The Air Force suggested that, "the pilot probably suffered from vertigo and crashed into the Lake."[43]

Dr. Paul R. Hill, a well-respected leading research scientist and development engineer and manager for NASA, and the National Advisory Council for Aeronautics, addressed the basic science and technology of the extraordinary performance capabilities of UFOs in his book, *Unconventional Flying Objects: A Scientific Analysis*.[44] Hill, who placed the UFO phenomenon through rigorous scientific scrutiny, concluded that UFOs, "obey, not defy, the laws of physics."[44a]

U.S. and Soviet Space UFO Incidents

Controversial reports of U.S. and Soviet astronaut UFO encounters exist in the literature, some of which include uncorroborated claims. These include:

1. Astronauts Buzz Aldrin and Neil Armstrong, who are alleged to have said "enormous spacecraft are out there" and that "they're on the moon watching us," during their historic Apollo 11 moon landing.
2. "All Apollo and Gemini flights were followed, both at a distance and sometimes closely, by space vehicles of extraterrestrial origin-flying saucers, or UFOs."[45]

Such reports have been denounced by the astronauts and NASA. Probably the most intriguing testimony by an astronaut was provided by Gordon Cooper who flew in both the Project Mercury and Gemini space program missions. In a 1973 interview, Cooper stated:

> I was a witness to an extraordinary phenomenon, here on this planet earth. I saw with my own eyes a defined area of ground being consumed by flames, with four indentations left by a flying object which had descended in the middle of a field. Beings had left the craft (there were other traces to prove this). They seemed to have studied topography, they had collected soil samples and, eventually, they returned to where they had come from, disappearing at enormous speed. At Edwards Air Force Base I was having some of the cameramen film precision landings. A saucer flew right over them, put down three landing gears, and landed out on the dry lakebed. They went out with their cameras towards the UFO. It lifted off and flew off at a very high rate of speed. I had a chance to hold it [the film] up to the window to look at it. Good close-up shots. There was no doubt in my mind that it was made someplace other than on this earth. In my opinion they were worried it would panic the public if they knew that someone had vehicles that had this kind of performance. So they started telling lies about it.[46]

Edgar Mitchell, Ph.D., the sixth man to walk on the moon on the Apollo 14 mission said:

> Yes, there have been ET visitations. There have been crashed craft. There have been material and bodies recovered. There has been a certain amount of reverse engineering that has allowed some of these craft, or some components, to be duplicated. And there is some group of people that may or may not be associated with the government at this point, but certainly were at one time, that have this knowledge. They have been attempting to conceal this knowledge or not permit it to be widely disseminated.... People in high level government have very, very little, if any, valid information about this. Most have no more knowledge than the man in the street.... [As to] the question, "How could it be kept secret?" It hasn't been kept secret. It's been there all along. But it has been the subject of disinformation in order to deflect attention and create confusion so the truth doesn't come out. I believe it is a very important effort that we get Congressional oversight of all this.[46a]

Dr. Garry Henderson, a research scientist for General Dynamics, verified that astronauts were under orders to not discuss their UFO sightings and mentioned that NASA "has many actual photos of these crafts, taken at close range by hand and movie camera."[46b]

Russian cosmonaut Vladimir Kovalyonok, while in space on a Saljut VI Mission, in 1981, reported observing an object that had an elliptical shape that tracked their spaceship.

> It only flew straight, but then a kind of explosion happened. It was very beautiful to watch, like golden light. This was the first part. Then, one or two seconds later, a second explosion followed somewhere else and two spheres appeared, again golden and very beautiful. After this explosion I just saw white smoke, then a cloud-like sphere.[47]

In another incident, Cosmonaut Gennadij Strekhalov, during a MIR mission, in 1990, reported the sudden appearance of a "perfect sphere" that resembled a "Christmas tree decoration." According to Strekhalov, the object was "beautiful, shiny, and glittering," but after ten seconds the sphere disappeared.[47a]

During mission STS-48 of Space Shuttle Discovery, on September 15, 1991, video showed a flash of light and several objects flying in an artificial or controlled manner as the astronauts worked outside the craft. A luminous object, "slowly" moving, changed direction, and accelerated away immediately following a flash of light. As soon as the object left, a streak of light moved through the area where the object had been located. NASA explained the objects as ice particles reacting to engine jets. NASA engineer and UFO skeptic James Oberg, maintained that the illumination conditions and thruster firings likely produced the events. In contrast, Dr. Jack Kasher, a professor of physics and astronomy, who analyzed the movement of the objects, argued against Oberg's explanation. Similarly, Richard Hogaland, author of *Dark Mission: The Secret History of NASA*, wrote: "Oberg's rebuttal relies on false reasoning, misrepresentation of facts and exclusion of contradictory data to build his weak case."[48] Computer scientist Lan Fleming also analyzed the movements of the objects and the flash of light that preceded the abrupt change in the course of the objects and concluded that the exhaust plume from one of the shuttle's reaction control system rockets could not have produced the flash of light. A video[49] of this incident can be found at: www.youtube.com/watch?v=ZNoXnDJKdWo

Physician and retired NASA astronaut Story Musgrave, a crew member aboard the space shuttle STS-80 Mission, commented on an object that suddenly appeared beneath the shuttle:

> I don't know what it is. Whether it's a washer, debris, ice particles, I don't know. But it's characteristic of the thousands of things which I've seen. What is not so characteristic is it appears to [have] come from nowhere. You would think that if it's facing the dark side or facing a side towards you which is not reflecting the sun, you would think that you would see something there. It's really impressive.[50]

Musgrave was adamant that the object appeared to be under intelligent control and that it tracked the shuttle. On a speaking tour, at the end of his lecture, Musgrave showed a slide of a drawing of the characteristic "Grey" alien and stated: "These guys are real, I guarantee it."[50a]

Physical Trace Evidence

Evidence from alleged UFO landing sites has been documented in the form of depressions in the ground, damaged vegetation, altered soil properties, and radioactivity. Tangible objects, although extremely rare in occurrence, have also been reported in the form of magnesium particles. Mentioned previously, the Sturrock Panel felt that existing physical evidence to support the ETH was inconclusive, but considered several unique UFO cases worthy of further scientific study. Among the unexplained physical evidence noted in the report[51] included:

1. Physical effects on witnesses, such as burns, or sensations of heat, and eye problems, possibly due to microwave energy, although "a few cases seem to point toward high doses of ionizing radiation, such as X-rays or gamma rays."
2. Radar detections of UFOs.

Based on the evidence reviewed, the panel of scientists concluded:

1. The UFO problem is not simple and should receive more attention, with an emphasis on physical evidence.
2. Regular contact between UFO investigators and the scientific community would be helpful, as also would institutional support.
3. The possibility of health risks associated with UFO events should not be ignored.[51a]

Ted Phillips, Director of The Center for Physical Trace Research (CPTR), who participated in the Vanguard Satellite Tracking Program and as a field engineer on the Minuteman Missile Project, and who investigated more than 500 UFO cases concluded, "After thirteen years of investigation, the data indicates a non-terrestrial origin."[52] In an article titled, "Ted Phillips' Physical Trace Catalogue," Paul Fuller reproduced cases from Ted Phillips' Physical Trace Catalogue, a few of which are included below:[52a]

> **Case 195p, March 15th, 1965, Fort Myers, Florida.** Jim Flynn, 45, saw a lighted object while hunting (88 feet in diameter, windows 21 inch wide). A humming sound was heard. When Flynn got to within 8 feet of the object, a beam of light was projected towards him which caused unconsciousness for 24 hours. He had lost vision

in the right eye, and saw poorly with the left. Sawgrass was burned in a circle 72 feet in diameter, the ground was turned up, and trees were burned.

Case 152: May 12th, 1962, Argentina, Pampa Province. V. and G. Tomasini and H. Zenobi saw an object on the ground 350 feet away. It looked like a railroad car and was illuminated. As they approached it, the object ascended, crossed low over the road, rose with a flame and separated into two sections that flew away in separate directions. A humming noise was heard. It was seen on the ground for one minute. A circle was burned, insects were carbonized, and the ground was petrified.

Case 134s: October 1959, Sweden, Mariannelund. The electrical power in the three witnesses' houses failed; when they ran outside they saw a blinding white light as a UFO stopped and hovered. The oval object, about 12 feet long and 8 feet high, slowly descended and turned to the right, hitting and smashing a portion of a maple tree. It then descended towards the ground. The witness, located 10 feet from the UFO, looked through a large window and saw two small occupants, with large eyes and the heads were high-crowned. It was found that a gray-white substance covered power lines.

Case 521: July 22nd, 1955. Cincinnati, Ohio. Mr. E.M., while mowing his lawn, kneeled down near a peach tree, when suddenly "a peculiar liquid substance dark red in color began pelting me and the tree." He looked up and saw a pear-shaped object about 1,000 feet high moving slowly. As he watched, his hands and arms began to burn. When he examined the peach tree the next day, he found that most of the leaves had turned brown and fallen, the twigs and limbs were brittle, the peaches seemed "petrified" and the trunk had turned so hard that a nail could be driven in only with great difficulty. The grass below the tree had also died.

Approximately twenty percent of the 4,000 cases in Phillips' Physical Trace Database include reports of humanoid beings as part of the witnesses' UFO encounters. Fuller concluded: "How much weight can we place on such accounts? Are all these cases hoaxes or do some of these cases represent encounters with objectively real but poorly understood natural phenomena?"[52b]

The Falcon Lake Landing

In 1967, a UFO encounter by Stephen Michalak of Winnipeg occurred in Whiteshell Provincial Park, where he observed two red, glowing, disc-shaped objects descending from the sky. One craft stopped and hovered while the other landed about 150 feet from him. He smelled a sulfur-like odor and heard a hissing sound. After approximately 30 minutes, a door opened, which revealed a brilliantly lighted interior. As he neared the craft, he heard voices coming from inside. Upon reaching the door, he looked inside and saw a panel of different-colored lights, and other light beams crossing in different directions. He then moved back when the panels suddenly moved together, hiding the door, which he described as "highly polished colored glass with no breaks or seams in its surface." When he touched the polished surface, his glove melted. Suddenly a small vented opening emitted heat that set his shirt on fire as the craft then ascended out of sight. He sought treatment for a headache, nausea, and burns on his chest, but for several days after the incident, Michalak was unable to eat, his blood lymphocyte count significantly decreased, and continued to feel weak and dizzy.

Timothy Good reviewing the case in his book *Above Top Secret,* wrote: "A hematologist's report indicated that Michalak's blood had 'some atypical lymphoid cells in the marrow plus a moderate increase in the number of plasma cells.'"[53] Although Michalak was examined by over twenty doctors, a diagnosis could not be made. However, Dr. H. Dudley, the former Chief of the Radioisotope Laboratory, U.S. Naval Hospital, believed the symptoms presented as a "classic picture of severe whole body exposure to radiation with X or gamma rays."

Eventually, Michalak returned to the landing site, where he found an outline of the object and the remains of his shirt. When the Royal Canadian Air Force searched thc site to collect samples, their representative described "a very evident circle" and found a high level of radiation in some samples, considering the site to be "a possible health hazard." An investigator for the Department of Health and Social Welfare also recorded a "significant level of radium 226" at the landing site.[53a]

Trans-en-Provence

Considered one of the most significant UFO incident's in France, Renato Nicolai, a technician, while working on his property saw "a somewhat bulging disk like two plates glued to each other by the rim, with a central ring some eight inches wide," which landed only fifty meters from him. As he approached the object, it flew away, leaving two round depression marks approximately eight feet in diameter, and two circular areas. He remarked that the object had two round protrusions under it that looked like landing gears. The site was inspected and soil and vegetation samples were collected for analysis by a unit of the French space agency (GEPAN) organized to investigate UFO reports. The investigators concluded:

1. A strong mechanical pressure, probably due to a heavy weight, caused the depression on the ground surface.

2. The soil was heated up to between 300 and 600 degrees C. (572 and 1112 F.)
3. Trace quantities were found of phosphate and zinc.
4. The chlorophyll content of vegetation in the immediate vicinity of the ground traces was reduced thirty percent to fifty percent, inversely proportional to distance, and "signs of premature senescence."
5. It was possible to qualitatively show the occurrence of an important event, which brought with it deformations of the terrain caused by mass, mechanics, a heating effect, and perhaps certain transformations and deposits of trace minerals.[54]

Toxicologist Bounias reported the results of an analysis he conducted of alfalfa at the landing site:

> From an anatomical and physiological point, they had all the characteristics of leaves of an advanced age that doesn't resemble anything that we know on our planet. The glucide and amino-acid content of very young leaves had been changed to become nearer the content characteristic of old leaves.[55]

Bounias rejected the hypothesis that the changes could have been caused by a deliberate act involving chemical poisons. Biochemical analysis indicated that "something did happen" and that the "influence of the unidentified source decreased with increasing distance from the epicenter."[55a]

In a paper by J. Jacques Velasco titled, "Report on the Analysis of Anomalous Physical Traces: The 1981 Trans-en-Provence UFO Case,"[56] samples analyzed from the landing site were independently analyzed by four laboratories and compared to reference samples collected outside the trace. These analyses concluded that a physical phenomenon interacted with the environment at the site, "producing abrasions, thermal impact and unexplained effects on plants." Velasco said, "the laboratory conclusion that seems to best cover the effects observed and analyzed is that of a powerful emission of electromagnetic fields, pulsed or not, in the microwave frequency range."[57] In 1983, GEPAN conducted an analysis of the landing site and concluded that leaves lost thirty percent to fifty percent of their chlorophyll and had aged in ways that could not be duplicated in the laboratory. GEPAN's final conclusion was that the damage was probably caused by "pulsed microwaves."[58]

The Valensole Case

In 1965, an incident in France included hard traces, botanical data, and physiological data, as well as detailed descriptions of beings associated with a UFO. Near the village of Valensole, farmer Maurice Masse observed an object descend from the sky and land in a field 200 feet away. He reported an oval-shaped structure resting on four legs with two beings in front of it, which he described as humanoid-looking "small boys," about four feet tall, and dressed in tight gray-green clothes. Masse portrayed them as having oversized heads with sharp chins, large and slanted eyes, and making a "grumbling" noise. Curiously, one of the beings pointed a small device at Masse, paralyzing him, and then entered the craft and flew away. Masse required twenty minutes to recover his mobility. The object left a deep hole and a moist area on the ground that soon hardened like concrete. Plants were affected by the proximity of the phenomenon, decaying in direct proportion to their distance from the center of the craft, and analysis found a higher amount of calcium at the landing site than elsewhere. Geometrically spaced indentations also covered the area. Leading UFO researcher, Dr. Jacques Vallée, interviewed Masse and concluded: "Throughout these discussions with Mr. Masse, I had the feeling that I was in the presence of a very intelligent man, capable of deep emotions and rational thought."[59]

The Lonnie Zamora Incident

The Lonnie Zamora incident on April 24, 1964, in Socorro, New Mexico, involved the observation of an object described by Officer Zamora as "like aluminum; it was whitish against the mesa background, but not chrome," and shaped like a letter "O" with four legs.[60]

Another witness, Larry Kratzer, described the object while taking off as follows: "a round, saucer- or egg-shaped object ascended vertically from the black smoke. After climbing vertically out of the smoke, the object leveled off and moved in a southwest direction." He said the object had a row of "portholes" across the side and a "red Z" marking toward one end. Zamora's description of the takeoff mentioned the absence of sound, the appearance of rapid acceleration, and it seemed to "rise up, and take off immediately across country."[60a] A memo from a FBI Special Agent in Charge to FBI Director, J. Edgar Hoover, obtained under the Freedom of Information Act (FOIA), described the scene of the reported landing: "noted four small irregularly shaped smouldering areas and four regular depressed areas approximately sixteen by six inches rectangular-type pattern averaging about twelve feet apart."

Hector Quintanella, head of the Air Force Project Blue Book, wrote, "there is no doubt that Lonnie Zamora saw an object which left quite an impression on him. There is also no question about Zamora's reliability. This is the best documented case on record."[61]

Despite the selected "physical trace" cases above, Carl Sagan thought that no "trace evidence" had been subjected to serious scientific scrutiny. Sagan wrote:

> Some enthusiasts argue that there are "thousands" of cases of "disturbed" soil where UFOs supposedly landed, and why isn't that good enough? It isn't good enough because there are ways of disturbing

> the soil other than by aliens and UFOs—humans with shovels is a possibility that springs into mind. One ufologists rebukes me for ignoring 4,400 physical trace cases from 65 countries. But not one of these cases, so far as I know, has been analyzed, with results published in a peer-reviewed journal in physics or chemistry, metallurgy or soil science, showing that the "traces" could not have been generated by people.[62]

Analysis from reported UFO landing sites of soil and vegetation have revealed some atypical results, but no indisputable proof to validate a non-earthly origin.

Radar-Visual Sightings

Radar sightings of UFOs, described as "bizarre blips," have been reported to appear on military and civil radar screens and execute maneuvers beyond our technical capability. Speeds of over several thousand miles per hour have been described, and many radar "blips" have been simultaneously witnessed as objects visually by observers on the ground and in the air.

In the book titled, *The Flying Saucerer*, author Arthur Shuttlewood claims he once met a retired RAF wing commander who estimated he had witnessed about 700 cases of "radar visual" UFOs or simultaneous observation of UFOs by witnesses on the ground and air.[63] Up until 1997, the GEPAN reported 101 (21 percent) out of 489 cases involving simultaneous radar and visual confirmation. Evidence from the U.S. Air Force Blue Book contained 363 aircraft cases of which also 21 percent involved both radar and visual confirmation. The NICAP reported 81 cases of radar tracking of UFOs, most of which were simultaneous with visual sightings, and a number of which involved use of interceptors.[64]

Unusual radar returns can be due to defracted layers of warm air known as "radar angels" or equipment malfunction. Despite this possibility, many credible radar-visual cases where the UFO was observed from both the ground and air, and confirmed by several different radar systems for hours have been documented. For example, anomalous radar returns concomitant with other UFO incidents investigated by the University of Colorado's, Condon Report, was published in a document titled, "Scientific Study of Unidentified Flying Objects." Several incidents mentioned in this report are addressed as follows:[65]

One of the most interesting radar-visual incidents occurred in Britain, in 1956, when an object tracked on radar at 4,000 mph was observed by both personnel in a control tower and crew of a C-47 aircraft. According to the radar operator, "there was no slow start up or build up to this speed—it was constant from the second it started to move until it stopped." The object's unusual behavior initiated orders to send two interceptors to investigate. When the pilot locked his guns, the UFO vanished and then reappeared behind the plane. Suddenly, a second UFO appeared on radar, which was confirmed by the crew. The pilot tried to evade the UFOs but was not successful, as they maintained the same distance and location behind the plane. Eventually, the two UFOs, still being tracked by radar, hovered before traveling in excess of 600 mph and disappearing. The Condon Report concluded:

> The preponderance of evidence indicates the possibility of a genuine UFO in this case. This is the most puzzling and unusual case in the Radar-Visual files. The apparently rational, intelligent behavior of the UFO suggests a mechanical device of unknown origin as the most probable explanation of this sighting.[65a]

In 1957, the flight crew of two airliners over Chesapeake Bay observed a luminous white object traveling at very high speed that was tracked on radar. Interestingly, both visual and radar sightings ended at the exact same time. According to one pilot, "the object dissolved right in front of my eyes." The Condon Report concluded: "There was no known natural or astronomical object...to have caused such a mirage," and the whole incident "was difficult to explain."[65b]

Of the numerous reports of UFO reports from sea, a few incidents stand out above the rest. One involved Harry Jordan, who served in the Operations Intelligence Division on several ships and was trained on Radar and Electronic Counter Measure equipment in the U.S. Navy during the 1960s. He presented testimony of his experience while stationed on the U.S.S. *Franklin D. Roosevelt* at the Senate UFO Hearing in 1998.[66] While on duty, off the coast of Sardinia, he made radar contact with an object that dropped from an "altitude of 80,000 to 65,000 feet in about 20 seconds where the contact then hovered for about ten minutes." Upon informing the Captain, the decision was made to launch Phantom F4Bs to investigate. When the jets were within 200 miles of the object, Jordan stated:

> The object closed from a distance of 600 miles from the ship to right above us in about 10 minutes. The bogey was traveling around 3,600 miles an hour at an altitude of 30,000 feet. I never saw any heat signature. Someone in CIC yelled out, "damn it, what the hell is that!" I recall vividly when it was first determined how unusual the situation had been. My division C.O. (Commander Gibson) asked me what I had put in my log if anything. He said to me "Jordan, this never happened." (I was reminded of that comment when I first saw the movie *Red October*.) I replied, "Yes sir." I never mentioned anything to fellow sailors or anyone else until years after my Honorable Discharge from the Navy.[66a]

From the Project Blue Book files another bizarre Radar-Visual sighting was investigated in 1957 above the Kirkland Air Force Base in New Mexico.[67] A radar operator reported a blip that indicated a plane falling at a dangerous angle. Ground observers described it as a green object "the shape of an automobile on end" that hovered a few hundred feet above the runway. Radar operators as well as eye witnesses then observed the object "ascend abruptly at an estimated rate of 4,500 feet per minute," before it disappeared from radar and sight. However, twenty minutes later the object reappeared and began to follow a C-46 aircraft for about 15 miles. According to a radar operator, "the object turned north to hover over the outer marker for approximately one -and-a-half minutes and then faded from scope."[67a]

Since 1982, twelve French aeronautical cases reported to GEPAN/SEPRA included a few radar-visual cases.[67b] One especially interesting incident occurred on January 28, 1994, near Paris. An object was observed by several crew members above a cloud layer at an altitude of over 11,000 feet, which was described by the captain as resembling a gigantic disk with an estimated diameter of about 1,000 meters (approximately 3,280 feet), and thickness about 100 meters (approximately 328 feet), with slightly "fuzzy edges." The witnesses suddenly lost sight of the object when the edges appeared to go out of focus and the object disappeared. Corresponding radar information by the military air traffic control tracked the object's velocity from 110 knots to zero.[67c] Thus there was excellent correspondence between radar and visual observations. Additional radar-visual sighting incidents are mentioned in Pilot Sightings that follows.[68]

Pilot Sightings

Pilot and aviation professionals have reported safety-related incidents of spherical UFOs often described as lights, metallic or glowing, objects. The reports are consistent in showing that UFOs demonstrate complex maneuvers at high rates of speed and unusual movements regarded as a hazard by aircrew who encounter them. In fact, 15 of 44 aviation safety-related UFO cases described by the National Aviation Reporting Center on Anomalous Phenomena (NARCAP) involved near-mid-air collisions defined as collision headings of less than 1,000 feet of separation.[68a]

The NARCAP, founded in 1999 by Dr. Richard Haines, senior aerospace scientist at NASA's Ames Research Center and chief scientist for the NARCAP, and Ted Roe, was developed because "the aviation industry is operating under a bias that is causing an under-reporting of safety-related encounters with UAP. Without this data, effective procedures have not been implemented and there is a real threat to aviation safety."[69] For example, an examination of 120 UFO cases by NARCAP Research Associate, Dr. Teodorani, titled, "A Comparative Analytical and Observational Study of North American Databases on Unidentified Aerial Phenomena," suggested:

1. "A misunderstanding has contributed to a 'blind spot' in research that is overlooking unusual atmospheric phenomena not detectable on radar."
2. "Spherical UFOs radiate energy and could be a threat to vital aviation systems."[70]

In an article by Haines titled, "Aviation Safety in America: A Previously Neglected Factor," an analysis of over 100 reports of UFOs that he and others collected and analyzed suggested that UFOs are "associated with a very high degree of intelligence, deliberate flight control, and advanced energy management."[71]

Based on over 3,000 cases of unusual visual and radar sightings of unexplained aerial phenomena, Haines concluded:

Aerial cases documented involve multiple factors:

1. "Sightings of long duration, allowing for accurate voice transmissions and the refinement of the initial identification.
2. Multiple witnesses—co-pilot, crew, passengers, other aircraft in different locations, and occasionally observers from the ground.
3. Onboard radar and ground radar recording the presence of a physical object, often corresponding exactly to the visual sighting.
4. Direct physical effects on the aircraft, such as equipment malfunction.[71a]

In a report by former Gen. Jose Periera of Brazil, commander of the Brazilian Air Force, in 1986, several Brazilian air force jets chased a UFO for 30 minutes. Periera stated:

> We have the correlation of independent readings from different sources. These data have nothing to do with human eyes. When, along with the radar, a pilot's pair of eyes sees that same thing, and then another pilot's, and so on, the incident has real credibility and stands on a solid foundation.[72]

In a 2012 study by Dominique F. Weinstein titled "Aviation Safety and Unidentified Aerial Phenomena: A Preliminary Study of 600 Cases of Unidentified Aerial Phenomena (UAP) Reported by Military and Civilian Pilots," the author reviewed evidence of pilot encounters with UFOs over a 64-year time period.[73] Of 600 reported cases, 443 cases (74 percent) were described as "objects" (42 percent) circular-shaped, and in 162 cases (27 percent), pilot observation was confirmed by ground and/or airborne radar. Weinstein concluded that the most frequent events with potential impact(s) on aviation safety were as follows:

1. "UFO approached aircraft on a collision course" (78 cases).
2. "UFO circled or maneuvered close to aircraft" (59 cases).

Further, in 81 cases (14 percent) pilots reported alleged EM effects on one or more aircraft systems, such as radio and compass systems, which were the predominant systems affected. According to Weinstein, "This analysis confirms the potential impact on aviation safety and the need for a serious study of these phenomena by governmental aviation departments and the International Civil Aviation Organization of the United Nations."[73a]

In a remarkable incident over Alaska, in 1986, the crew of a Japanese 747 plane, while flying from Paris to Narita, Tokyo, observed two UFOs that suddenly appeared and paralleled their plane. Each had "two rectangular arrays" of what appeared to be glowing nozzles or thrusters, though their bodies remained obscured by darkness.

> It was about seven or so minutes since we began paying attention to the lights when, most unexpectedly, two spaceships stopped in front of our face, shooting off lights. The inside cockpit shined brightly and I felt warm in the face.[74]

When the two UFOs left, a much larger disk-shaped object began to follow them and matched their direction and speed. The two objects then suddenly appeared only 500-1,000 feet in front of the plane, and activated "a kind of reverse thrust, and [their] lights became dazzlingly bright."[74a] Terauchi described the UFOs maneuver:

> The thing was flying as if there was no such thing as gravity. It sped up, then stopped, then flew at our speed, in our direction, so that to us it [appeared to be] standing still. The next instant it changed course. In other words, the flying object had overcome gravity.[75]

Captain Terauchi believed to have seen an outline of a gigantic spaceship on his port side that was "twice the size of an aircraft carrier" that followed "in formation," throughout a 45-degree turn, a descent from 35,000 to 31,000 feet, and a 360-degree turn. Following this maneuver, the crew lost sight of the object. An FAA investigation concluded there was, "not enough material to confirm that something was there," and though they were "accepting the descriptions by the crew," they were "unable to support what they saw."[76]

On April 20, 2004, a Mexican Air Force airplane, under the command of Mayor Magdaleno Jasso Núñez, while flying a mission to identify drug dealer flights in Mexico, detected unknown traffic at 10,500 feet over Ciudad del Carmen, Campeche airspace.[77] Upon approaching the craft, it immediately escaped at a tremendous speed and was detected by radar. Suddenly, more unknown objects arrived and radar detected the presence of nine new, unknown objects of the same size and characteristics that appeared out of "nowhere." Despite the presence of eleven objects close to the plane, and tracked on radar, the crew was not able to visualize them. The UFOs suddenly surrounded the plane at close range, which radar picked up as eleven objects in a circle formation around their plane. A few minutes later, all objects disappeared. The incident was taken very seriously by the Department of Defense Staff and after several weeks of investigation they decided, under the command of General Clemente Vega Garcia, to contact researcher and TV journalist Jaime Maussan to investigate the incident. The outcome of this investigation was highlighted by General Vega:

> This new era of relationship among the Mexican UFO witnesses, skywatchers, ufologists and our military forces will try to establish and give form to a new legislation in our law system focused to be prepared for any incident involving these unidentified flying objects, our people, our commercial and military airplanes for learning and understanding what are we going to do and how are we going to confront this reality.[77a]

In an interview by UFO Evidence, Director Jean-Jacques Velasco, a member of the French CNES who lead the SEPRA, related an interesting incident involving a pilot-radar confirmation of a UFO. It involved a crew member in an Airbus while over Paris, who reported a "strange object." According to Velasco, "the machine appeared as a kind of dark bell," and then a few seconds later, the object assumed the "shape of an egg." The observation lasted only one minute, but the military radars recorded the phenomenon for several minutes."[78]

In another incident, Lieutenant John W. Kilburn and others aboard a British jet aircraft reported a silver disk-shaped object moving back and forth that began to hover as it rotated. Lieutenant Michael Swiney and crew took off to investigate in a Meteor jet and reported seeing three white circular objects in front of the plane. Swiney recalled the incident in an interview:

> It was something supernatural. I immediately thought of course, of saucers, because that's actually what they looked like. They were not leaving a condensation trail as I knew we were. They were circular and appeared to be stationary. We continued to climb to twice that height [to 30,000 feet] and as we did they took on a slightly different perspective. For example the higher we got they lost their circular shape and took on more of a 'flat plate' appearance. At one time the objects, which were still very much in view, appeared to go from one side of us to the other, and to make quite sure it was not an illusion caused by us in our aeroplane moving to one side, I checked that we were absolutely still on a very steady heading, and sure enough they had moved across to the starboard side of the aircraft.[79]

The next day, crew of the aircraft carrier U.S.S. *Franklin D. Roosevelt* observed a fast-flying, silver sphere-shaped object following NATO ships, which was photographed by journalist Wallace Litwin. The pictures have never been made public. The Air Force project chief, Captain Ruppelt stated, "[The pictures] turned out to be excellent. Judging by the size of the object in each successive photo, one could see that it was moving rapidly."[79a]

The section below summarizes several cases from the Appendices of Haines (2000) where the witness description of the UFO indicates a singular light or a spherically shaped object:[80]

1. May 1952: 600 miles off Jacksonville, Florida: The crew on Pan-American Airlines Flight 203, while over the San Juan Oceanic Control, noticed a white light that suddenly moved directly ahead of the plane and increased in size. According to the captain, "the light began to get bigger and bigger until it was ten times the size of a landing light of an airplane." The Captain later told the Air Force investigator, "I always thought these people who reported flying saucers were crazy, but now I don't know."
2. March 1954, Ft. Lauderdale, Florida: Capt. Dan Holland, was flying a U.S. Marine jet of the Third Marine Aircraft Wing at 26,000 feet when he observed a "round unidentified object" about twice the size of his own plane that fell vertically "like a falling star." The captain stated:

   It suddenly stopped 3 or 4 thousand feet above us. It looked like a gleaming white ball with a gold ring around the lower ⅓ of the ball... Then the thing accelerated faster than anything I've ever seen before and disappeared to the East at an amazing speed in about 15 seconds. We were doing over 400 and it made us look slow. I always thought anyone who said he saw a flying saucer should have his head examined, but I'm damned convinced now that saucers exist.
3. November 1956, 60 miles from Mobile, Alabama: Captain W. Hull, while flying Capital Airlines flight 77 from LaGuardia Airport, New York to Mobile, Alabama, saw a "brilliant" object falling when it suddenly stopped in front of their plane. According to Hull:

   It was an intense blue-white light, approximately 7 or 8 times as bright as Venus. I knew that could not possibly be an airplane. The object began to move up and down while making sharp turns (90-degree angle) and then shot out over the Gulf of Mexico, rising at the most breathtaking angle and at such a fantastic speed that it diminished rapidly to a pinpoint and was swallowed up in the night.
4. April, 1966, Near Ocala, Florida: Several crew members, Frank Stockton, the executive assistant to the Governor of Florida, Governor Haydon Burns, a State Patrol Officer, and several newspaper reporters, experienced a UFO encounter at 6,000 feet during their flight from

Orlando to Tallahassee. Two dumbbell-shape yellow-orange spheres of light followed them on the right side of their plane for about forty miles. Governor Burns asked his pilot to "turn into it" and as the pilot did, the objects rose at a steep angle and disappeared.

5. April 1973, N. Farmington, Missouri: While flying a Piper Cherokee at 3,500 feet, two co-pilots saw a "strange light off the left wing tip." One pilot said the light was bright white with an occasional orange tinge that appeared to "give off heat waves." As they approached the runway, a white beam of light was emitted from the object as it moved directly ahead of his aircraft. According to the co-pilot, it then "immediately stopped, reversed its direction and flew away from us at a high rate of speed."
6. June 11, 1978, Los Angeles, California: A private pilot and flight instructor, while flying a Cessna 150 observed a small spherical craft traveling at a speed of about 200-300 mph. The pilot recalled: I turned right to follow the object and by the time I turned it was climbing to my altitude and was on a westerly course in a matter of seconds. It went by us very fast and turned in front of us to the south at a range of about 2-3,000 feet. Then it took up an easterly heading on our left doing a complete circle around us quite a few times. On one of the object's easterly passes I could see that it definitely was a solid metallic aircraft of ovoid shape having a definite axis about which it moved...with a continuous highly reflective surface with no visible seams, markings, bolts.... (It) was no more than 3 feet in length and slightly smaller in height.
7. February, 1985, Charleston, West Virginia: Capt. Mark Savage was piloting a Beechcraft King Air TC263 with eight passengers when a "large white circle" began to follow the plane. It performed three separate 360- degree vertical loops around the plane while remaining in formation that was witnessed by all on the plane. After inquiring the tower about the object, Savage said it made a "full, 360-degree horizontal orbit around his airplane, followed by two more similar maneuvers while continuously pacing the plane." The UFO then accelerated very rapidly and disappeared.
8. August 13, 1959, Roswell and Corona, New Mexico: Jack Goldsberry was piloting a Cessna 170 at 8,000 feet, when he reported observing "three elliptical-shaped, 10-20 foot diameter, gray, fuzzy-edged objects in close formation" directly ahead of him. The three objects circled his aircraft several times and then disappeared. After landing at the air base, he was interrogated for several hours by an officer who handled UFO sighting reports and was told "to say nothing of the incident to anyone except (to) his wife."

9. May 26, 1979, Central Utah: Pilot James Gallagher recalled a UFO encounter while flying at 10,000 feet in a light airplane near the Challis National Forest:

   I looked up in front of me and saw these five orange objects in a horizontal formation in front of me and then they tilted—like an airplane would dip its wings—and I thought it was (lights on) some kind of aircraft. Then they spread out and I knew damn well it wasn't an aircraft. My magnetic compass started spinning and my automatic direction finder started spinning. At that point they were in a straight line formation and then they just blinked out. I did have trouble receiving on the radio because of heavy static and my engine started running rough.
10. October 18 1973, near Mansfield, Ohio: An Army helicopter encountered a near midair collision with a UFO. The crew observed a red light flying over 600 knots approaching on midair collision course. Just before impact, a solid cigar-shaped, gray-metallic, domed object stopped and hovered above and in front of the helicopter. It had a red light at the nose, a white light at the tail, and a green beam emitted from the bottom. The beam focused on the windshield bathing the cockpit in intense light. No noise or turbulence was heard. After a few seconds, the object accelerated away toward Lake Erie.
11. October 5 1996, Pelotas, Brazil: Haraldo Westendorf, while flying his small plane, observed a spinning cone-shaped object, which he described as about 225 feet high and 325 feet in diameter. While circling the object, he noticed a hole on the top of the object, from which a saucer-shaped object about 30 feet in diameter emerged. The saucer took off at about Mach 10, or ten times the speed of sound, and was followed by the object, which also accelerated away at tremendous speed. The entire incident was witnessed by three ground-based air traffic controllers, among others, but the government's air defense system radar center did not record the object.
12. British Airways pilot Graham Sheppard stated: "I must have spoken to 20 pilots who have had sightings but all are adamant they do not want publicity." Additionally, on February 18th, 2013, a group of former pilots held a meeting in Washington, D.C. to recount their experiences with UFOs and demanded the U.S. government reopen an investigation of the phenomenon.

Major UFO Incidents

Washington, D.C., 1952

On July 19, 1952, an air traffic controller at National Airport in Washington, D.C., informed his supervisor, the Chief Civil Aeronautics Administration Air Traffic Controller at National Airport, Harry Barnes, of "blips" on his radar screen where no planes were located. A few hours later, pilot Howard Dermott on Capital Flight 610 reported an unidentified light following his plane. A few days after the incident, Barnes stated:

> We knew immediately that a very strange situation existed. Their movements were completely radical compared to those of ordinary aircraft. They moved with such sudden bursts of intense speed that radar could not track them continuously. Other air towers in the area began tracking "unknowns," which were also observed from the ground and in the air for several hours, as one controller said, "They're flying at over 1,000 miles an hour!" The next day radar tracked UFOs performing, according to an Air Force weather observer, extraordinary "gyrations and reversals, traveling over 900 mph."[81]

Sightings and trackings occurred on several occasions during the week but then resulted in a massive UFO wave the following weekend. In one incident, as a fighter closed on UFOs, the objects turned and surrounding it in seconds. A little later the pilot said, "We are closing in at five miles," and, "It looks like a lit cigar," and then, "As soon as we started to gain on them, they vanished."

Harry Barnes publicly confirmed that radar tracks of unknown targets correlated exactly with visual reports of glowing, oval-shaped objects provided by the Air Force interceptor pilots ordered to pursue them. He stated:

> I challenge anyone to present verifiable evidence that the U.S. government, or any other government, was flying an aircraft in 1952, which could travel thousands of miles per hour, instantly make a right-angle turn, then continue on its way unfazed by the impossible violent maneuver.

This activity, verified by expert radar operators, took place on several occasions over Washington, D.C. in 1952. Barnes further confirmed that the UFOs had performed 90- and 180-degree course changes, traveled at nearly 7,000 miles per hour, and made instantaneous reversals.[81a]

The Air Force held a press conference in response to public demand for an explanation during which time Capt. Roy James stated that "temperature inversions," which is an increase in temperature with height, caused the radar blips. This explanation led to headlines stating, "SAUCER" ALARM DISCOUNTED BY PENTAGON; RADAR OBJECTS LAID TO COLD AIR FORMATIONS."

This conclusion, however, was rejected by those who had seen the objects either in the air or on radar. The Air Force held another press conference when Major General Roger M. Ramey, Director of Operations, and Major General John A. Samford, Director of Intelligence stated: "The Air Force has run down thousands of sightings in recent years, but only twenty percent remain unexplained," and "The recent blips and lights can be attributed to weather inversions."

Years later, Capt. Dick Foley, who intercepted the UFOs, said that when he closed in on one, which he described as a "shiny discus-shaped vehicle," two identical objects moved alongside him, one on each wing. He added, "They had no wings and no cockpit or windows," and estimated their size to be about forty feet in diameter and ten feet wide. He said the UFOs "disarmed my guns and then in a few minutes all three of them accelerated, climbed, and left me like I was tied to the dock. So I told the controllers, and went home." A detailed discussion of the Washington, D.C. incident can be found in a book by Kevin D. Randle titled, *UFOs Over the Capitol.*[81b]

Rendlesham Forest, Suffolk, England, 1980

In December 1980, Rendlesham Forest, located near RAF Woodbridge in Suffolk, England, was the scene of reported sightings of unexplained lights and the alleged landing of one or more craft by many U.S. Air Force personnel over several days. The incident began when strange lights were seen descending into the forest by several military personnel. Upon searching for an aircraft, they saw lights moving through the trees, and a bright light discharged from an unidentified object. Sgt. Jim Penniston later claimed to have encountered a "craft of unknown origin" and to have made detailed notes of its features, touched its "warm" surface, and copied the symbols on its body. Penniston claims to have received a binary code (*i.e.*, thousands of sequential ones and zeros) by telepathy from the UFO which has been subject to different translations among researchers who believe there may be significant relevance associated with this message. He reported seeing a triangular landing gear on the object, which left depressions in the ground that were later identified, as well as burn marks and broken branches on nearby trees. The servicemen, who returned to the site the next day with radiation detectors, noticed a flashing light across the field followed by lights in the sky which released a stream of lights towards the ground. In June 2010, retired Colonel Charles Halt signed a notarized affidavit, summarizing the events, stating his belief that the UFOs were extraterrestrial.[82]

> I believe the objects that I saw at close quarter were extraterrestrial in origin and that the security services of both the United States and the United Kingdom have attempted—both then and now—to subvert the significance of what occurred at Rendlesham Forest and RAF Bentwaters by the use of well-practiced methods of disinformation.

Two book titled, *Left at East Gate: A First-Hand Account of the Rendlesham Forest UFO Incident, Its Cover-up, and Investigation,* and *Encounter in Rendlesham Forest: The Inside Story of the World's best-Documented UFO Incident,* provide a comprehensive treatment of Great Britain's "Roswell."[82a, 83]

Shag Harbour, Nova Scotia, 1967

A fishing village in Nova Scotia was the scene of an incident that began when about ten people saw a low-flying lit object crash into the Gulf of Maine near Shag Harbour. Assuming an aircraft had crashed, military police officers arrived at the scene, but the object reportedly sank. Two days after the incident, divers surveyed the sea floor but found no trace of an object. Further evidence from military and civilian witnesses implies that a highly secretive military search involving the Royal Canadian Navy and U.S. Navy ships occurred in Shag Harbour. According to one military witness, he was briefed that the object had originally been picked up on radar coming out of Siberia, and after crashing in Shag Harbour, it traveled underwater up the coast and positioned itself on top of a submarine magnetic detection grid ,where it was supposedly met by a second vehicle. Navy ships were allegedly involved in an attempt to recover the object. One American diver, known as "Harry" in the book titled, *Dark Object* (2001),[84] stated that the object wasn't from planet Earth. "Harry" claimed photographs were taken by the divers and some foam-like debris was recovered. Another military witness claimed there were actually two objects that were monitored by radar and sonar for three days while the objects were underwater until a Soviet submarine entered Canadian waters near Nova Scotia. When the ships left to intercept the submarine, the objects took off. However, no official documentation exists to support witness stories of a search near Nova Scotia, or of the diver's claims, with the exception of archived records that indicate a substantial amount of search and monitor activity in the Shelburne area during that time period. Canada's Department of National Defense has officially stated that this sighting remains unsolved.[84a]

Roswell, New Mexico, 1947

When an object crashed near Roswell, New Mexico, in July 1947, the Roswell Army Air Field stated they recovered a "flying disk." The following day Commanding General Roger Ramey said a weather balloon was recovered, which was dramatized by a press conference that showed debris supposedly from the balloon. Little debate of the incident occurred until 1978 when Stanton Friedman interviewed Major Jesse Marcel, who participated in the recovery effort, said the military covered up the recovery of an alien spacecraft. Other witnesses contradicted the weather balloon rationale by providing anecdotal evidence of a military operation that recovered alien craft and bodies, and alleged witness intimidation. According to Marcel, the debris was "strewn over a wide area," and described weightless "I"-beams with unknown symbols along the length, in two colors, that would "neither bend nor break."

Marcel also described metal debris the thickness of tinfoil resistant to damage. In 1989, mortician Glenn Dennis claimed alien autopsies were carried out at the Roswell base. In the book, *A History of UFO Crashes* (1995), researcher Kevin Randle reported that military radar had tracked a UFO over southern New Mexico for four days and that on the night of July 4, 1947, radar indicated the object had gone down about thirty to forty miles northwest of Roswell.[85] The authors said eyewitness William Woody, who lived east of Roswell, recalled a "brilliant object descending to the ground" that night.[85a]

Through the years, the incident has been dramatized in various media forms and summarized in two reports by the U.S. General Accounting Office in 1995 and 1997. The "official" government report was that the recovered material was debris from a once-top-secret weather balloon operation called Project Mogul, and reports of alien bodies were likely poor recall from witnesses who observed injured or killed personnel.[86] The debate as to what actually occurred in Roswell will likely linger for some time to come.

Stephenville, Texas, 2008

The Stephenville incident on January 8, 2008, involved many witness reports of a large object in the sky that hovered above the town before taking off at a tremendous speed. The MUFON presented a report of the sighting by Glen Schulze and Robert Powell, titled, "Special Research Report Stephenville, Texas," that incorporated an analysis of radar records from the Federal Aviation Administration, the National Weather Service, and witness testimony.[87] The authors concluded that radar confirmed witness observations of an object and that, on two separate occasions, radar picked up an object traveling at about 2,000 mph, and at other times at a slow pace. They also concluded that the UFO was not a "known aircraft." Pilot Steve Allen observed the object from the ground and described it as half-mile wide with strobe lights about a half-mile apart that changed pattern. He reported that two vertical flames about a quarter-mile apart were emitted for several seconds and when pursued by two fighter jets, it disappeared at a speed estimated at 3,000 mph. He stated, "I don't know if it was a biblical experience or somebody from a different universe or whatever but it was definitely not from around these parts."[87a]

Belgium, 1989-1990

From October 1989 throughout 1990, hundreds of reports by thousands of witnesses of very large triangular-shaped objects were observed in Belgium and documented by the Belgian Society for the Study of Space Phenomena, who published comprehensive reports on the UFO wave. Air Force jets chased objects that were simultaneously tracked by both air and ground radar. The Chief of Operations of the Royal Belgian Air Force, Colonel Wilfred De Brouwer, established a Task Force Unit to investigate the sightings. The first important incident involved a multiple-witness observation of a strange aircraft that was summarized by professor of physics, Auguste Meessen:

> On November 29, 1989, a large craft with triangular shape flew over the town of Eupen. It was stationary in the air above a field which it illuminated with three powerful beams. The beams emanated from large circular surfaces near the triangle's corners. In the center of the dark and flat understructure there was some kind of red gyrating beacon. The object did not make any noise.[88]

Reported sightings during 1989-1990 were characterized as a dark, triangular object with white lights at the corners and a red flashing light in the middle. Many of the objects hovered, with some then suddenly accelerating away at a terrific speed. The UFO wave climaxed with a simultaneous radar and visual confirmation, and a jet-scramble incident on the night of March 30-31, 1990, observed by hundreds of people. A preliminary report prepared by Major P. Lambrechts of the Belgian Air Force General Staff stated:[88a]

> The observation of UFOs during the night of March 30 to 31, 1990, dismisses several hypotheses such as optical illusions, balloons, meteorological inversions, military aircraft, and holographic projections. The aircraft had brief radar contacts on several occasions, but the pilots at no time established visual contact with the UFOs. Each time the pilots were able to secure a lock on one of the targets for a few seconds, there resulted a drastic change in the behavior of the detected targets. During the first lock-on, their speed changed in a minimum of time from 170 to 1,100 mph and from 9,000 to 5,000 feet, returning then to 11,000 feet in order to change again to close to ground level.

The Minister of Aeronautics, Brigadier General Otávio Moreira Lima stated:

> Between 20:00 hrs. (5/19) and 01:00 hrs. (5/20) at least 20 objects were detected by Brazilian radars. They saturated the radars and interrupted traffic in the area. Each time that radar detected unidentified objects, fighters took off for intercept. Radar detects only solid metallic bodies and heavy (mass) clouds. There were no clouds nor conventional aircraft in the region. The sky was clear. Radar doesn't have optical illusions.[89]

Air Force Major Ney Cerqueira, in charge of the Air Defense Operations Center said:

> We don't have technical operational conditions to explain it. The appearance and disappearance of these objects on the radar screens are unexplained. They are Unidentified Aerial Movements. The lights were moving at a speed ranging between 150 to 1,000 mph.[89a]

In response to public pressure, an official investigation and report of the incident concluded: "It is the opinion of this Command that the phenomenon is solid and reflects intelligence by its capacity to follow and sustain distance from the observers, as well as to fly in formation, and are not necessarily manned craft."[89b] Although this incident remains unexplained, Meessen accepted a proposed hypothesis that some of the radar contacts were really "angels" caused by a rare meteorological phenomenon. Meessen explained how the high velocities measured by the Doppler radar of the F-16 fighters might result from interference effects, but pointed out that another radar trace had no explanation. Regarding the visual sightings of this event by the gendarmes and others, he suggested that they could possibly have been caused by stars seen under conditions of "exceptional atmospheric refraction."[89c] Because the majority of the sightings described triangular-shaped objects, many researchers speculated that these were caused by either stealth fighters or some other advanced secret military aircraft. However, no known aircraft to this day has been able to fly in the manner reported for the Belgian UFOs. In a letter to French researcher Renaud Marhic, the Minister of Defense at the time of the UFO wave, Leo Delcroix, wrote:

> Unfortunately, no explanation has been found to date. The nature and origin of the phenomenon remain unknown. One theory can, however, be definitely dismissed since the Belgian Armed Forces have been positively assured by American authorities that there has never been any sort of American aerial test flight.[89d]

Given the possibility of advanced secret technology having been responsible for the reported sightings, De Brouwer was assured by the U.S. Air Force in a 1990 memo titled, "Belgium and the UFO Issue," that no U.S. aircraft was in the area at the time of the reported sightings. If the witness accounts of the UFOs maneuverability are accurate, such as remaining motionless, noiseless, and then able to accelerate to thousands of miles per hour, it is difficult to comprehend how the craft could have been of earthly origin, especially since for over twenty years since the incident, no aircraft has demonstrated such advanced technology (at least to the public). A detailed personal account of the UFO incident in Belgium can be read in a chapter by General Wilfried De Brouwer titled, "The UAP Wave over Belgium," in Leslie Kean's book.[90]

Phoenix, Arizona, 1997

The Phoenix Lights incident involved a series of widely sighted UFOs observed in the skies in and around Phoenix, Arizona, on March 13, 1997.[91] Lights of varying descriptions were seen by thousands of people from Nevada, through Phoenix, to Tucson, Arizona. There were allegedly two distinct events involved in the incident:

1. A triangular formation of lights seen to pass over the state.
2. A series of stationary lights seen in the Phoenix area.

Despite the U.S. Air Force explanation that the second group of lights were flares dropped by an aircraft on training exercises, witnesses claim to have observed a very large square-shaped UFO. Initial reports indicated an object of six points of light, followed by a report of eight lights, with a separate ninth, aligned with the eight. The formation was seen again over the Gila River and a few minutes later, the craft was over Phoenix, where thousands observed the object. Later that night, people in Rainbow Valley reported a distinct "V" formation although several light descriptions like a "V," circular, and crescent were also reported. The enormous object, which was low enough to have mountains behind it in pictures, provided photographic experts a scale to estimate its altitude, and the distance from the camera. This resulted in the craft's estimate as being one mile or more in length. The velocity of the craft varied from Mach 2-3 to just 10-15 mph and was reported to remain motionless for several minutes over Sky Harbor Airport in Phoenix. The object was also reported to change shape, speed, and color. Another witness estimated the craft at two miles wide with dozens of bright lights along the edges, and a row of windows with "silhouettes of people." Two airplane pilots, who observed the object at different times and places, described a craft of "immense size," measuring up to a mile long.

The Phoenix lights case is not without controversy. In May 1997, Luke AFB Public Affairs Office stated that Air Force personnel who investigated the case claimed that "flares dropped from an A-10 Warthog" caused the numerous reports of night lights. The case remains a mystery and a source of continuing debate. Lynne D. Kitei, author of the book, *The Phoenix Lights: A Skeptics Discovery That We Are Not Alone* (2010), provides a comprehensive review of this fascinating case.[91a]

Hudson Valley, New York, 1983

A luminous boomerang-shaped object as large as a football field was reported by thousands of witnesses flying over southern New York State (Hudson Valley) in March 1983. The large object, which had the appearance of "grey metal," moved very slowly, and was only 50-100 feet above street level. Freddy Vicente, while driving on the Taconic State Parkway, said, "a circle of twelve or more clearly oversized lights glided past my windshield and out of sight into the night."[92] The Federal Aviation Administration attributed the sightings as light aircraft flying in formation, a possibility that many eyewitnesses firmly discounted. Some people "screamed out in fear at the sight while others felt awe and even an attraction to it, especially those who sensed a wordless communication from the object not to be afraid." Several support groups were developed for people claiming to have been contacted by ET beings, including a monthly gathering called the UFO Roundtable.[92a]

Chicago, O'Hare International Airport, 2006

On November 7, 2006, several airline employees observed a "round, revolving, grey, metallic-appearing object" hovering for about 20 minutes above an airline gate at O'Hare International Airport less than 2,000 feet above ground level. The object, estimated by witnesses to range from approximately 20-80 feet in diameter, was not detected on radar. Witness testimony by separate individuals included the following:

1. From a dead stop, suddenly you saw the motion. You saw it go up those few hundred feet. But it was so fast you couldn't even process it until it was gone. There was no acceleration. No noise that I could tell.
2. The object had an odd visual effect to it...the sort-of-mirror-like-yet-sort-of "fuzzyish" quality...but I did think it was rotating rapidly and counter-clockwise.
3. It was very obviously a solid object.
4. It surely did leave a hole in the cloud, and it went from no movement to incredible speed in a split second. There was no noticeable acceleration, just gone. And no sonic boom. Upon departing through a cloud at a steep angle, a round hole in the cloud remained for about 15 minutes.[93]

A detailed analysis of this incident, conducted by Dr. Haines and associates from the NARCAP, in 2007, concluded that the object, "possessed a high energy density that caused a hole to be produced in the cloud," and that the object observed "remains unknown." The NARCAP recommended that the U.S. government conduct research of "electromagnetic phenomena" to avoid the "risk of grave consequences."[94]

UFOs and Nuclear and Missile Sites

In a book titled, *UFOs and Nukes: Extraordinary Encounters at Nuclear Weapons Sites*,[95] leading UFO researcher Robert Hastings summarized his work over the past forty years interviewing over 140 former and retired U.S. military personnel and nuclear weapons specialists of their UFO encounters. One interesting case occurred on June 24, 1984, when security guards at the Indian Point Nuclear Power Plant, near Peekskill, New York, reported seeing a UFO over the plant, about 300 feet above the exhaust funnel of one of the plant's three nuclear reactors for approximately 15 minutes. Security guards who saw the UFO described them as "huge in size, diamond-shaped and approximately 450 feet in length." The object's color changed from first white, to blue, red, green and then to amber. Police Sgt. Karl Hoffman said the UFO had a "dozen white lights" in V-formation that slowly moved towards the power plant. According to Hastings:

> Hundreds of ex-military men have slowly but surely come forward to confirm their involvement in, or knowledge of, one UFO-related incident or another at U.S. nuclear weapons sites. One obvious interpretation of UFO activity at ICBM sites is that someone or something was monitoring, on an ongoing basis, the nuclear standoff between the U.S. and the Soviet Union during the Cold War era.[95a]

In an article titled, "New Revelations: Two ex-U.S. Air Force Security Policemen Discuss UFO Activity at Nuclear Weapons Sites" (2012),[96] Hastings disclosed an incident reported to him by former U.S. Air Force Security Policeman Sgt. Richard E. Walker who was responsible for guarding nuclear weapons at K.I. Sawyer AFB in Michigan from 1973 to 1976. The following presents the author's account of Walker's experience:

> The UFO continued its slow approach and then hovered over the flight line and the Weapon Storage Area. At the time, K.I. Sawyer had nuclear weapons in there and on the B-52 bombers that were on alert on the flight line. As the object continued to hover over the base, the radio chatter from all of the security personnel increased. I remember that several of them began to say something to the effect, "Do you see that?" as the object began to get brighter and brighter. It hovered for about one or two minutes, over the bomber alert area, when it suddenly split into five separate objects, which departed in several different directions at an incredible rate of speed.[96a]

Hastings commented that the UFOs' behavior, in the form of splitting into smaller objects, was "identical to one reported by former RAF Bentwaters deputy base commander, now-retired USAF Col. Charles Halt, relating to the famous Rendlesham Forest UFO incidents of December 1980." In another incident, he shared a UFO encounter by retired U.S. Air Force Security Policeman Anthony W. Keel, while stationed at Ellsworth AFB, South Dakota in September 1991:

> We both saw and verified a blue, pulsating light near the site and called it in. The light was about the size of a large helicopter, was semi-circular and oblong, and made not the faintest of noise. The closest we were able to get was about one-quarter to one-half mile from it. We were debriefed by the Flight Security Controller and Flight Chief and were told not to make written statements.[97]

In one of the most significant documented UFO incidents on record, Hastings presented excerpts of an interview with David Schuur, a Minuteman missile crewmember in the 455th/91st Strategic Missile Wing at Minot AFB in the early 60s, regarding a UFO incident at a nuclear missile base. Schuur stated:

> When the object passed over our flight, we started receiving many spurious indications on our console. The object was apparently sending some kind of signals into each missile. Not every missile got checked [out] by the object, but there were several that did, maybe six, seven, or eight. Maybe all ten got checked, but I don't think so. As this thing was passing over each missile site, we would start getting erratic indications on that particular missile. After a few seconds, everything reset back to normal. But then the next missile showed spurious indicators, so the object had apparently moved on to that one, and did the same thing to it and then on to the next one, and so on. It was as if the object was scanning each missile, one by one. The Inner Security and Outer Security [alarms were triggered] but we got those all the time, for one reason or another. However, on this particular night, we had to activate the "Inhibit" switch because we got "Launch in Progress" indicators! After a few minutes, the UFO passed to the northwest of us and all indicators reset to normal.[97a]

Hastings considered the UFO-nuclear connection a message:

> Demonstrations designed to scare the hell out of the command-level personnel in both countries. Similarly, the ongoing missile shutdown incidents were meant to demonstrate a different but equally-effective technological tool at our visitors' disposal.[97b]

A remarkable incident similar to the one that occurred at Minot AFB took place at a nuclear missile site in the Ukraine in October 1982.[97c] Another tremendous flying disc was believed to have activated several nuclear missiles, which were then ready to launch. George Knapp, an investigative reporter secured documents that revealed the Soviet Ministry of Defense acknowledged the object hovered for two hours at a height, which prevented attack from planes or missiles. The activated missiles went into "countdown mode" despite the fact, according to the Minister of Defense, that nobody entered the launch code sequence needed for takeoff. After fifteen seconds, the missiles deactivated. Following the incident, Major Mikhail Kataman, a guidance system expert, officially stated for the record that the missiles' security systems were disabled by a "powerful electromagnetic pulse." As in the Minot AFB incident, several missiles were "activated" by a UFO. Hastings interpreted the incidents at Minot AFB and the Soviet Union as follows:

> While I am of the opinion that those who pilot the UFOs are visitors from elsewhere, I think they have engaged in an ongoing surveillance of, and interference with, our nuclear weapons to send the message that we are playing with fire. That the use of nuclear weapons poses a threat to human civilization if not the continued existence of our species itself.[97d]

At an army missile base in the district of Kapustin Yar, Russia, on the night of July 28-29, 1989, seven military witnesses observed three objects a few miles away. According to one witness, Ensign Valery N. Voloshin:

> While the object was hovering over the depot, a bright beam appeared from the bottom of the disc, where the flash had been before, and made two or three circles, lighting the corner of one of the buildings. The movement of the beam lasted for several seconds, then the beam disappeared and the object, still flashing, moved in the direction of the railway station. After that, I observed the object hovering over the logistics yard, railway station, and cement factory. Then it returned to the rocket weapons depot, and hovered over it at an altitude of 60-70m [200-240 feet.]. The object was observed from that time on, by the first guard-shift and its commander. At 1:30 hrs., the object flew in the direction of the city of Akhtubinsk and disappeared from sight. The flashes on the object were not periodical, I observed all this for exactly two hours.[98]

In August 1973, the test launch of a Minuteman intercontinental ballistic missile from Vandenburg Air Force base was closely monitored by a UFO on radar and tracked at an altitude of around 400,000 feet as it hovered close to the missile's nose cone. The object, estimated to be ten feet high and forty feet long, was tracked by two separate radar systems, which also picked up at least three other unknown objects in that area. Author Shuttlewood stated that, "radar picked up an inverted saucer-shaped object to the right and above the descending nose cone and watched it across the warhead's trajectory to a point which was below and to the left of it..."[99]

The results of a study by Dr. Donald A Johnson, who analyzed the number of UFO sightings by counties with and without a nuclear a plant concluded that there is an "association between the presence of a nuclear facility and the rates of both UFO sightings and close encounters." More specifically, he found that there is an excess of 3,051 UFO reports for nuclear site counties above what would have been predicted based on the non-nuclear counties. For close encounters, he reported in excess of 568 close encounter reports over what should have been expected based on other UFO reporting dynamics. According to Johnson, this result suggests, "nuclear facilities attract UFOs."[100]

Discussion

The UFO evidence presented in this chapter introduces an associated question that is difficult to ignore. That is: Does the collective evidence provide undeniable confirmation that non-human intelligent beings are operating UFOs and interacting with humans?

The evidence is not convincing enough for the skeptical community to support the widely-held viewpoint that UFOs are intelligently controlled physical craft of extraterrestrial or extra-dimensional origin. In contrast, many ufologists believe that compelling UFO evidence indicates that non-human intelligent beings are operating UFOs and interacting with humans. This perspective is primarily based on the following:

1. UFOs extraordinary aerial maneuvers appear to defy gravity and inertia.
2. Varying sizes, shapes, and "shape-shifting" behavior.
3. Revealed government/military declassified UFO documents.
4. Psychological and physiological effects on humans.
5. Interference with airplane systems, and nuclear missiles at bases in the U.S. and Russia.
6. Witness encounters of "high strangeness" with physical craft and their occupants, among others.

Alternatively, in light of the somewhat controversial and largely anecdotal nature of the evidence cited, the often limited and inadequate application of acceptable scientific methods to study the phenomenon, along with a touch of UFO hoaxes, and "confirmation bias," have led the vast majority of scientists to regard the UFO evidence as too unreliable to believe alien beings have visited Earth.

While controversy exists as to whether the quality of evidence provides undeniable proof that NHI governs the phenomenon, the evidence clearly verifies the existence of very strange aerial events, which appear as a form of technologically advanced physical objects of unknown origin. Based on consistent, longstanding witness testimony worldwide, it is difficult to deny that physical objects are performing inexplicable maneuvers in our skies. Nick Pope, who worked for the British Government's Ministry of Defense (MoD) and spent several years investigating reports of UFO sightings for the MoD, proposed that some UFOs may be extraterrestrial life from other planets in physical craft visiting Earth. Pope stated:

> The records of UFO reports describe many examples of craft that are silent, divide into smaller segments, and zip away noiselessly at amazing speeds. Not only do ordinary people report them, but so do military personnel.[101]

Pope's statement, which does not rule out the possibility of natural atmospheric/meteorological phenomena, and/or advanced secret military technology as the source of some unexplained UFOs, fails to provide evidence that NHI governs its behavior. So are these objects natural phenomenon, man-made craft, and/or NHI visiting Earth? Given the limited physical UFO evidence to adequately study, the lack of comprehensive and rigorous scientific investigations of the phenomenon, and the less than enthusiastic interest on the part of the general scientific community to conduct UFO research, it would seem that an explanation of the nature and origin of the phenomenon is unlikely any time soon.

The issue of the validity of evidence remains at the heart of the UFO phenomenon. The general scientific community, who tend to ignore theories not consistent with accepted norms, dispute evidence which support the UFO phenomenon. That is, evidence must be subjected to scientific study capable of reproduction and authentication before concluding that an alien intelligence is operating UFOs. Authenticity of evidence relates to the question of how conventional research can be designed to determine the nature and processes behind alleged UFO experiences. However, approaching the UFO phenomenon from a research perspective is difficult because of the lack of physical evidence to analyze. Compounding this issue is the problem associated with the phenomenon's behavior, which does not appear to conform to known scientific principles such as gravity and inertia. Consequently, it would seem that we must wait until newly developed methodological approaches can improve our ability to effectively collect and analyze the UFO evidence before the scientific community can accept the final conclusion with confidence.

CHAPTER FIVE

Theories and Cases of High Strangeness

Overview

The more one gets involved in the UFO phenomenon, the more perplexing it becomes. Especially puzzling are the reported strange alleged UFO encounters of various kinds by people from diverse occupations and educational levels from all corners of the world, which appear to defy logical explanation. Several UFO databases established by the NUFORC, CPTR, MUFON, and NICAP, and related literature, are filled with unusual alleged "close encounter" cases in which the UFO is reported to appear under intelligent control. The phenomena consists of reports of strange flying physical craft that demonstrate an ability to suddenly appear and disappear, change shape, accelerate at a tremendous speed, and to merge and split apart. Such reported incidents suggest that the UFO phenomenon's maneuverability may defy laws of gravity and inertia, which seem illogical given our current understanding of scientific principles and physical laws. Additionally, among a group of people, some may see a UFO while others don't, some report gaining psychic ability after a UFO encounter, and some believe to have telepathic communications with the UFO occupants, among other incidents characterized as incidents of "high strangeness." While bizarre UFO incidents may lend hints to their possible nature or origin, a number of UFO theories have been proposed that include the extraterrestrial, extra-dimensional, atmospheric phenomenon, paranormal manifestations, advanced secret technology, a manifestation of a psycho-cultural phenomenon, and time travel to explain the nature and origin of this perplexing phenomenon (See Chapter Six: UFO Theories).

It appears that the intelligence (if there is one) behind the phenomenon is hesitant to interact with humans on a personal level unless one accepts the alleged "alien abduction" phenomena as a form of such "interaction" (See Chapter Seven: The Alien Abduction Phenomenon). Leading UFO researcher and author, Jacques F. Vallée, believes that people are experiencing "something that has physical and psychological components" which he termed as "high strangeness."[1] Accordingly, Vallée believes that the UFOs "absurd behavior" is one reason many scientists reject the UFO phenomenon.

Not surprisingly, given the apparent "strangeness" of the phenomenon, any proposed hypothesis to explain it will almost certainly be met with a high degree of skepticism. Analogous examples of "strange" ideas that have eventually come to pass over time, can easily be drawn from history, as evidenced by disbelief when scientists proposed the Earth was round, our planet orbits around the sun, and that we will someday walk on the moon. Apparently, there exists a great distance in time between many seemingly implausible hypotheses and their acceptance once proven through scientific study and human endeavor. Within this historical context, is it possible that the "high strangeness" associated with the UFO phenomenon provides evidence of its nature and origin? Consistent with Carl Sagan's position that "extraordinary claims require extraordinary evidence," it would seem appropriate to explore whether proposed extraordinary hypotheses should also require "extraordinary evidence" to prove. Accordingly, could the phenomena's apparent unusual behavior suggest an extra-dimensional hypothesis (EDH), an atmospheric phenomenon such as plasma, a type of psychic/consciousness connection, a yet to be discovered natural phenomenon, or advanced secret military technology?

The Extra-Dimensional Hypothesis

Although the extraterrestrial hypothesis (ETH) has remained the predominant explanation for UFOs by ufologists, some have abandoned it in favor of the EDH. The greater acceptance of the EDH increased with the publication of the book by Dr. J. Allen Hynek and Jacques Vallée, which proposed the hypothesis in *The Edge of Reality: A Progress Report on Unidentified Flying Objects*,[2] and in Jacques Vallée's book *Messengers of Deception: UFO Contacts and Cults*.[3] Strangely, the EDH states that the phenomenon represents visitations from other "realities" or "dimensions" that accompany our own. This hypothesis, which evolved from the bizarre behavior of UFOs, is thought to have a paranormal and dimensional aspect to it that can't be ignored. Could one possible "strange" hypothesis include parallel universes, or other time-like dimensions beyond the space-time reality we ascribe too? Or could the strangeness of their behavior be explained on the basis of differences between the time-space continuum of UFOs and us?

Some have accepted the EDH, as an alternative to the ETH, since an anti-gravity or speed-of-light travel required as part of the ETH, seem implausible. The EDH may also be more suitable to some, since it circumvents the debatable issue pertaining to the necessary use of propulsion as the EDH holds that UFOs are devices that travel between different realities or parallel universes. According to principles in theoretical physics, a parallel universe or different dimension can be manifested via traversable wormholes that connect two different universes, having two different locations, times, and dimensions. In other words, an alternate reality may coexist with our own. A few physicists have speculated that the shape-shifting UFOs may represent the energy change occurring around the UFO as it "moves between dimensions." For example, a three-dimension cross section of a four-dimension tube would appear spherical. That is, it would appear as a different shape in our three-dimensional space as it moved.

Related to this concept is the "multiverse" theory, which attempts to resolve a mathematical contradiction between two theories in physics: quantum mechanics and the theory of relativity. Leading theoretical physicist, Stephen Hawking, in his book, The Grand Design,[4] proposed that one can have different "universes" in one ultimate existence, a "multiverse." This theory proposes that the universe can be explained in terms of very small strings that vibrate in invisible dimensions. If it exists, it could explain everything in the universe from particle physics to the physical laws that govern our universe. According to physicist B. Green, "there are a couple of multiverses that come out of our study of string theory, *i.e.*, there are many entities allowed for by the theory."[5] This implies that we may be "living in one dimension, while other surfaces with other beings on it exist out in space." Could this theory, or an alternative theory that explains the existence of the "multiverse," explain the physical force responsible for causing and regulating the UFO phenomenon?

When I think of high strangeness associated with UFOs, I often recall an excerpt from J. Allen Hynek's speech, "What I Really Believe About UFOs," presented at the 1977 International UFO Congress:[6]

1. We must ask whether the diversity of observed UFOs all spring from the same basic source, as do weather phenomenon, which all originate in the atmosphere.
2. We must not ask what hypothesis can explain the most facts, but we must ask, which hypothesis can explain the most puzzling facts?
3. Do we have two aspects of one phenomenon or two different sets of phenomena?
4. I hold it entirely possible that a technology exists that encompasses both the physical and the psychic, the material and the mental. There are stars that are millions of years older than the sun. There may be a civilization that is a million of years more advanced than man's. I hypothesize an "M&M" technology encompassing the mental and material realms. The psychic realms, so mysterious to us today may be an ordinary part of an advanced technology.

Jacques Vallée, a proponent of the EDH, initiated the idea that UFO events were as much "psychic" in nature as "physical." While the UFO gives the appearance as a physical object, Vallée believes that either through "very clever deception or very advanced physical principles," the UFO "triggers psychic effects either purposely or as a side effect of its manifestations, which are too common to be ignored." While a UFO observation does not make someone "psychic," he is convinced that the phenomenon somehow incorporates "heightened awareness of synchronicities, paranormal sounds and lights and occasionally absurd coincidences similar to those described in the poltergeist literature." Vallée stated:

> There is a system around us that transcends time as it transcends space, *i.e.*, the system may well be able to locate itself in outer space, but its manifestations are not spacecraft in the ordinary "nuts and bolts" sense. The UFOs are physical manifestations that cannot be understood apart from their psychic and symbolic reality. What we see in effect here is a control system which acts on humans and uses humans.[7]

Ufologists have attempted to understand what happens during a close encounter with a UFO. One very "strange" experience reported that defies explanation is the apparent distortion of time or an overwhelming feeling of isolation. However, once the UFO leaves, the unusual feeling disappears. Is it possible that the UFO may be creating a different local state of space-time experienced by the witness? If so, it may account for the altered state of consciousness reported by many who have had a close encounter with a UFO, since normal time-space would end for them as they experience the altered time-space of the UFO. This effect may explain some of the more unusual aspects of UFO encounters, such as environmental sound disappearing, feelings of isolation, time slowing down, and electrical interference. Are there rationale explanations for the apparently "incomprehensible" events related to the UFO phenomenon?

Cases of "High Strangeness"

Not surprisingly, given the apparent "strangeness" of the phenomenon, any proposed hypothesis to explain it will almost certainly be met with a high degree of skepticism. According to *Conspiracy Journal* Editor Tim Swartz, there are many incidents that demonstrate that the UFOs can alter the physical nature of their craft and/or give the appearance to do so. A few such cases are described below:[8]

On June 29, 1954, the crew of a British Overseas Airways Corporation plane flying over Goose Bay, Labrador at 19,000 feet noticed an object about five miles away described as a large pear-shaped UFO flying in formation with six smaller objects. According to the Captain, as the plane neared the object, the smaller UFOs formed into a line, merged into the larger object, and then disappeared. Following the incident, the Captain stated:

> They were obviously not aircraft as we know them. All appeared black and I will swear they were solid. There was a big central object that appeared to keep changing shape. The six smaller objects dodged about either in front or behind.[8a]

In another case, a Pastor, while traveling with his family, observed a silver aluminum object flying above the mountains, which he described as the "shape of a box and about the size of a small private plane." The object then morphed into what he described as a "round bottom cup shape without the handle," proceeded to "just cruise around," and then suddenly disappeared. Another "strange" incident in 2005 involved a man waiting at a traffic light who noticed a bright silver, metallic UFO in the sky in front of his car. The man recalled it as a "thin, cigar-shaped" object with "rounded ends." A few seconds after it appeared, the object "changed shape with the front end moving slightly inward so that the object took on more of a boomerang shape with one side shorter than the other." Suddenly, the UFO appeared to "ripple," become "fuzzy" at the edges, and then disappeared.

Another unusual incident involving a "shape-shifting" UFO occurred at the Nellis Air Force Base Bombing and Gunnery Range Complex, Nevada, in 1994, that was tracked on radar and videotaped. The witnesses reported it changed from a "disc-shaped" object into a "small jet with round stubby wings, and then into three-balls." Another unusual encounter, in February 2010, involved a man who noticed a circular object hovering in the sky that began to descend slowly towards him in an irregular manner. The object was estimated at 100 feet long with blue and red lights along its bottom. Shortly after landing, a white apparition exited from the ship and floated towards him across the lawn. The witness stated: "It was about 4 feet high and seemed to be translucent and moved very slowly towards us. I was transfixed because it made a droning noise, which sounded like "my, my." Credence to this report was provided by a witness who claimed to have seen the ship accelerate rapidly at a 45-degree angle and disappeared from sight.[9]

Still another reported bizarre UFO encounter occurred in November 1979, when Robert Taylor, while walking in the woods near his home, observed a silent and stationary spherical object in the sky that he described as similar to "black sand paper," with a "row of small, circular windows around the centre." Various sections of the object were transparent and seemed to change shape. As he approached the object, two smaller spheres were released from the main object and attached themselves to his legs. The objects then discharged a pungent odor that made him nauseous and then unconsciousness. Upon waking, he had great difficulty walking, but managed to return home. An investigation revealed indentations in the area of the reported incident, none of which matched any forestry equipment or cars.

In another incident, in 1982, while driving from Los Angeles to San Francisco, two individuals sighted a fifty-foot-wide ball that looked like a living creature, described as a "series of lights, merging and rotating into each other, surrounded by a fuzzy mist." The object descended towards them, changed color, and then emitted a beam of light at their car. After a temporary blackout, they were "babbling" to each other in some unknown language for about ten to fifteen minutes when the strange experience ended.[9a]

A strange incident occurred in December 1958, when two men driving in the Swedish forest noticed a glowing craft with three legs, over 12 feet long, resting nearby on the ground. Four beings, each about 3 feet tall, blue-grey in color, and virtually amorphous, with no visible limbs, head, or any other recognizable features, were seen in front of the craft. The men described them leaping around their craft at first, but when they somehow perceived the two men, three beings approached them and attached themselves to the men, causing a suction force attempting to bring the men towards their craft. In the ensuing struggle, the men smelled an overpowering odor from the beings. During their attempt to escape, one of the men's arms allegedly entered inside the body of the creature, which had no effect. As his struggle succeeded, he was able to return to the car and sound the horn loudly, causing them to release one of the men. The beings then entered the craft, which rose up into the sky with a high-pitched noise and sped away.[9b]

In recent years, attempts have been made to investigate the popularized UFO incident in Varginha, Brazil, in 1996. The book titled, *UFOs Crash in Brazil*[10] by orthopedic surgeon and UFO researcher Dr. Roger Leir, includes interviews with military officials, hospital surgeons, and witnesses, which form the basis of his report. Briefly, the incident began when the North American Aerospace Defense Command tracked a UFO over the western hemisphere, followed by rumors of mass UFO sightings throughout southern Brazil in the days after. The incident climaxed when witnesses reported seeing a malfunctioning "submarine-shaped craft" moving slowly about twenty feet above the ground. The next day, strange creatures were reported wandering around the town in a "confused state," which prompted calls to the police that they were being visited by "monsters." Based on witness testimony, two creatures were captured and one was shot dead. The other injured creature was reportedly transferred to a hospital. Leir recalled instructions by an officer to prepare for surgery to repair a fractured leg on the alleged "bipedal" being, described as being about 5 feet tall, with large red eyes, a thin neck, and dark brown skin. After surgery, the surgeon noticed the aliens eyes fixated upon him, when he then began to feel '"hammer-like blows" to his head and chunks of information entering his mind, which he described as "thoughtgrams." The surgeon has never revealed the full extent of what the alien creature told him, except that its race felt sorry for us because we are detached from our spiritual selves and unaware of the amazing things we can accomplish that its race possesses. According to Leir, the surgeon complained of headaches for the two weeks following the event and was extremely emotional when recalling this part of the story.[10a]

While some people perceive the Varginha case with high skepticism, there is some evidence to support the incident. Ubirajara Rodriguez, an attorney and Varginha UFO case expert, obtained a copy of the death certificate of a Corporal Marco Cherez, an officer who died three weeks after he supposedly touched the creature. His death certificate states the cause of death as being from a "toxic substance." In the weeks that followed the event, a surprise visit was made to Brazil by Warren Christopher and Daniel S. Goldin who were, at the time, the U.S. Secretary of State, and Director of NASA, respectively. Dr. Leir was shown several authenticated documents concerning agreements between Brazil and America that allowed for "any material coming from space that is found in Brazil to be turned over to the government of the United States."[10b] Additionally, there are hundreds of witnesses across Varginha, who firmly believe that extraterrestrials crash landed in their city.

Thousands of residents in Voronezh, Russia, reportedly observed several appearances of UFOs over a six-day period in September 1989, which included several landings witnessed by over forty people. In one incident, a forty-five-foot-wide red light descended from the sky and hovered over a park. Suddenly, a door opened and a ten foot tall being with no neck and three eyes, wearing a silver outfit and bronze-colored boots appeared. The door then closed and the craft landed. The being verbalized and a rectangular object suddenly appeared on the ground. When one 16- year-old boy cried out in fear, the being's eyes discharged a light at the child causing temporary paralysis. The craft disappeared, but then reappeared a few minutes later. The being now held a long tube at its side that he pointed at the boy, who became invisible. The being then reentered the sphere, and as the object flew away, the boy reappeared. After taking off, the craft instantaneously disappeared in the sky. An investigation revealed that the radioactivity level at the landing site was double the background level. Traces were also found where the craft's legs stood, along with an area of flattened grass and soil.[11]

In a bizarre space incident in 1984, three cosmonauts of the Soviet space station, Salyut 7, reported the station completely surrounded in a blinding bright orange light resulting in temporary blindness.[12] As each cosmonaut looked out the window, they reported seeing the faces of seven angels outside. They told ground control their faces and bodies looked human, they had large wings behind their backs, and luminous halos above their heads. The angels kept up with the movement and speed of the space station for ten minutes before disappearing. The cosmonauts agreed that their long time in space and related stress of the mission more than likely caused this mass hallucination. After another eleven days in space, the crew was joined by three more of their colleagues from the Soyuz T-12 space craft. Soon, thereafter, the crew again reported to ground control that the space station was bathed in the same orange light. Incredibly, now all six cosmonauts reported seeing seven angels all resembling humans, but with wings. Each angel was reported as a large plane and was smiling. Again, keeping up with the movements and speed of the space station for a short while, they eventually just disappeared. How could the second crew be suffering from the stress of long-term space travel as they had just arrived? All six cosmonauts saw this event take place with no explanation as to why the same experience occurred the second time. Following this incident, which was classified as top secret, the cosmonauts were subjected to psychological and medical tests, which were all normal. NASA psychologists speculate that such "psychic" incidents reported by pilots and astronauts may be due to such factors as pressure and temperature fluctuations, and shortage of oxygen, etc.[12a]

Another strange incident involved the crew and passengers of an Aeroflot flight in 1984.[13] They reported seeing an enormous "yellow star" that projected a beam of light towards the ground, and then into the aircraft cabin forming a "green cloud." The object, which paralleled the plane, discharged several different colored lights and changed shape as if to mimic the plane. The crew reported it became a "wingless cloud-aircraft with a pointed tail." The "cloud" continued to escort the plane for over an hour until it began to descend to land. Strangely, ground radar had picked up two blips trailing behind the aircraft, and while these targets were reported to be "solid," the radar reflection of the aircraft kept fading in and out. As another plane approached the UFO, the object emitted a light that struck the two pilots. Several days later, one of them was taken to hospital where he later died from a type of blood cancer. A similar disease reportedly caused the other pilot to be disabled his entire life.[13a]

There are also many reports of UFOs mimicking human behavior. In several cases, high-powered lights have been flashed at luminous UFOs, resulting in the UFO responding by blinking back in similar sequences. UFO occupants have also been reported to employ paralyzing beams. In one incident in 1947, a geology professor on a rock-hunting expedition in Italy approached a red, lens-shaped object, about thirty feet wide and twenty feet high. He saw two small, green-skinned humanoid creatures and shouted out to them, asking them who they were. One creature then touched its belt which released a beam which dislodged the pick from his hand as he fell to the ground unable to move. The beings took the pick and returned to their craft which accelerated out of sight.[13b]

The "UFO Ranch"

A book pertaining to the many UFO sightings, and related personal experiences, theories, and cases, in the Uintah Basin in Nevada, authored by plant physiologist, Dr. Frank Salisbury, titled, *The Utah UFO Display: A Scientist's Report*,[14] is an interesting read. Associated with the unique aspect of this area is the well-known popularized ranch located in Uintah County bordering the Ute Indian Reservation. This ranch has been called the "UFO ranch" due to the longstanding strange events reported by hundreds of people over the past fifty years. These events included UFO sightings, animal mutilations and disappearances, poltergeist events, sightings of Bigfoot-like creatures, and physical effects on plants, soil, and humans. A brief summary of the results of an investigation conducted at the "UFO ranch" by researchers Kelleher and Knapp are below:

> One hundred incidents include vanishing and mutilated cattle, UFOs or orbs, large animals with piercing yellow eyes that they say were not injured when struck by bullets, and invisible objects emitting destructive magnetic fields. The National Institute for Discovery (NIDS), founded by Robert Bigelow, who bought and investigated the ranch, admitted to "difficulty obtaining evidence consistent with scientific publication" even though the NIDS scientists admitted to have seen balls of light, unknown creatures and UFOs, and mutilated animals.[15]

Tom Gorman, who bought the ranch in 1994, reported seeing floating spheres of different sizes and colors. The family contends that the blue spheres, which seemed to induce waves of fear in them, convinced them to sell the ranch. Some of the reported strange incidents at the ranch included:

1. Glowing blue orbs which may be ball lightning that caused fear.
2. Cattle were slaughtered with precision as evidenced by the removal of an ear, excision of genitals, and removal of the anus.
3. A variety of UFOs in the form of black triangles, and a large refrigerator-shaped object that hovers and disappears.
4. Reptilian creatures and humanoids that exit UFOs.
5. Balls of light that enter and exit a lake.
6. A portal lights up and humanoids exit it.
7. Voices speak from the air in an unintelligible language.[16]

A NIDS scientist who investigated the reported strange experiences at the ranch stated:

> It isn't as simple as saying that ETs or flying saucers are doing it. It's some kind of consciousness, but it's always something new and different, something non-repeatable. It's reactive to people and equipment, and we set up the ranch to be a proving ground for the scientific method, but science doesn't seem amenable to the solution of these kinds of problems.[16a]

A summary of the NIDS results provided by Dr. Salisbury, based on the analysis of witness interpretations of their experiences at the ranch, were prepared by Junior Hicks who cataloged about 400 incidents.[16b] Most incidents were UFO sightings, with thousands of other cases considered unreported.

The most significant results are summarized below:[17]

1. About 35 percent of cases involved silver or metallic objects.
2. About 22 percent of the UFOs were disks, 18 percent were doomed, and 42 percent were round or egg-shaped.
3. UFOs hovered, moved slowly, and accelerated rapidly.
4. The vast majority of UFOs were silent. A few generated different sounds.
5. About two fifths of the objects were 10-100 feet in diameter.

Salisbury considered the reported UFO sightings at Uintah Basin as "actual events" that "consist of some natural phenomenon that science does not yet comprehend. He believed that a reasonable explanation is the "extraterrestrial-machine hypothesis with its dimensional complications."[18]

One obvious question is what is so unique about the Basin to allow this highly strange phenomenon to flourish in the manner reported over so many years? Are there other Uintah Basin's to study for research purposes? And if not, why not?

Discussion

Individual accounts from highly credible individuals include reports of bizarre aerial maneuvers, close encounters, and telepathic alien communications, among other incidents characterized as "high strangeness." Collectively, they represent poorly understood events inconsistent with known physical laws and psychological behavior. If proven valid, do such incidents of "high strangeness" characterize a new area of science or are we simply dealing with creative hoaxes, a psycho-cultural phenomenon, confabulation, delusional behavior, or an unknown phenomenon? Or is some form of NHI interacting with humans? Do such reported incidents provide any unique insight to support the extraterrestrial or extra-dimensional hypotheses?

A paradox exists when we evaluate the evidence of "high strangeness" which, if true, suggests UFOs are capable of mitigating gravity and inertia, and of modifying space-time. An alternative explanation is that we may be dealing with an unknown phenomenon capable of producing these bizarre events in people's minds, or both. While it would be a giant leap to claim to know the nature of the phenomenon, as many ufologists contend they do, the answer may evolve from the work by researchers who study the source of reported cases of "high strangeness." Until the nature and origin of the phenomenon is established (if ever), hypotheses will continue to be proposed to explain such reports, but will remain only as hypotheses associated with probabilities, until an organized UFO study is begun to more seriously investigate the phenomenon using several multidisciplinary-based research approaches (See Chapter Nine: The UFO Phenomenon: A New Approach).

Maybe Carl Sagan's statement that "somewhere something incredible is waiting to be known" will be realized through a better understanding of the "high strangeness" associated with the UFO phenomena.

CHAPTER SIX

UFO Theories

Overview

The vast majority of UFO reports investigated have been explained as natural or man-made phenomena with many unresolved cases serving as the foundation for several theories that attempt to explain this longstanding mystery.[1]

1. Natural or man-made phenomena.
2. The extraterrestrial hypothesis (ETH)—UFOs are physical craft governed by non-human intelligence (NHI) from another solar system.
3. The extra-dimensional hypothesis (EDH)—NHI is operating physical craft from another dimension or parallel universe.
4. The psycho-cultural hypothesis (PCH).
5. The "paranormal" or experiences that are beyond science's ability to explain or measure.
6. Atmospheric phenomenon like plasma.
7. Time travel-UFOs are from our future.

Given the above context, keep in mind that there exists a great distance in time between many seemingly implausible theories and their acceptance once proven through scientific study. Consistent with Carl Sagan's position that "extraordinary claims require extraordinary evidence,"[2] it would seem appropriate to explore whether extraordinary theories require extraordinary evidence to prove.

The Extraterrestrial and Extra-Dimensional Hypotheses: A Debate

Although the ETH has remained the predominant explanation for UFOs, some UFO researchers have abandoned it in favor of the EDH which implies that beings coexist with us in a parallel reality, as discussed in Chapter Five:

Theories and Cases of High Strangeness. Strangely, the EDH states that the phenomenon represents visitations from other "realities" or "dimensions" that accompany our own (see *The Edge of Reality: A Progress Report on Unidentified Flying Objects*[3] and *Messengers of Deception: UFO Contacts and Cults*[4]). Could one possible "strange" hypothesis include parallel universes, or other time-like dimensions beyond the space-time reality we ascribe to, or could the strangeness of their behavior be explained on the basis of differences between the time-space continuum of UFOs and us?

Within the abstract field of quantum physics, the branch of physics dealing with physical phenomena at microscopic levels, the controversial existence of alternate realities has been promoted as a possible explanation for the UFO phenomena. Though theoretical in nature, the EDH may help explain the accounts of missing time and time distortion among other forms of "high strangeness" often experienced in a close UFO encounter. Based on anecdotal testimony, many quantum mechanical theorists believe the UFOs apparent ability to defy laws of gravity and inertia, may require different scientific methods and principles to prove the existence of a parallel reality or "muiltiverse." J. Vallée, who proposed the EDH hypothesis, provided rationale for why UFOs are not extraterrestrial:

1. Unexplained close encounters are far more numerous than required for any physical survey of the earth.
2. The humanoid body structure of the alleged "aliens" is not likely to have originated on another planet and is not biologically adapted to space travel.
3. The reported behavior in thousands of abduction reports contradicts the hypothesis of genetic or scientific experimentation on humans by an advanced race.
4. The extension of the phenomenon throughout recorded history demonstrates that UFOs are not a contemporary phenomenon.
5. The apparent ability of UFOs to manipulate space and time suggests radically different and richer alternatives.[5]

Vallée contends that these points, in addition to the alien abduction phenomenon, argue against the possibility that UFOs are extraterrestrial in origin. He suggested that if aliens did naturally evolve to a humanoid shape, they might modify their bodies using genetic engineering to enhance their ability to work and survive in space. Alternatively, he believes that UFOs that exist in higher dimensions, "which is all around us," can somehow be "retrieved and manifested in one's mind as physical events (*e.g.*, UFOs).[6]

If you accept the ETH then you must explain the associated question as to how they overcome vast distances that seem incomprehensible to journey? The popular theories that propose that some UFOs represent intelligent life visiting Earth do not address the manner in which they get "here" from "there."

Except in theory, we are oblivious to accomplishing interstellar travel. But that's a start. Several physicists have proposed theories such as the velocity-of-light constraint, wormholes, multiverse, and superstring, to explain interstellar travel, but there is still much speculation on their existence. It is presumptuous to believe, however, that any one of these theories is not viable since history is filled with "impossible" ideas that eventually became true. Is it possible that there are energy sources and/or interstellar gateways yet to be discovered that may provide the means to travel among the stars within a reasonable time frame? If the reported inexplicable behavior of UFOs is valid, as described by hovering, accelerating from a standstill position to over several thousand miles per hour, and performing angular turns at tremendous speed, then an argument may be made for a technology and/or energy source that can provide the means to travel vast distances in space. Alternatively, if the theoretical "wormhole" actually exists, allowed for by Einstein's Theory of General Relativity, interstellar travel may be accomplished by the curvature of space-time which connects two distant locations or times. Accordingly, the ETH has become more likely through alternative theories that make the "they can't get here from there" argument for the ETH more persuasive.

One theoretical approach proposed by Thorne and Sagan concerns the possibility of "wormholes" that may provide a shortcut through space-time.[7] The possible existence of traversable wormholes would allow travel from one part of the universe to another part of that same or different universe very quickly. Dr. Paul Hill, a former NASA researcher and engineer, who developed a theory of UFO propulsion based on the effects of relativity, also believes that "interstellar distances are not insurmountable."[8] Consequently, could the UFO phenomenon be based on this hypothetical interpretation of quantum mechanics? According to theoretical physicist Stephen Hawking, wormholes may exist in quantum form which provides tunnels that link separate locations to enable interstellar time travel from other civilizations in the universe. Hawking stated:

> Down at the smallest of scales, smaller even than molecules, smaller than atoms, we get to a place called the quantum foam. This is where wormholes exist. Tiny tunnels or shortcuts through space and time constantly form, disappear, and reform within this quantum world. And they actually link two separate places and two different times.[9]

Based on his experiences investigating hundreds of UFO reports as a scientific adviser to several studies undertaken by the U.S. Air Force to scientifically analyze UFO-related events, Dr. J. Allen Hynek was in a unique position to provide keen insights of the ETH and EDH. According to Hynek, there is "sufficient evidence to defend both the ETH and EDH hypothesis."[10] Evidence for the ETH include radar and physical-trace cases, while evidence to support the EDH included the aspect of "materialization and dematerialization," "telepathic communication," the "kinematic behavior of UFOs," "levitation of cars or persons," and the "development by some of psychic abilities after an encounter." Based on the ETH and EDH, he questioned whether we have "two aspects of one phenomenon or two different sets of phenomena."[10a] Hynek discussed his position of the phenomenon at the 1978 UFO Hearing held at the United Nations stating: "It is a phenomenon so strange and foreign to our daily terrestrial mode of thought that it is frequently met by ridicule and derision by persons and organizations unacquainted with the facts." Further, in a paper presented to the Joint Symposium of the American Institute of Aeronautics & Astronautics, Hynek wrote:

> I ask you to explain quantitatively, not qualitatively, the reported phenomena of materialization and dematerialization, of shape changes, of the noiseless hovering in the Earth's gravitational field, accelerations that, for an appreciable mass, require energy sources far beyond present capabilities, even theoretical capabilities, the well-known and often reported electromagnetic interference effect, the psychic effects on percipients, including purported telepathic communications.[10b]

As most theories serve as a source of debate, the ETH is no exception. For example, in contrast to positions that support the ETH, arguments against it were presented by Dr. Hynek at the 1983 MUFON Symposium:

1. Failure of sophisticated surveillance systems to detect incoming or outgoing UFOs.
2. Isolation of the UFO phenomenon in time and space.
3. The space unworthiness of UFOs.
4. The problem of astronomical distances.[11]

Nick Pope, a Scientific Officer in Great Brittan's Ministry of Defense (MoD) who was responsible for the government's UFO reports, advocated for the ETH based on the inexplicable UFO cases he reviewed such as the "Rendlesham Forest Incident."[12] Additionally, Jean-Jacques Velasco, the head of the official French UFO investigation SEPRA, stated that fourteen percent of the 5,800 cases studied were "utterly inexplicable and extraterrestrial in origin."[13] Yves Sillard, the head of the new official French UFO investigation, GEIPAN, and former head of the French space agency, supported Velasco's conclusion. Additionally, the 1999 French COMETA, composed of high-level military analysts/generals and aerospace engineers/scientists, concluded:

> ...that the physical reality of UFOs, under control of intelligent beings, is "quasi-certain." Only one hypothesis takes into account the available data: the hypothesis of extraterrestrial visitors. This hypothesis is

> of course unproven, but has far-reaching consequences. The goals of these alleged visitors remain unknown but must be the subject of speculations and prospective scenarios.[14]

Several European countries who conducted a secret joint study in 1954, also declared that UFOs were extraterrestrial. German rocketry pioneer Hermann Oberth, who headed the study, stated "these objects (UFOs) are conceived and directed by intelligent beings of a very high order. They do not originate in our solar system, perhaps not in our galaxy."[15] Adding to the ETH/EDH debate, astrophysicist Dr. Peter A. Sturrock, stated:

> Discussions of the UFO issue have remained narrowly polarized between advocates and adversaries of a single theory, namely the extraterrestrial hypothesis. This fixation on the ETH has narrowed and impoverished the debate, precluding an examination of other possible theories for the phenomenon.[16]

The general scientific community, who regards the ufology discipline as a "pseudoscience," is highly skeptical of any extraordinary theory such as the ETH or EDH to explain the UFO phenomenon. Despite the well-accepted notion that intelligent life forms likely exist in the universe, most scientists dismiss the possibility that UFOs are ET, since "they can't get here from there." Skeptics of the UFO phenomenon often defend their position and debunk ufology, and by default, the ETH and EDH, by citing Dr. Carl Sagan's position on the validity of UFOs, as mentioned previously:

> Reliable cases are uninteresting and the interesting cases are unreliable. Unfortunately there are no cases that are both reliable and interesting. There was no strong evidence that aliens were visiting the Earth either in the past or present.[17]

Stephen Hawking, also argued that UFOs have ordinary explanations.[18] Similarly, Dr. David Morrison, director of the Carl Sagan Center for Study of Life in the Universe at the SETI Institute, and senior scientist at the NASA Astrobiology Institute, stated:

> No one has ever found a single artifact, or any other convincing evidence for such alien visits. As far as I know, no claims of UFOs as being alien craft have any validity. The claims are without substance, and certainly not proved.[19]

The leading argument against the ETH is that it is just too far to travel here. For example, if we engage in some light math, traveling at the speed of light of about 186,000 miles per second, would still take about 4 years to reach our closet star, Proxima Centauri, 4.24 light years distance or 26 trillion miles away. Alternatively, it would take the shuttle space craft traveling at 25,000 mph over 100,000 years to land on an orbiting planet of this star system. And if beings on such a planet wanted to come here traveling 600,000 mph or 200 miles per second, it would take over 4,000 years! The enormous distance between planets and solar systems make interstellar travel impractical, particularly because of the incredible amount of energy required using conventional means. More specifically, 7 × 1019 Joules of energy is needed to send the space shuttle on a one-way, 50-year, journey to the nearest star.[20] Not only are the distance and required energy major obstacles to interstellar travel, interstellar gas is another. The significant heating effect from hydrogen and other atoms as the craft approaches the speed of light will melt it. Despite these impeding factors, the ETH remains one of the most popular theories to explain the origin of UFOs and has become more likely through alternative theories, such as, the wormholes, multiverse, and superstring that may allow for interstellar travel.

Additionally, official statements by NASA and the White House, concomitant with the absence of "proof" in the search for extraterrestrial intelligence, have also argued against the validity of the UFO-ETH connection. For instance, in November 2011, the White House released an official response to petitions asking the U.S. Government to acknowledge formally that aliens have visited earth and to disclose any intentional withholding of government interactions with extraterrestrial beings. The official response stated:

> The U.S. government has no evidence that any life exists outside our planet, or that an extraterrestrial presence has contacted or engaged any member of the human race. There is no credible information to suggest that any evidence is being hidden from the public's eye.[21]

Similarly, NASA's position in 2006 was that the ETH to explain UFOs has a "lack of empirical evidence." Scientists have been searching for intelligence in our galaxy for decades and, to date, no signal from any extraterrestrial stellar system has ever been "officially" detected. Scientific studies have also examined UFO reports with none concluding that any were caused by ET spacecraft. The UFO Subcommittee of the American Institute of Aeronautics and Astronautics (AIAA), for example, reported that, "we know of no means for the UFOs to beat the laws of physics (*i.e.*, relativity) and cross the vast distances of interstellar space, unless they can somehow bend space and time as has been suggested." However, the AIAA concluded that about a third of the cases could not be explained and worthy of further study.[22]

Psychological and Sociological Theories

Psycho-social theorists have provided several reasons to explain UFO and alien abduction reports and beliefs. Overall, they contend there must be either a conscious or subconscious recall from various media forms or a heightened level of gullibility influenced and reinforced by the strong social context of the UFO phenomenon. Carl Gustav Jung, the psychotherapist and psychiatrist who founded analytical psychology, advocated the psycho-cultural hypothesis (PCH) and paranormal theory to explain the UFO phenomena.[23] The PCH regards the UFO phenomenon as a cultural phenomenon in which the belief in UFOs developed out of our societies interest with space-flight reinforced by media hype of aliens and flying saucers. Although Jung believed that UFOs might be psychological manifestations, he did rule out the possibility of intelligently controlled physical objects.

Another proponent of the PCH, neurologist Dr. Steven Novella, president and co-founder of the New England Skeptical Society, considers the UFO phenomenon an example of "modern mythology," which evolved out of "popular culture" facilitated by the media. Supportive evidence for this notion is largely based on the evolution of how aliens have evolved over time. Novella provides examples of how witness reports changed from "hairy dwarfs to giant insects" to the current "grey" alien which appeared after the famous Betty and Barney Hill abduction case in 1961. Novella wrote:

> Once certain details become a standard part of the mythology, they are often then retrofitted into older stories. The famous Roswell Incident, for example, existed for almost thirty years, from 1947 until the 1970s, without any mention of alien bodies. It was only after the little grays emerged that testimony arose of witnesses seeing similar aliens in Roswell in 1947.[24]

Further support for the PCH was provided by Bartholomew and Howard, who described the airship sightings of 1896-1897 as analogous to current UFO descriptions.[25] Interest in "flying machines" at that time resulted in "sightings of unidentified lights or objects in the sky that were quickly interpreted as the expected airships" by credible witnesses. The authors contend that "media hype" was responsible for changing human behavior in accordance with the PCH. Further, the objects reported at that time were consistent with 19th century portrayals with "flapping wings and bulbous fuselages," rather than the modern-day descriptions of UFOs.[25a]

Some theories propose that UFO experiences may represent psychological abnormalities resulting from Temporal Lobe Epilepsy, or Fantasy-Prone Personality Syndrome, among other psychologically based conditions. Accordingly, the experience is "real" to the individual. While most theories of this kind involve neurological and biochemical explanations, the "psychoanalytic" explanation cites stress-related effects and disordered personality types as a basis to explain reported UFO experiences. Further, if the UFO sighting occurred long ago, the witness may also add information that did not occur, which psychologist's term "confabulation," (*i.e.*, filling in memory gaps and paraphrasing of events). Confabulation can range in credibility from relatively mild to more severe forms which can be bizarre.[26] While memory distortion as manifested in "confabulation" is a normal memory process, certain forms of brain damage can result in a person making inaccurate statements without trying to be deceptive. If those who suffer from altered states of consciousness also have a strong belief in UFOs, the probability of perceiving a UFO may be enhanced. That is, psychological processes may simulate the appearance of UFOs and their occupants. Does this imply that all who recall UFO experiences have a form of brain damage that manifests in so-called "bizarre" confabulations or a type of "normal" memory distortion? Not likely. If memory distortions fail to explain UFO experiences, then perhaps it can be explained by the PCH. Alternatively, can the PCH be interrelated with confabulation, confirmation bias, or delusions to explain some, if not all, individual UFO reports?

A strong argument against the PCH is that many UFO sightings involve multiple witnesses, and simultaneous radar-visual sightings. Accordingly, while it is acknowledged that some encounters may contain a psychological component, it is unlikely that all UFO sightings can be explained solely on the basis of the PCH and related psychological explanations.

Paranormal

The paranormal theory, while interesting to contemplate, resides at the fringe along the UFO theory continuum, especially since the "paranormal" may not be measurable and explained using the scientific method. Given the "high strangeness" of the UFO phenomenon, any proposed theory to explain unusual aerial events will almost certainly be met with a high degree of skepticism. Within this context, is it possible that the "high strangeness" associated with the phenomenon provides evidence of its nature and origin? This theory, regarded as "pseudoscience" by mainstream science, suggests that UFOs are paranormal manifestations, which evolved from the reported "high strangeness" associated with the phenomenon. This is evidenced by witness reports of "shape-shifting" UFOs, their apparent ability to materialize and dematerialize, reports of aliens floating through structures, and telepathic communication with aliens associated with many UFO encounters. Some UFO researchers make analogous assumptions between the behavior of UFOs and their occupants and other "paranormal" areas of study, which include apparitions, the Men-in-Black phenomenon, and demons.

A proponent of the paranormal theory, journalist and ufologist John Keel used the term "ultraterrestrials" for UFO occupants he believed to be "shape-changing, non-human" beings.[27] Interestingly, a large segment of UFO literature is associated with the occult and the metaphysical, like invisible beings, demons, and ghosts, and many UFO reports recount alleged incidents that are similar to demonic possession and psychic phenomena. According to Keel, in some UFO encounters, people are not able to identify the site of their experience, as evidenced by reports that landmarks, roads, and highways seem to vanish.[27a] Keel believes that a close-encounter experience commonly begins with a sudden flash of light, which changes color, or a humming/buzzing sound, followed by a type of paralysis associated with hallucinations and lost time for up to several hours. An apparent physical object also begins to form, such as an unusual flying machine or an entity of some kind.

Some people have reported encounters with strange creatures and a variety of paranormal events, especially poltergeist phenomena associated with luminous phenomenon or physical UFOs. Some develop psychic powers such as telepathy and psychic healing, or report visits by threatening "Men in Black," who apply pressure in an effort to silence them, or they see apparitions which sometimes attack them. UFO researchers have also reported paranormal-type experiences after they began to study the UFO phenomenon manifested by UFO sightings or abductions, harassment by mysterious persons, and paranormal experiences. Additional evidence to support the paranormal theory is provided in a discussion of the highly unusual UFO experiences associated with the "UFO Ranch" (*i.e.,* Skinwalker ranch) located in the Uintah County of Utah. This interesting case is discussed in Chapter Five: Theories and Cases of High Strangeness.

Plasma

What is plasma and its possible relationship to the UFO phenomenon? Plasma, which carries electrical current and generates magnetic fields, "comprises more than ninety-nine percent of the visible universe, and permeates the solar system, interstellar and intergalactic environments."[28] Similar to ball lightning, plasma is an atmospheric phenomenon not fully understood by modern science. Theoretically, the phenomenon of ionized and excited atmospheric molecules around a UFO also ties together a number of related mysteries about the phenomenon:

1. General nighttime appearance of the UFO.
2. Many colors.
3. Self-illuminating character.
4. Fuzzy appearance.
5. Indiscernible outline with the appearance of a physical object/craft behind the light.

This evidence, which is similar to witness descriptions of the appearance and behavior of UFOs, reinforces the notion that many people who encountered a UFO may have experienced a plasma-related phenomena. Extensive research on plasma by Dr. V.N. Tsytovich, a scientist at the General Physics Institute, Russian Academy of Science, while working with colleagues there and at the Max-Planck Institute for Extraterrestrial Physics in Garching, Germany, studied the behavior of complex mixtures of inorganic materials in plasma and concluded that plasma exhibited:

1. Gradual growth.
2. Splitting into two or more separate parts.
3. Dissolution to invisibility.
4. Disparate bright lights merging into larger formations (often reported as small craft joining the mother ship and forming a row of portholes).
5. Disappearance, accompanied by a smell.
6. Rotation, nonlinear motion.
7. Weak thermal radiation.
8. Beamed light emissions.[28a]

Interestingly, most, if not all, of these behaviors have been similarly described by witnesses during UFO encounters. The beamed light emissions, reported by witnesses of UFOs, were explained by the Russian scientists as "discharge, or leakage paths" that allow the plasma to "float off" and to change direction, seemingly at will. Findings similar to those reported by Tsytovich were made by astrophysicist Dr. Massimo Teodorani and his associates, who researched anomalous plasma formations in the valley of Hessdalen, Norway, where for more than two decades people reported pulsing lights that change shape. The phenomenon observed by the team of scientists was partitioned into two groups:

1. Thermal plasmas (95 percent).
2. Unidentified solid objects (5 percent).

The researchers concluded:

1. Most of the luminous phenomena are thermal plasma.
2. The light balls are constituted of many small components that are vibrating around a common center.
3. The light balls are able to eject smaller light balls.
4. The light balls change shape all the time.
5. They are able to divide themselves into several parts.
6. They have the ability to penetrate solid objects.
7. They emit a wide range of electromagnetic waves.[29]

Evidence to support a "plasma"-based theory was provided in a report from Project Condign (1997-2000), a secret UFO study of over 10,000 sightings occurring over a thirty-year span (1967-1997), undertaken by the British

Government's Defense Intelligence Staff. The study concluded that UFOs are "highly charged atmospheric plasmas"[30], which can cause neurological effects on humans who encountered them.[31] The project concluded:

1. Seventy-five percent of people felt odd or dizzy or reported tingling sensations.
2. Sixty-five percent saw vivid images and/or said they experienced pleasant vibrations.
3. Forty percent said they experienced fear or terror.

Interestingly, witnesses having a close UFO encounter often report similar effects.[31a]

Ball lightning, an atmospheric electrical phenomenon, which usually appears as a luminous spherical object, that varies from a few inches to several meters in diameter and is capable of flying in formation and forming patterns of several balls, produce a characteristic sphere or round shape of a reported UFO. These balls are also able to move synchronously and to join and then part again. When flying in formation, it gives the appearance of a solid craft.

It is important to note the striking similarities between the patterns of plasma behavior above and those reported by witnesses of UFO encounters described in chapter Three: UFO Behavior and Effects. The commonly shared characteristics of both, as described through anecdotal testimony, suggests that many reported UFO encounters may involve the interaction between humans and plasma energy! The UFO's ability to split, rotate, disappear, and emit light, may also contribute to the perception that it is under "intelligent control," a frequent conclusion by witnesses of UFOs. Thus, could all or some UFOs be plasma based? Are we dealing with one or more phenomenon such as plasma, the EDH, ETH, PCH, paranormal, and natural and/or man-made, or something yet to be discovered?

Physicists Tsytovich and Teodorani examined 120 UFO cases involving aviation safety issues, in 2009, and suggested that a "misunderstanding" has contributed to a "blind spot" in research that is overlooking atmospheric phenomena, like "plasmoids," as a basis for most UFO sightings, and that "spherical UFOs radiate energy and could be a threat to vital aviation systems."[32] Many pilots and aviation professionals have reported safety-related incidents/observations of spherical UFOs described as "lights," "metallic," or "glowing" objects. According to Teodorani, they perform "complex trajectories, high rates of speed, and unusual movements that are often regarded as a hazard by aircrews."[32a] For example, 15 of 44 aviation safety-related spherical UFO cases reviewed described near mid-air collisions.

Another explanation for the possible UFO-plasma phenomenon connection was proposed by neuroscientist Dr. Michael Persinger, called the "tectonic strain theory."[33] According to Persinger, this light energy results when layers of rock under the earth's surface are pushed into each other, as during tremors or earthquakes, causing energy to rise to the surface. This energy appears as a concentrated sphere of light, which moves erratically for a few seconds to several minutes. Persinger, who analyzed over 3,000 UFO sightings, found that many of them occurred weeks or months before the start of tremors. He also proposed that the luminous energy from tectonic fractures may cause witnesses close to the phenomenon to hallucinate or to temporarily blackout. He contends that, "the electromagnetic fields generate hallucinations in the temporal lobe, based on images from popular culture of alien craft, beings, communications, or creatures."[33a] This physiological effect may explain some, if not all, of the "high strangeness" cases reported by those who experience close encounters with luminous appearing objects. Persinger's claims regarding the effects of environmental geomagnetic activity on the production of UFOs, paranormal experiences, and physiological effects in humans are controversial and have not been replicated by independent investigators.

Theoretical physicist, Dr. Matti Pitkänen, who supports the "tectonic strain theory," suggests that UFOs might be "plasmoids," which he contends are "primitive life-forms" that could "easily follow the energy beam flowing from the spot of tectonic activity."[34] Pitkänen also believes that the "random variation of the beam direction" could explain the often reported "random butterfly-like motion of UFOs."[34a] In contrast, astronomer, Chris Rutkowski, contested Persinger's statistical methodology, which he feels confuses "correlation with causality."[35] Rutkowski also criticized Persinger's theory, since it fails to adequately account for UFO sightings in regions distant from tectonic fractures.[36]

Paul Devereux, co-founder and the managing editor of the academic publication *Time & Mind–the Journal of Archaeology, Consciousness and Culture*, and a Research Fellow with the International Consciousness Research Laboratories (ICRL) group at Princeton University, believes most UFOs are earthlights:

1. Over forty percent of UFO sightings occur on or close to geological faults (*i.e.*, electromagnetic activity).
2. Earthlights exhibit intelligence as reflected in their apparent ability to respond to the movements and thoughts of observers.[37]

Interestingly, paranormal activity is commonly reported during earthlight activity, and both UFO and poltergeist activity seem to increase during enhanced geomagnetic activity.[38] While there are obvious similarities between earthlights and UFO reports, the earthlight theory may not explain all UFO sightings, since UFOs are seen in seismically inactive areas, and the largest earthlights are generally only several feet across, whereas some UFOs have been described as over several hundred feet in diameter.

In support of Devereux's extraordinary claim that "earthlights exhibit intelligence," and Pitkänen's belief that plasma is a "primitive life-form," theoretical physicist David Bohm reported that once "electrons were in plasma, they stopped behaving like individuals and started behaving as if they were a part of a larger and interconnected whole."[38a] He reported having an impression that plasma was "alive" and had some "traits of living things."[38b] The debate on the existence of plasma-based life forms has been going on for more than twenty years, ever since some models showed that plasma can mimic the functions of a primitive cell. This luminous energy, believed to be discharged into the atmosphere, was duplicated by Dr. Brian Brady who exposed quartz rock to a pressure of 23,000 pound per square inch, resulting in a discharge of small lights.[39]

Such luminous energy, described in shape, such as a ball and pillar, may constitute some percentage of UFO reports.[40] Earthlights seen in daylight can also appear shiny and metallic and are likely to have a spherical, oval, or disc form. Multiple earthlights have also been reported to fly together, divide and merge, and move in a coordinated fashion. Interestingly, these descriptions are also commonly reported by those who report a typical UFO.

Plasma research is still in its early phases, and it is premature to verify such astonishing conclusions. An interesting article by David Pratt, titled, "UFOs: The Psychic Dimension," presents examples of UFO encounters associated with "earthlights" or possible plasma energy, some of which are presented below:[41]

> In northeastern Oklahoma, 10 to 15 people observed an orange-yellow light, 1-2 feet in diameter, which suddenly appeared about 30 feet away in the middle of the road. It was "throbbing and slowly rolling along the ground." The light rose up to about 10 feet above the ground, split into 2 sections, and shot into the woods in both directions at once.
>
> In 1975, a teacher saw a dark cloud, 1-2 feet in diameter hovering above his house. While floating, it changed shape from a "small globular mass to a larger ovoid, and finally morphed into a dark, multi-curved, vaporous form, about 6 feet high and 1.5 feet wide." Strangely, the cloud "seemed to inhale, pursed its 'lips', and directed a stream of water towards him and the car, soaking both." A minute later the spray stopped, and the cloud vanished.
>
> In 1951, U.S. soldiers in Korea observed a glowing, disc-shaped UFO moving in their direction. One of the soldiers shot it and heard the sound of metal hitting metal. The object "went wild" and began to move erratically and flash its light off and on. The men then heard a sound like the revving of a generator, and were swept by some form of a ray, which produced a burning, tingling sensation. A few days later, they were evacuated as they were too weak to walk.
>
> In 1965, a "metallic lifeform" appeared in Rio Vista, California, described as cigar-shaped, about 5 feet in diameter and 12 to 15 feet long. A few hundred people observed the glowing red object move

> noiselessly a few hundred feet above the treetops. Some people shot at the object, which resulted in a "metallic twang" and caused the object to flare up bright red.

Another type of natural atmospheric event associated with thunderstorm activity known as "sprites" may also be responsible for some UFO sightings. A sprite, elicited by lightning between an underlying thundercloud and the ground, is composed of "electrical discharges that occur high above thunderstorm clouds."[42] Sprites are reddish-orange in color with bluish hanging tendrils below, and usually occur in clusters of two or more at an altitude ranging between thirty and sixty miles. According to Colin Price, director of the Geophysics and Planetary Sciences Department at Tel Aviv University, "these bizarre flashes of light can even appear to purposefully dance in the sky, thus giving the impression that there is some sort of intelligence behind them."[42a]

Given the unique similarity in the reported appearance and behavior of both atmospheric "plasma" and UFOs, the obvious question is whether or not all or part of the small percentage of unexplained UFOs can be accounted for by this natural phenomenon. It is imperative that future research focus on this connection to establish the percentage of UFO reports attributed to this atmospheric phenomenon.

Time Travel

According to the time travel theory, UFOs are visitors from our own future. Some UFO researchers believe those from our future are returning to their past for needed DNA. Part of the rationale for this theory evolved from the descriptions of the frail humanoid "grey" beings, usually seen during reported alien abductions. It is speculated that their apparent fragile condition requires them to interbreed with humans to modify their genetic material. The alien-hybrid babies reportedly seen during the abduction scenario also lend support for this theory. Additionally, based on anecdotal evidence, "normal" appearing humans within physical craft have identified themselves as from our future.

While highly controversial on many levels, the obvious initial question to address is whether time travel is possible. This naturally incorporates the theory of general relativity, which suggests that if you move fast enough through space, the observations that you make about space-time differ from the observations of others moving at different speeds. The concept of time travel is highly debatable, since the solutions to the equations of general relativity that describe space-time remain tentative. Many in the scientific community also believe that traveling back in time is highly unlikely due to problems of "causality." The classic example of a problem involving causality is the debated "grandfather paradox,"[43] which asks: what if you went back in time and killed your grandfather before your father was born? While this incident would be expected to upset the balance of current-day affairs, some scientists believe that such a paradox could be avoided by the notion of "branching parallel universes." That is, the theory of general relativity permits time travel avoiding this paradox. In other words, when the past is changed by killing someone, a new universe is created, with the original one the same and the new one containing the modification.

An important viewpoint that challenges the time travel theory is provided by one of the most brilliant theoretical physicists in history, Stephen Hawking, who stated:

> Einstein's general theory of relativity seems to offer the possibility that we could warp space-time so much that we could travel back in time. However, it is likely that warping would trigger a bolt of radiation that would destroy the spaceship and maybe the space-time itself. I have experimental evidence that time travel is not possible.[44]

Consequently, if Hawking is correct, UFOs are not from our future. Alternatively, if he's wrong, maybe they are?

Discussion

Many who believe that some UFOs are physical craft from another solar system or space-time, do so based on pure faith and the human tendency to want to believe in something. That is, scientific verification of a theory often takes a back seat to those who tend to formulate conclusions in a biased fashion. The motivation to do so may be based on the accepted premise that the existence of intelligent life in the universe is extremely high, and possibly even a touch of wishful thinking. Could this possibly explain why many who observe an unusual object in the sky will interpret it as an ET craft, while others who see the same object will consider it to be of earthly origin?

In the absence of definitive proof, several UFO theories will continue to facilitate the longstanding debate of the true nature and origin of the phenomenon. And in the absence of such proof, no one theory will be accepted by the scientific community and skeptics alike who generally accept one or more alternative theories, such as natural and man-made phenomena, advanced secret technology, and the psycho-cultural hypothesis, among others, to explain the phenomenon. While some theories may sound more plausible than others, theories alone do not provide the definitive proof that explains the force that controls and regulates this phenomenon.

CHAPTER SEVEN

The Alien Abduction Phenomenon

Overview

One's interpretation that UFOs are extraterrestrial in origin provides the foundation for understanding the alien abduction phenomenon (AAP); *i.e.*, conscious or hypnotic induced memories of being taken by alien beings and subjected to biological procedures. If you consider that UFOs are extraterrestrial craft, the AAP is plausible, but if you believe that UFOs are nothing more than natural or man-made phenomenon, then the AAP may be explained by one or more "non-alien" theories such as the false-memory syndrome, sleep paralysis, psychological disorders, or the psycho-cultural hypothesis, among others. Even if aliens are not abducting humans, the AAP is still an extraordinary mystery worthy of further study. And if aliens are abducting humans, how do we prove it?

The absence of irrefutable evidence to support the belief by many UFO researchers that an alien intelligence has visited Earth, also applies to the AAP. The strongest evidence to support the AAP is the consistency of the experience by those claiming to have been abducted (Hopkins[1], 1987; Jacobs[2], 1992; and Mack[3], 1995). This anecdotal evidence, concomitant with the controversial physiological effects that may accompany the AAP like scars and implants, and the absence from expected locations at the time of abduction, verified independently in a few cases by Mack[3a] (1995), provide the primary evidence to support the AAP. Abduction researchers also report that alien abductions occur in different members of the same families at different stages of their lives. Comparative studies by Dr. T. Bullard of hundreds of individuals claiming to have been abducted also suggest that the same episode recur in eighty percent of "high informative" cases.[4]

Since the scientific community considers the UFO phenomenon highly unlikely, the AAP, by default is also considered a remote possibility. This is based, in large part, on the absence of compelling physical evidence to validate that UFOs are extraterrestrial craft. The lack of objective evidence in the form of corroborating physical evidence for firsthand accounts of alien abductions, and no witness accounts of an abduction also serve to invalidate abduction claims, and provide support for one or more "non-alien" related AAP theories mentioned above. The scientific community also dismisses the AAP on the basis of research-supported psychological explanations, which include biased or inaccurate memory, unreliable perception, social pressures motivating lies, and hypnotists influencing highly suggestible witnesses. Scientists, for instance, claim that a person's memory can restructure situations the abductee has seen in the media that pertain to alien abductions and UFOs. Another concern is that the subject desires and expects the abduction event and the hypnotist leads the "suggestible" person to that conclusion. In contrast, several abduction researchers, such as history professor Dr. David Jacobs, psychologist Dr. Leo Sprinkle, psychiatrist Dr. John Mack, and ufologists Thomas Bullard and Budd Hopkins, among others, support the validity of the AAP. In 1992, a five-day conference, chaired by M.I.T.'s Professor of Physics, Dr. David Pritchard, and Harvard Professor of Psychiatry, Dr. John Mack, was held at M.I.T. to examine "the findings of various investigators studying people who report experiences of abductions by aliens, and the related issues of the phenomenon." The conference proceedings can be reviewed in a book by C. Bryan, titled, *Close Encounters of the Fourth Kind: A Reporter's Notebook on Alien Abduction, UFOs, and the Conference at M.I.T*[5], which recounts cases of being taken aboard extraterrestrial spacecraft and examined by aliens. Additional information on the AAP may be obtained from the following sources:

1. International Center for Abduction Research (www.ufoabduction.com).
2. Alien Abduction Experience and Research (www.abduct.com/books/b29.php).
3. Alien Abduction articles on UFO Evidence (www.ufoevidence.org/topics/Abduction.html).
4. Abduction Information Center (www.virtuallystrange.net/aic).

The Alien Abduction Experience

Abduction reports consistently include features that seem implausible, such as moving through walls, levitation, the ability to immobilize a person, and mental communication with alien beings. Procedures that seem to involve biological research are the focus of most alleged abduction experiences. Based on anecdotal hypnotherapy-induced recall from abductees, Dr. David Jacobs, a leading abduction researcher, contends that the abduction experience, "is precisely orchestrated, and the procedures are predetermined. The beings are task-oriented and there is no indication whatsoever that we have been able to find any aspect of their lives outside of performing the abduction procedures."[6]

These procedures, conducted on a table with a bright light overhead, most often involve the reproductive system, and the sinus cavities. Rodeghier (1994)[7] and Mack (1995)[8] described the most frequent features of the abduction experience:

1. Taken against one's will to an unfamiliar environment by a being described as technologically superior and non-human.
2. Subjected to invasive medical procedures.
3. Expresses strong emotion related to this experience.

A study of 150 abduction reports found tables mentioned in 39 percent, computer/TV screens in 13 percent, computers in 12 percent, chairs in 8 percent, counters or shelves in 7 percent, cabinets in 7 percent, and benches in 4 percent.[9] According to Bullard (1989), additional experiences often reported by the abductees involve:

1. Sexual liaisons.
2. They forget the majority of their experience.
3. Are returned to earth, occasionally in a different location from where they were allegedly taken.
4. May have a feeling of oneness with God, or their abductors.
5. Must cope with the effects of the experience (*e.g.*, psychological, physical, and social).[10]

Based on his research with reported abductees, Dr. Jacobs described a typical abduction experience:

> In a common abduction, humans are taken out of their normal environment by aliens. The people are rendered passive and cannot resist. They are taken aboard a UFO, their clothes are removed and they are made to lie on a table. A series of physical, mental, and productive procedures are then administered to the subjects. People's physical bodies are probed and examined. Sperm is taken, eggs are harvested. The aliens perform staring procedures during which they gaze into abductees' eyes at a distance of only an inch or two. These "mindscan" procedures appear to be neurological manipulations which give the aliens the ability to "enter into" peoples' minds. After the table procedures, abductees report that they are sometimes taken into other rooms where they are required to have skin on skin contact with unusual looking babies. Abductees say that these babies seem to be crosses between humans and aliens. They call them "hybrids." Abductees also see hybrid toddlers, older youth, adolescents, and adults. Sometimes abductees report that they are required to perform tasks, that they are "tested" in some way. They say that machines

> are brought in to examine them. They sometimes are required to have a form of sexual intercourse with other humans, and sometimes with adolescent and adult hybrids. They are returned to their normal environment and within seconds, they forget what has just happened to them.[11]

As mentioned in Jacobs' statement above, a common feature of the AAP reported by abductees is the procedure termed "Mindscan" in which the alien stares into their eyes, which elicit various emotional states and visual images. Mindscan has been associated with "harvesting" by which the alien causes sexual stimulation prior to an internal procedure to recover an egg or sperm. Some abductees report that hybrids have had on-going, complex, contact with them since they were children.[11a]

Hypnotherapy and the Alien Adduction Phenomenon: The Debate

Despite the use of hypnosis as an effectiveness treatment for several health-related problems and procedures, such as digestive, insomnia, and anesthesia, and the acceptance by the American Psychological Association (APA) of its value in clinical use (APA, 2006), hypnosis is considered a controversial method for eliciting memory recall in those who allege to have been abducted by aliens. Hypnotherapy has also been criticized for its limited effectiveness recovering lost or hidden memories, and the likelihood of "suggestibility" by extrinsic influences on those undergoing hypnosis. In other words, one's altered state of mind during hypnosis may be responsible for the creation of an abduction scenario. Psychologists Loftus and Clark, commented that, research on hypnotically induced memory reveals that, "hypnosis does not result in increased memory accuracy but merely increased output. Hypnotically induced testimony has been ruled inadmissible in most courts, because it greatly increases the witness's vulnerability to suggestion and because it is based on a false theory of memory."[12] This position, substantiated by experimental research on recovered and false memories due to hypnosis, has raised serious questions of the accuracy of the abduction experiences retrieved under hypnosis. In contrast, hypnosis has been considered a reliable and often necessary tool by abduction investigators to help facilitate memory recall of abduction events that may otherwise remain uncovered (B. Hopkins, 1987; D. Jacobs, 1992; J. Mack, 1995).

Researchers who use hypnosis to investigate alleged alien abduction experiences contend they purposely lead the subject away from the abduction narrative, and suggest a more rational explanation, which is often "met with great resistance." Dr. Jacobs who supports the use of hypnosis in his AAP research stated:

> Hypnosis properly used by asking the right questions in the right way at the right time can elicit information that surpasses consciously recalled material in its detail and accuracy. Research, however, has demonstrated that confabulation is as possible under hypnosis as it is in ordinary memory and that, in some cases, while memory recall is increased under hypnosis, so is inaccurate recall.[13]

While the majority of alien abductees recall their abduction(s) through hypnosis,[14] some abductees claim to have conscious memories without hypnosis (B. Hopkins, 1987; D. Jacobs, 1992; J. Mack, 1995). Due to the extensive use of hypnosis, the abduction narratives are frequently explained by skeptics as false memories and suggestions by the hypnotherapist.[15] A frequent claim by skeptics is that abductees often seek hypnotherapists to resolve issues, such as missing time or unexplained physical symptoms that often involve two phases:

1. An information gathering stage, in which the hypnotherapist asks about unexplained illnesses or unusual phenomena during the patients lives caused by the alleged abduction.
2. Hypnosis and guided imagery to facilitate recall. It is believed that this process increases the possibility that this discussion will be introduced into later abduction "memories."[16]

While Jacobs cites this as a limitation to support alien abductions, he contends: "we must do the best with what we have."[17]

Dr. Thomas Bullard, who conducted a large-scale comparative analysis of about 300 alleged alien abduction cases concluded: "whether hypnosis shapes and implants memories, or breaks through a surface screen memory to reveal the true appearance of the beings, the AAP remains a question in need of resolution."[18] Additionally, in an article by psychologists Newman and Baumeister (1996), the APP was explained on a cognitive basis, which involves the "integration and elaborations of hallucinations" aided by hypnosis.[19] Thus the "pitfalls" of hypnosis are believed to contribute to the AAP. However, since about thirty percent of abduction reports are obtained without hypnosis (Mack, 1995)[20], a non-hypnotic explanation must be made to account for their reports. Additionally, Baumeister (1989) ruled out psychological interpretations such as lies, attention-seeking behavior, mental illness, and desire for victim status as possible causes for abduction reports.[21] Such conflicting evidence makes it more difficult to explain the abduction experience.

The Alien Abduction Phenomenon: Studies and Theories

Arguments Against the Alien Abduction Phenomenon

Probably the most compelling argument against the AAP is that they are elaborations of the experience of sleep paralysis. A sleep-paralysis episode is characterized by a person waking up paralyzed, sensing a presence in the room, and feeling fear. That is, when a person awakes from the lightest sleep stage, the paralysis continues for a few minutes and the dream content may continue as the person awakens, leading to hallucinations. It is thought that sleep paralysis, which may be responsible for historical reports of succubi, incubi, and other demons, is believed to be the basis of the AAP as influenced by current popular culture and stories of aliens.

Psychologist Dr. Richard McNally contends that reports of alien abductions are the result of "sleep paralysis" and the product of "fantasy and of suggestion."[22] Similarly, a study by Susan Blackmore and Marcus Cox (2008) concluded that reports of alien abductions are related to sleep paralysis and subsequent "hallucinations linked to pathologic neurophysiology."[23] Supporting evidence against the AAP was also provided by Spanos et al. (1993), who revealed similarities between the alien abduction experience and sleep paralysis:

1. Most abductions occurred at night.
2. Almost 60 percent were sleep related.
3. About 25 percent of the most intense experiences involved symptoms similar to sleep paralysis.[24]

Psychologist, Dr. Susan Clancy, based on personality tests in her population of abductees, contends that the AAP can be explained in terms of "sleep paralysis with hallucinations, the availability of cultural scripts, and the development of false memories through hypnosis and other guided imagery techniques."[25] She also concluded that abductees score higher on a characteristic called "schizotypy" (*i.e.*, being prone to fantasy and magical thinking). Alien abductees, in contrast to the general population, also demonstrated greater difficulty distinguishing real from imagined events, and were more likely to believe in the paranormal. Clancy concluded that in most cases, the "traumatic experience was consistent with sleep paralysis."[25a]

Another argument against the AAP is that memory recall occurred after the reported experience from the majority of those who had no conscious memory of the abduction. Some people, however, do report conscious recall of their alien abduction experience. In a study from the *Journal of Abnormal Psychology* (2002) titled, "Memory Distortion in People Reporting Abduction by Aliens," false memory creation was examined in people who reported having been abducted by aliens.[26] Those who reported recovered and repressed memories of alien abduction were more prone than control participants to exhibit false recall and recognition. Clancy also believes that the person not prone to paranormal thinking, will likely interpret it as a momentary "perceptual aberration," but to the "paranormally inclined," the experience "perfectly fits the alien abduction."[26a] Additionally, Carl Sagan suggested that alien abduction represent a form of mass psychosis, hysteria, or hallucination.

The common perspective held by many who reject the AAP pertain to the patterns of beliefs of extraterrestrial visitations. This pattern, reinforced by representations of the UFO subject through the media, the Internet, and various books and magazines, affects our objectivity interpreting a strange experience. That is, some people may choose to make this experience fit in with their belief in UFO and alien abductions. A psychologically-based explanation for the abduction experience is termed "confabulation" which is mixing fantasy with reality to the extent that it becomes difficult to differentiate one from the other. That is, those with fantasy-prone personalities are susceptible to memory distortions influenced by science fiction. This psycho-social mix results in today's alien abduction experience as opposed to other creature-like experiences consistent with stories in the past, like demons and incubus.

D. V. Forrest (2008) concluded that several predisposing factors, such as sleep paralysis, a history of being hypnotized, and preoccupation with the paranormal and extraterrestrial, are largely responsible for the belief held by those who feel they were abducted by aliens.[27] In a study of 18 abductees that included an age and gender matched control group, C. C. French et al., (2008) concluded that abductees show higher levels of dissociativity, absorption, paranormal belief, paranormal experience, self-reported psychic ability, fantasy proneness, tendency to hallucinate, and self-reported incidence of sleep paralysis.[28] This finding supports previous research, which suggest that abductees have a different psychological profile compared to control participants.

Additional evidence cited to reject the AAP, is that no photographs or films of an abduction have ever been made, despite the efforts of some abductees to document their experiences on videotape. Videotaping in bedrooms where regular abductions supposedly occur has only delayed abductions, until people get tired of setting up the camera or the abductee sleeps somewhere else. Further, attempts by abductees to steal souvenirs while on the alien craft are usually unsuccessful, or if a souvenir is supposedly brought back, it later can't be found.[29] Such events also support a psychological or psychic experience rather than a real alien abduction incident.

Arguments in Support of the Alien Abduction Phenomenon

A comprehensive overview of the APP may be found in the book, *The Abduction Experience: A Critical Evaluation of Theory and Evidence,* by psychologist and UFO researcher Dr. Stuart Appelle. The author, who addressed several hypotheses to explain the APP that include, "deception, fantasy-proneness, hypnotizability, false-memory syndrome, personality, sleep phenomena, psychopathology," among others, concluded "no theory yet enjoys enough empirical support to be accepted as a general explanation for the abduction experience."[30] According to Mack (1995), neurophysiological explanations, such as sleep paralysis and temporal lobe epilepsy, proposed as a basis for the AAP (Spanos et al. 1993; Persinger 1992; Blackmore 1994), have "either failed to find such pathology among abduction experiencers or have chosen to overlook important aspects of the phenomenon."[31] A study by McLeod, Corbisier, and Mack (1996) presented evidence that abduction experiences cannot be readily explained by "hypnotic elaboration, masochism, and fantasy proneness," since approximately thirty percent of abduction accounts are obtained without hypnosis.[32] Further, the authors concluded:[32a]

> Unlike masochists, the vast majority of individuals reporting abduction experiences do not seek to reexperience them, and that individuals reporting abduction experiences are not more hypnotizable or fantasy prone than the general population.

In a clinical study of abductees, R. Laibow reported several discrepancies between the expected data and the observable phenomena which support the AAP:

1. Absence of psychopathology coupled with the high level of functioning found in many abductees.
2. Highly dissimilar people produce strikingly similar accounts of abductions by UFO occupants, despite the widely divergent cultural, socioeconomic, educational, occupational, intellectual, and emotional status of abductees.
3. A significant percentage of abduction reports are recalled consciously prior to the use of hypnosis.[33]

In a study of over 800 alleged abductees, Dr. Mack concluded, "the majority of abductees do not appear to be deluded, confabulating, lying, self-dramatizing, or suffering from a clear mental illness."[34] Additionally, Dr. Appelle confirmed, "assessment by both clinical examination and standardized tests has shown that, as a group, abduction experiments are not different from the general population in terms of psychopathology prevalence."[35] Several researchers also emphasized that since abductees do not suffer from psychopathology, there is no a priori reason to reject their reports because their personality characteristics make them less reliable than other reporters of the phenomena.[36, 37]

Budd Hopkins, author of several books about the AAP and founder of the Intruders Foundation, a non-profit organization created to document and research alien abductions, and who has worked with over 500 abductees, contends that "alien abductions" are the source of the UFO phenomenon.[38]

According to Hopkins, "most times a UFO is seen, it marks the start or end of an abduction." He cites "scoop marks" and unexplained scars where abductees remember having undergone operations as primary evidence to support what he believes is an "ongoing genetic experiment by aliens."[38a] Similarly, D. Jacobs, director of the International Center for Abduction Research, claimed that humans are "victims of a widespread program of physiological exploitation, with breeding and hybridization program." Jacobs, who conducted over 1,000 hypnotic regressions with abductees and firmly believes the AAP is real, stated:

> I tried to be as objective and as agenda free as possible. The majority of evidence for the alien abduction phenomenon is from human memory derived from hypnosis. It is difficult to imagine a weaker form of evidence. But it is evidence and we have a great deal of it.[39]

Dr. Mack, who was initially skeptical of the AAP and of the belief held by abductee proponent B. Hopkins, eventually believed it to be a real event. Based on research with 200 abductees, Mack addressed themes of spirituality and modern world views as the foundation of the AAP and concluded that the AAP was valid, but not directly related to the physical universe. He stated:

> It belonged to the spiritual realm: a different plane of reality, accessible only through a widening of conscious perception. There was nothing to suggest that their stories were delusional, a misinterpretation of dreams, or the product of fantasy. None of them seemed like people who would concoct a strange story for some personal purpose.[40]

This perspective was in sharp contrast to those who support the AAP, such as Hopkins and Jacobs, who advocate the physical reality of aliens. In an article titled, "A Brief Review of Issues Relating to the Reality of the Abduction Phenomenon" (1995), Mack wrote:

> We are dealing here with a profound mystery that has potentially vast implications for our contemporary world. For I have no basis for concluding as yet that anything other than what experiencers say happened to them actually did. The experiential data, which, in the absence of more robust physical evidence, suggests that abduction experiencers have been visited by some sort of "alien" intelligence which has impacted them physically and psychologically.[41]

Dr. Jacobs, based on his research, believes that the objective of the abduction scenario relates to an alien program of producing offspring to create a Hybrid Race. He contends: "No significant body of thought has come about that presents strong evidence that anything else is happening other than what the abductees have stated."[42] While highly speculative in nature, and uncorroborated by supporting evidence, Jacobs has been criticized for inducing his beliefs through the hypnosis process leading to abduction accounts. An argument against this position is that similar abduction accounts have been made by those through conscious recall.

Author and ufologist Jenny Randles contends that, during the abductions, information that corresponds to some major change on earth that the entities desire to assist us in dealing with, is subconsciously implanted to be "activated" by the entities at some later time.[43] Despite the absence of undeniable objective evidence to support the AAP, UFO researcher and historian Richard Dolan believes the AAP to be a real event. In an interview with Alfred Lambremont Webre, Dolan stated:

> Extraterrestrial (ET) abductions are one of the most explosive aspects of the entire ET situation. There is no indication that the abducting grey ETs are promoting ET disclosure or that the human power structure is promoting disclosure.[44]

UFO researcher J. Vallée also considers:

> The symbolic display seen by the abductees is identical to the type of initiation ritual or astral voyage that is embedded in the occult traditions of every culture. The structure of abduction stories is identical to that of occult initiation rituals. The UFO beings of today belong to the same class of manifestation as the occult entities that were described in centuries past.[45]

Alien abduction researcher and self-reported abductee, Dr. Karla Turner, who authored several books on the abduction phenomenon, concluded that the creation of a hybrid race is just a small part of the alien agenda. She wrote:

> Aliens can control what we think we see. They can appear to us in any number of disguises and shapes; Aliens can take us–our consciousness–out of our physical bodies, disable our control of our bodies, install one of their own entities, and use our bodies as vehicles for their own activities before returning our consciousness to our bodies; Aliens can be present with us in an invisible state and can make themselves only partially visible; Aliens show a great interest in adult sexuality, child sexuality, and in inflicting physical pain on abductees; Abductees recall being instructed and trained by aliens. Abductees report being taken to facilities in which they encounter not only aliens but also normal-looking humans, sometimes in military uniforms, working with the alien captors. Some abductees report being told or shown the small Gray "workers" are mass-produced android robots, not soul-bearing individuals and thus not "alive" as we understand the term.[46]

In a 2013 questionnaire-based study to determine common characteristics of the abduction experience, Kathleen Marden and Denise Stoner compiled fifty samples from alien abduction experiencers (AE) and twenty-five non-abduction experiencers (NAE) that pertained to their demographics, memories, emotional responses, physiological responses, and psychic phenomena. The most significant outcomes of this study are summarized below:[47]

1. The majority of abduction experiencers believe that their alien contact occurs periodically throughout their lifetime.
2. A highly significant (83 percent) number of individuals from the AE Group stated that they had awoken with unexplained marks on their bodies, whereas only 20 percent of the NAE group replied in the affirmative. Long, thin bruises were most often found on women's calves, thighs, or buttocks, suggesting finger marks. Scoop marks were reported on arms, ankles, behind knees, or on feet. Puncture wounds were found on hands and rib cages, although one woman reported a vaginal puncture wound. Burn marks were on upper backs and sunburn-like rashes were reported, sometimes on the entire body. Several participants mentioned plastic-like filaments, the size of a strand of hair, coming from various locations on their bodies.
3. The vast majority were revisited—some more than ten times—and were taken from their homes to an alien craft. Often the abduction experiencers sensed an impending visitation by alien entities before it occurred. A new psychic awareness emerged in most experiencers and about half now have healing abilities.
4. A statistically significant effect was found in the AE Group (88 percent) versus the NAE group (32 percent) who reported telepathic communication with their visitors.

In those reporting conscious recall of their abduction experience, Marden and Stoner reported the following interesting results:[47a]

1. 88 percent stated that their abduction memories were consciously recalled; 56 percent through dreams; 36 percent through hypnosis; 16 percent through other means, such as flashbacks.
2. 67 percent stated that they consciously recalled (not with hypnosis) the observation of an unconventional craft at less than 1,000 feet prior to an abduction.
3. 56 percent stated that they consciously recalled (not with hypnosis) the observation of non-human entities immediately prior to an abduction while they were outside their home.
4. 76 percent indicated that they were not alone when they were taken.
5. 62 percent of the witnesses had conscious recall for at least part of the experience.

6. 43 percent stated that witnesses reported the observation of a UFO near their house, vehicle, tent, among others, prior to or during their abduction.
7. 58 percent stated that they are aware of having been examined on an alien craft.

The study results reveal that the majority of the respondents had conscious recall of at least one abduction experience and were not alone when it occurred.[47b] More than half remembered observing a craft at less than 1,000 feet and non-human entities before at least one abduction experience. While reports of abduction experiences indicate that the majority of abductions occur from their bedrooms and have no witnesses, the results suggest that this conclusion may be inaccurate.

Psychologist Dr. Don Donderi, who evaluated six abduction cases he personally investigated, along with several cases reported by other researchers, concluded that alien abductions are real events. This notion is based on what he considers "consistent multiple accounts of remembered experiences," which he feels "cannot be explained away as psychological abnormalities because the people who remember being abducted are not psychologically abnormal."[48] Based on this analysis, he concluded:

> Based on the consistency of the evidence, its congruence with other aspects of the experience, and its congruence with non-hypnotically obtained evidence, I think that hypnotically recovered abduction memories following a close encounter and missing time are accurate (within the limits of memory accuracy) accounts of what happened during the period of missing time. I think that the six cases, as well as many others, show that extraterrestrial occupants have abducted people into UFOs, examined them, interacted with them in other ways, and then, after one or two hours, returned them to Earth.[48a]

Discussion

In the absence of compelling, irrefutable empirical evidence to support the AAP, the conclusion that aliens have abducted humans, should be regarded as tenuous at best. There are numerous obstacles to accepting the authenticity of the AAP as a real event. The anecdotal evidence, elicited by hypnosis or conscious recall, makes it difficult to accept the AAP with certainty. The AAP, which includes accounts of telepathy with alien being, movement through walls, and hybrid aliens, among others, seem implausible. These reported events alone, as strange as they are, do not necessarily rule out the possibility that aliens are abducting humans. However, one can't ignore that memory can be biased or faulty; perception ambiguous and unreliable; social pressures and social gain can motivate convincing lies; and that hypnotists can influence susceptible witnesses. Consequently, there is reason to strongly suspect that the AAP may represent a form of an individual and psycho-cultural anomaly.

The inaccuracies of memory recovered from hypnotherapy must be considered in evaluating abduction reports and the AAP. Hypnotic regression as a method to recover memories has been established as a means to generate false memories (Scheflin and Shapiro, 1989).[49] Physical evidence in the form of scars are also not convincing enough to support the AAP. Even Dr. Mack admits that the scars are "usually too trivial by themselves to be medically significant" and that the evidence overall is "maddeningly subtle and difficult to corroborate with as much supporting data as firm proof would require."[50] Thus the physical evidence is not sufficiently robust to substantiate the abductees' reports. Therefore, in order to accept the AAP as a real event, I propose that the following corroborating evidence be required:

1. Verification by independent research investigations of multiple-witness accounts of independent abduction incidents.
2. Verification by different investigators, which document the validity of the reported "alien hybrid baby."
3. Replicated scientific results and conclusions by different investigators, which document reported "alien implant" devices to be of unknown composition and functionality.

Regardless of the actual reason(s) for the AAP, it remains a unique mystery that requires further study to better understand. However, since information reported on the AAP has been polarized and sensationalized, the vast majority of scientists are reluctant to do so. Additionally, as in the case of Dr. Mack who was forced to engage in a legal battle to maintain tenure status at Harvard due to his views on the AAP, researchers do not want to possibly jeopardize their reputations and careers.

Despite these obstacles, I would consider many investigative psychologists and sociologists to regard the AAP an interesting research topic because of its role in the person's life, the association between the similarity among subjective reports and memory processes, and possible psycho-cultural influences. Such research may contribute towards our better understanding of certain aspects of the human mind, such as accuracy of encoded memory, and the reliability of hypnosis and other altered states. Or, are aliens abducting humans?

CHAPTER EIGHT

Exopolitics

Overview

The Freedom of Information Act (FOIA) is a federal law that provides disclosure of prior documents not submitted to the public by agencies of the U.S. Government, such as the Departments of State, Federal Bureau of Investigation (FBI), the National Security Agency (NSA), the Defense Intelligence Agency (DIA), and the Central Intelligence Agency (CIA), among others. Consequently, declassification of some UFO documents has been made public in the United States. Over the past decade, many other countries have also established organizations dedicated to collecting and declassifying UFO reports and official communications on the subject, like the United Kingdom, Russia, Ecuador, France, Denmark, Brazil, Sweden, Canada, and others.

These documents, which only a small percentage are of significant importance, make it clear that many countries considered the UFO phenomenon a vital matter. A comprehensive review and chronological history of the position on UFOs by the military, government, and scientific community, which include pertinent declassified U.S. Government documents prepared by high-ranking officials, such as the "1947 Twining Memo," "USAF Intelligence Report," "U.S. Air Force Bases," "UFOs Over Belgium (1989-1990)," "Chadwell Memos (1952)," and "Halt Memo (1981)," among others, can be found in Richard Dolan's book titled, *A.D. After Disclosure: The People's Guide to Life After Contact.*[1] An article titled, "Exopolitics: Discipline of Choice for Public Policy Issues Concerning Extraterrestrial Life" by Michael E. Salla also provides a summary of the political-legal-UFO interrelationship.[2] Additionally, Clifford Stone's book, *UFOs are Real*, address documents obtained under FOIA requests, which demonstrate the existence of various classified programs and incidents that deal with the UFO phenomenon.[3] A comprehensive review of the CIA-UFO relationship may be found in an article titled, "CIA's Role in the Study of UFOs, 1947-90," prepared by Gerald K. Haines, a historian for the National Reconnaissance Office, who studied secret CIA files for an internal study that examined the agency's involvement in UFOs through the 1990s.[4]

Additionally, the Citizens Against UFO Secrecy (CAUS), in 1977, formed in response to the FOIA, made requests, and filed law suits against the NSA and the CIA as part of their objective to have government agencies disclose their knowledge of UFOs, but with limited success. The CAUS found these departments "evasive" in responding to their requests.

Over the past decade, many ufologists have focused on "exopolitics" as an approach to the study of the UFO phenomenon. According to M. Salla, a researcher in this area, exopolitics is a concept "implicit in terms such as the "Flying Saucer Conspiracy," "UFO Cover-up," and "Cosmic Watergate," that have been a standard part of UFO literature for over five decades." Salla wrote:

> Those explicitly supporting exopolitics as a distinct disciplinary approach to the extraterrestrial hypothesis (ETH), contrast it to the empirical study of UFO sightings focusing on improved investigative techniques and analysis of the best available evidence substantiating the reality of the UFO phenomenon and the ETH. While UFO studies has been dominated by physical scientists with an affinity for quantitative analysis of empirical UFO data, exopolitical researchers tend to have social science backgrounds where qualitative analysis of the UFO data and the ETH occurs more often.[5]

Declassified UFO Documents

Among the websites below, of particular interest is the information on the CIA's website (www.foia.cia.gov/collection/ufos-fact-or-fiction) that provides over 200 documents of firsthand accounts from personnel and press-related coverage of UFO incidents. A few of the most significant UFO documents from the U.S. Government obtained under the FOIA include:

1. A UFO incident at the US/UK air base near Rendlesham forest led to an investigation by base personnel.
2. Belgian airspace was frequently visited by large triangular objects, observed visually, and by ground and airborne radar.
3. The attempted intercept of a UFO by Iranian aircraft, who disabled their instruments and weapon systems, among others.

Many ufologists consider these documents as objective, strong supporting evidence that physical craft operated by alien beings have visited Earth, and that world governments have conspired to cover-up such visitations.

Declassified UFO documents may be found in the following websites:

1. www.theblackvault.com/m/articles/view/All-UFO-Documents-From.
2. www.ufoevidence.org/topics/Documents.html.

3. www.ufocasebook.com/fbi.html.
4. majesticdocuments.com/official/foia.php.
5. www.presidentialufo.com/foia-files.
6. www.nsa.gov/public_info/declass/ufo/.
7. www.dod.mil/pubs/foi/homeland_defense/UFOs/.
8. vault.fbi.gov/UFO.
9. www.foia.cia.gov/collection/ufos-fact-or-fiction.
10. www.nationalarchives.gov.uk/ufos/.

The documents addressed that follow, combined with the evidence presented in Chapter Five: Theories and Cases of High Strangeness and Chapter Six: UFO Evidence provide undeniable evidence of the existence of UFOs, but fail to provide irrefutable proof that NHI has, without a shred of doubt, visited Earth (in my humble opinion). But you be the judge.

Majestic 12 (MJ-12) Documents: The controversial Majestic Documents (and MJ-12) describe those individuals and agencies involved in the alleged extraterrestrial presence and government cover-up of UFOs. The controversy over the authenticity of the supposedly leaked government documents mentioning MJ-12, an alleged secret committee of scientists, military leaders, and government officials, formed in 1947 by President Truman to investigate the recovery of the alleged UFO crash in Roswell, New Mexico (July 1947), has persisted for decades.[6] Ufology researcher, Stanton Friedman, who advocates the legitimacy of the "Majestic Documents," maintains the existence of what he termed a "Cosmic Watergate," created to preserve secrecy over evidence supporting the extraterrestrial phenomenon and captured UFOs and their occupants.[7] An opposing viewpoint was provided by historian Gerald Haines, who wrote:

> A series of documents surfaced which some ufologists said proved that President Truman created a top secret committee in 1947, Majestic-12, to secure the recovery of UFO wreckage from Roswell and any other UFO crash site for scientific study and to examine any alien bodies recovered from such sites. Most if not all of these documents have proved to be fabrications. Yet the controversy persists.[8]

Leading UFO researcher Robert Hastings, who also considers the MJ-12 documents fraudulent, stated:

> No matter how many times certain researchers—who should know better—suggest or outright claim that they are legitimate, one glaring fact remains: Not a single "document" has a verifiable provenance, confirming its origin within the U.S. Government network of departments and agencies. The forensic and anecdotal data are damning.[9]

1. **The Twining Memo** (1947): The document titled, "AMC Opinion on Flying Disc," prepared by Lieutenant General N.F Twining, Head of the U.S. Air Materiel Command, was released under the FOIA in 1985. It was written in response to a directive from Air Force Intelligence and Brig. General George Schulgen about flying saucers, who wrote "saucers" were "real and not visionary or fictitious." Twining wrote:

   There are objects probably approximating the shape of a disc, and the reported operating characteristics such as extreme rates of climb, maneuverability (particularly in roll), and action which must be considered evasive when sighted or contacted by friendly aircraft and radar lend belief to the possibility that some objects are controlled either manually, automatically or remotely.[10]

2. **FBI Memo** (1948): According to UFO historian and researcher Richard Dolan, this FBI memo titled, "Protection of Vital Installations," which is as "extraordinary as the Twining Memo," was sent to the Director of the FBI by the San Antonio, Texas, field office. Excerpts from this memo follow:

   In July 1948, an unidentified aircraft was "seen" by an Eastern Airlines pilot and co-pilot and one or more passengers of the Eastern Airlines plane over Montgomery, Alabama. This aircraft was reported to be of an unconventional type without wings and resembled generally a "rocket ship." It was reported to have had windows, to have been larger than the Eastern Airlines plane, and to have been traveling at an estimated speed of 2,700 miles an hour. It appeared out of a thunderhead ahead of the Eastern Airlines plane and immediately disappeared in another cloud narrowly missing a collision with the Eastern Airlines plane. No sound or air disturbance was noted in connection with this appearance.[11]

   In every case but one the shape of the objects has been reported as round in a point of light with a definite area to the light's source. One report gives a diamond shape; another indicates that trailing lights are elongated. The size is usually compared to one-fourth the diameter of the full moon, and they have also been compared in size to a basketball with trailing lights the size of a baseball. On two occasions reports have been received of the sightings of multiple units. The only conclusions reached thus far are that they are either hitherto unobserved natural phenomena or that they are man-made. No scientific experiments are known to exist in this country which could give rise to such phenomena.

3. **USAF Intelligence Report** (1951): This report addressed a UFO encounter on July 9, 1951, by a fighter pilot who described a UFO:

...flat on top and bottom and appearing from a front view to have rounded edges and slightly beveled....as object dived from top of plane it was completely round and spinning in a clockwise direction.... Only 1 object observed. Solar white. No vapor trails or exhaust or visible system of propulsion. The object was traveling at a tremendous speed.[11a]

4. **Chadwell Memos** (1952): The high level of interest with UFO sightings reported during the NATO exercise, Operation Mainbrace, resulted in a memorandum prepared by the CIA's Assistant Director of Scientific Intelligence, Dr. H. Marshall Chadwell, to the CIA Director, General Walter Bedell Smith, a senior United States Army general who served as General Dwight D. Eisenhower's chief of staff. The memo titled, "British Activity in the Field of UFOs," was made public in 2001 via the FOIA. Chadwell wrote:

   At this time, the reports of incidents convince us that there is something going on that must have immediate attention. Sightings of unexplained objects at great altitudes and traveling at high speeds in the vicinity of major U.S. defense installations are of such nature that they are not attributable to natural phenomena or known types of aerial vehicles.[11b]

   Responding to a separate UFO incident in Yorkshire, U.K, Chadwell stated:

   In some RAF field, there was some sort of demonstration to which high officials of the RAF in London had been invited. During the show, a perfect flying saucer was seen by these officials as well as RAF pilots. So many people saw it that many articles appeared in the public press.[11c]

5. **U.S. Air Force Bases**: The Department of Defense and CIA documents reveal that military personnel sighted UFOs near nuclear-weapons storage areas and missile control facilities, many confirmed by radar, at several air force bases (AFB) during the '60s and '70s, such as, Loring, Wurtsmith, Malstrom, and Minot, among others. A 1975 NORAD Command Director's Log, provided by the National Investigations Committee on Aerial Phenomenon (NICAP), contains official documents of the various UFO incident reports:[11d]

   In a 1966 incident at Malstrom AFB, considered one of the most significant UFO events, UFOs sighted by security personnel were reported separately at the same time when Minuteman Strategic missiles were confirmed by the USAF to have shutdown within seconds of each other with no known cause. Sensors at the missile sites triggered an alarm which resulted in a Sabotage Alert Team's arrival at the site. The team reported a glowing orange disk-shaped object the size of a "football field," whose light illuminated the missile site. The object, confirmed by radar and approached by two interceptors, eventually disappeared from radar. An investigation of the incident established that the computer codes in the missile warhead had been altered; an outcome believed to be impossible to achieve.[12] (Information pertaining to the UFO-nuclear missile connection is addressed in Chapter Four: UFO Evidence.)

During several weeks in 1975, the Strategic Air Command at Wurtsmith AFB was placed on high alert because of repeated incidents of UFOs near atomic weapons areas. In response to these events, the Commander-in-Chief of NORAD sent a memo to NORAD units on November 11, 1975. It stated:

> Since 28 Oct 75, numerous reports of suspicious objects have been received at the NORAD CU; reliable military personnel at Loring AFB, Maine, Wurtsmith AFB, Michigan, Malmstrom AFB, Mt, Minot AFB, ND, and Canadian Forces Station, Falconbridge, Ontario, Canada have visually sighted suspicious objects. On October 27-28, 1975, Staff Sgt. Danny K. Lewis, 42nd Security Police Squadron, while on duty at the munitions storage area of Loring AFB, Maine, at 7:45 p.m. saw an apparent aircraft at low altitude along the northern perimeter of the base. Other witnesses were Sgt. Clifton W. Blakeslee and Staff Sgt. William J. Long. The craft had a red light and a pulsating white light.[13]

Excerpts from a statement of a UFO encounter by the pilot of a KC-135 at the Wurtsmith AFB in a "Memo for the Record," dated January 18, 1979, follow:

> We were returning from a refueling mission and during our first approach into the traffic pattern, RAPCON vectored us to check out a reported UFO in the area of the Wurtsmith Weapons Storage Area. I remember seeing lights similar to strobe lights which were flashing irregularly. After observing the lights we determined that there were in fact two objects and the irregular flashing appeared to be some sort of signal being passed from one to the other in an effort to maintain the same position. We were able to paint an object on the radar scope for about 10 seconds. I would guess that we stayed close to the UFO most of the time, approximately one mile away, and each time we attempted to close on the object it would speed away from us. Finally, we turned back in the direction of the UFO and it really took off back in the direction of the Bay area. I know this might sound crazy, but I would estimate that the UFO sped away from us doing approximately 1,150 mph. We continued in the direction of the Bay until RAPCON called us again and said they were painting a UFO four to five miles over the coast traveling in a westerly direction.

> They vectored us to the position of the UFO and we proceeded but at that point we were low on fuel and were forced to return to Wurtsmith. I remember that while on final approach we saw the lights again near the Weapons Storage Area. Following the mission we discussed the incident and about a week later, Captain Higginbotham was questioned by the Office of Special Investigations and cautioned not to discuss the incident.[14]

In another incident at Loring AFB, a message to the National Military Command Center in Washington, D.C. stated, "The A/C [aircraft] definitely penetrated the Loring Air Force Base northern perimeter and on one occasion was within 300 yards of the munitions storage area perimeter. Del Kindschi, a spokesman for NORAD, commented on this incident:

> The UFO was tracked on radar intermittently for six hours. The object zoomed from 26,000 feet to 45,000 feet, stopped a while, and then moved up very quickly to 72,000 feet. The first visual sightings were at 3:00 a.m. from Sudbury, Ontario, as brilliant lights that hovered low in the sky, then suddenly shot straight up at tremendous speed.[14a]

6. **Tehran, Iran** (1976): Considered to be one the most significant documented UFO incidents, the crew of an F-4 jet was chased by a UFO that moved at incredible speeds and disabled the plane's instrumentation. One of the pilots, Yaddi Nazeri, estimated the UFO velocity at 2-3,000 mph. At a Washington, D.C. press conference on November 12, 2007, sponsored by the Disclosure Project, Jafari said that the main object released four objects, one he tried unsuccessfully to fire on, another followed him back, and one landed on the desert floor.[15] (Details of this UFO incident may be found in Chapter Four: UFO Evidence.) The U.S. Defense Intelligence Agency provided an evaluation of this event:

   This case is a classic which meets all the criteria necessary for a valid study of the UFO phenomenon:

   A. The object was seen by multiple witnesses from different locations ... and viewpoints.
   B. The credibility of many of the witnesses was high (an Air Force general, qualified air crews, and experienced radar operators).
   C. Visual sightings were confirmed by radar.
   D. Similar electromagnetic effects were reported by three separate aircraft.
   E. There were physiological effects on some crew members (*i.e.*, loss of night vision due to the brightness of the object).

F. An inordinate amount of maneuverability was displayed by the UFOs.[15a]

7. **The 1981 Halt Memo**: A memo from Charles I. Halt, Lt. Col., USAF, Deputy Base Commander to the UK Ministry of Defense may be found at: www.ianridpath.com/ufo/appendix.html. This memo, released under the FOIA in 1983 by the U.S. Air Force to Robert Todd of the CAUS, was prepared in response to an incident described in Chapter Four: UFO Evidence, which involved reported sightings of unexplained lights and the alleged landing of one or more unknown craft in Rendlesham Forest, Suffolk, England, in December 1980. Given the relative importance of this extraordinary incident, within the context of UFO evidence, the entire memo is presented as follows:

   Early in the morning of 27 Dec 80 (approximately 0300L) two USAF security police patrolmen saw unusual lights outside the back gate at RAF Woodbridge. Thinking an aircraft might have crashed or been forced down, they called for permission to go outside the gate to investigate. The on-duty flight chief responded and allowed three patrolmen to proceed on foot. The individuals reported seeing a strange glowing object in the forest. The object was described as being metallic in appearance and triangular in shape, approximately two to three meters across the base and approximately two meters high. It illuminated the entire forest with a white light. The object itself had a pulsing red light on top and a bank(s) of blue lights underneath. The object was hovering or on legs. As the patrolmen approached the object, it maneuvered through the trees and disappeared. At this time the animals on a nearby farm went into a frenzy. The object was briefly sighted approximately an hour later near the back gate. The next day, three depressions 1.5 inches deep and 7 inches in diameter were found where the object had been sighted on the ground. The following night (29 Dec 80) the area was checked for radiation. Beta/gamma readings of 0.1 milliroentgens were recorded with peak readings in the three depressions and near the center of the triangle formed by the depressions. A nearby tree had moderate (0.05–0.07) readings on the side of the tree toward the depressions. Later in the night a red sun-like light was seen through the trees. It moved about and pulsed. At one point it appeared to throw off glowing particles and then broke into five separate white objects and then disappeared. Immediately thereafter, three star-like objects were noticed in the sky, two objects to the north and one to the south, all of which were about 10 degrees off the horizon. The objects moved rapidly in sharp, angular movements and displayed red, green and blue lights. The objects to the north appeared to be elliptical through an 8-12 power lens. They then turned to full circles. The objects to the north remained in the sky for an hour or more. The object to the south was visible for two or three hours and beamed down a stream of light from time to time. Numerous individuals, including the undersigned, witnessed the activities.[16]

8. **Belgium UFO** (1989-90): The Belgian UFO wave involved unknown objects that were tracked on radar, chased by Air Force F-16s, and photographed. Of the more than 13,000 witnesses on the ground, over 2,500 filed written statements of their experiences. Major P. Lambrechts of the Belgian Air Force General Staff included his account of the incident in a report titled, "Report on the Observation of UFOs During the Night of March 30-31, 1990." Lambrechts wrote:

> The speeds measured at that time and the altitude shifts exclude the hypothesis according to which planes could be mistaken for the observed UFOs. The slow moves during the other phases differ also from the moves of planes.... Though speeds greater than the sound barrier have been measured several times, not any bang has been noticed. Here also, no explanation can be given.[17]

When the pilots were debriefed, they emphasized it was impossible for them to accelerate as quickly as the UFO. Their account was confirmed by the plane's radar that indicated that the object was at 7,000 feet, climbed to 10,000 feet in a few seconds, and then dropped to only 500 feet in a few more seconds. During this maneuver, the UFO accelerated more than 1,000 mph. Colonel W. J.L. De Brouwer stated:

> We measured some exceptional acceleration which cannot be related to conventional aircraft...that is clear....The data on this performance which were registered during the lock-ons on the radar, was totally outside of the normal performance envelope of any airplane. (Additional information of this incident is addressed in Chapter Four: UFO Evidence.)[18]

9. **William B. Smith Memo** (1951): Of all the documents obtained through the FOIA, the "Smith Memo" is regarded by many ufologists as the most compelling evidence to support the belief that the government has covered up their knowledge of UFOs. This document, written by radio engineer W. Smith of the Canadian Department of Transportation to the Controller of Telecommunications, outlined five points obtained from discussions with U.S. officials working on the "flying saucers:"

   A. The matter is the most highly classified subject in the United States Government, rating higher even than the H-bomb.

B. Flying saucers exist.
C. Their modus operandi is unknown but concentrated effort is being made by a small group headed by Doctor Vannevar Bush.
D. The entire matter is considered by the United States authorities to be of tremendous significance.
E. The United States authorities are investigating along quite a number of lines, which might possibly be related to the saucers, such as mental phenomena.[19]

10. **One controversial official U.S. Air Force memo**, dated March 22, 1950, by Guy Hottel (Head of Field Office in Washington, D.C.) to FBI Director J. Edgar Hoover, has received considerable attention by the public in recent years. In reference to a UFO incident, it stated, the "saucers" were:

> ...circular in shape with raised centers, approximately 50 feet in diameter. Each one was occupied by three bodies of human shape but only three feet tall, dressed in metallic cloth of a very fine texture. Each body was bandaged in a manner similar to the blackout suits used by speed fliers and test pilots.[20]

The authenticity of the Hottel memo was questioned in a written statement by the FBI:

> It does not prove the existence of UFOs; it is simply a second- or third-hand claim that we never investigated. Some people believe the memo repeats a hoax that was circulating at that time, but the Bureau's files have no information to verify that theory. Sorry, no smoking gun on UFOs. The mystery remains...[20a]

Government Disclosure

In July 2012, the Ministry of Defense (MoD) in Great Britain released over 6,500 pages of UFO-related documents, policies on UFOs, and public sightings and drawings of UFOs from 1965 to 2008, many of which may be found at: www.nationalarchieves.gov.uk/ufos/. One document includes Prime Minister Tony Blair's briefings on UFO sightings in 1998, and the MoD concern about military jets crashing after reported UFO encounters. Further, the Condign Report (2000), a secret UFO study by the British Government's Defense Intelligence Staff in the late 1990s called, "Unidentified Aerial Phenomena in the U.K. Air Defense Region," concluded that while "no definitive conclusions could be drawn, it couldn't rule out the possibility that some unexplained losses of military aircraft may have been caused by unidentified objects and that military and civilian air crews should not attempt to out-maneuver a UFO."[21]

Obtained via the FOIA in 2006, a report by officials from the UK during the 1950s included their perspective on UFOs:

> That UFOs exist is indisputable. Credited with the ability to hover, land, take-off, accelerate to exceptional velocities and vanish, they can reportedly alter their direction of flight suddenly and clearly can exhibit aerodynamic characteristics well beyond those of any known aircraft or missile-either manned or unmanned. No artifacts of unknown or unexplained origin have been reported or handed to the UK authorities, despite thousands of UAP reports.[22]

An interesting document from a branch of the Defense Intelligence Staff at the MoD, in 1995, pertained to a government officials fear that if the MoD interest in UFOs was made public, it could lead to “disbelief and embarrassment, since few people will believe the truth that lack of funds and higher priorities have prevented any study of the thousands of reports received.”[22a]

Another U.K. document indicated the government’s interest in UFOs by the many roles and branches of the MoD assigned to address the phenomenon:

1. The Air Staff Secretariat at MoD “dealt with all public and Parliamentary correspondence on UFOs.”
2. The DI55—a branch of the Defense Intelligence Staff was “responsible for assessing UFO reports for information of intelligence interest until 2000.”
3. The “DAO/ ADGE1/CT & UK Ops—a section of the RAF/Air Staff was responsible for Air Defense radars when additional assessment was needed on reported UFO sightings.”[22b]

In March 2007, the French space agency disclosed its UFO files of over 100,000 pages of witness reports of UFO incidents, and photographs, videos, and audiotapes of over 1,500 sightings since 1954. Jacques Patenet, an aeronautical engineer who led a study of the “non-identified aerospatial phenomena,” stated that the UFO files “doesn’t demonstrate the presence of extraterrestrial beings. But it doesn’t demonstrate the impossibility of such presence either. The questions remain open.”[23] According to Patenet, almost twenty-five percent of the cases indicate “we are confronted with something we can’t explain.”[23a] The New Zealand military also released previously classified reports of about 2,000 pages of documents from 1954 to 2009, of UFO sightings and alien encounters by members of the public, military personnel, and commercial pilots.[24] In 1997, in response to civilian and military sightings, the Chilean Air Force formed the Committee for the Study of Anomalous Phenomena and the Peruvian Air Force set up a similar group in 2001. Several other South American countries also established comparable investigative groups, and Spain and Canada released documents in the 1970s and 1980s.

The Brazilian Government declassified over 4,000 pages of UFO documents (1950-1980s), which included a compelling disclosure of dozens of reports of a UFO incident on May 19, 1986, considered as the "Official UFO Night in Brazil." This case involved the detection of 21 spherical objects by radar and confirmed by civilian pilots.

Emphasizing the importance for government disclosure of UFOs is leading UFO researcher Robert Hastings, who wrote:

> As I see it, the ongoing UFO intervention in U.S. strategic affairs is now a tale that needs to be told, in unflinching terms, to our legislative assemblies, if possible, but from the rooftops if necessary. All bold endeavors bear both planned-for and unintended consequences. The inevitable admission by U.S. government officials that our nuclear weapons have long been monitored, and at times compromised, by those of unknown origin and objectives, is not without its perils. But the facts will—and should—become known, sooner or later, by one means or another, in a society such as ours. And that's a good thing. After all, isn't that how a democracy is supposed to operate?[25]

The Conspiracy Theory

The conspiracy theory implies that conclusive evidence, which demonstrates that UFOs are under intelligent control, is being suppressed by many governments, especially the U.S. Researchers have found some evidence of suppression of UFO incidents by governments but have found no compelling proof of a "conspiracy." Similarly, the recent UFO "disclosure" initiative, which has transitioned into "exopolitics," assumes that UFOs are extraterrestrial in origin, and that the government will officially reveal their presence. Many ufologists also maintain, on the basis of key witness testimony by retired military and government personnel and official declassified government/military UFO documents, that certain departments within one or more government agencies, such as, the CIA, FBI, and NSA, know what the phenomenon is, have remains of physical craft and their occupants, and have back-engineered technology from recovered UFOs. Interestingly, according to a 2002 Roper poll, seventy-two percent of Americans believe the federal government is suppressing information about UFOs. As a result, the conspiracy theory persists, despite the official U.S. government and NASA position on UFOs:

> No branch of the United States Government is currently involved with or responsible for investigations into the possibility of advanced alien civilizations on other planets or for investigating Unidentified Flying Objects (UFO's). The US Air Force and the National Aeronautics and Space Administration (NASA) have had intermittent, independent

> investigations of the possibility of alien life on other planets; however, none of these has produced factual evidence that life exists on other planets, nor that UFO's are related to aliens. From 1947 to 1969, the Air Force investigated UFO's; then in 1977, NASA was asked to examine the possibility of resuming UFO investigations. After studying all of the facts available, it was determined that nothing would be gained by further investigation, since there was an absence of tangible evidence.[26]

Not convinced by this official position, ufologists continue with "disclosure"-led campaigns, with the most recent by The Citizens Hearing on Disclosure in April-May 2013. Stephen Bassett, who led the Citizens Hearing on Disclosure, alleges the government has been tracking extraterrestrial crafts for decades and the evidence is "overwhelming—beyond any reasonable doubt, there's an extraterrestrial presence (and) almost certainly from another planet."[27] According to Dr. Steven Greer, founder of the Disclosure Project, there are over "500 government, military, and intelligence community witnesses" with "personal, firsthand experience with UFOs, ETs, ET technology, and the cover-up that keeps this information secret." Other notable individuals who have also stated that UFO evidence is being withheld from the public include Senator Barry Goldwater, Admiral Lord Hill Norton (former NATO head and chief of the British Defense Staff), Brigadier-General Arthur Exon (former commanding officer of Wright-Patterson AFB), Vice-Admiral Roscoe H. Hillenkoetter (first CIA director), astronauts Gordon Cooper and Edgar Mitchell, and former Canadian Defense Minister Paul Hellyer. Senator Goldwater stated:

> I think the government does know. I can't back that up, but I think that at Wright-Patterson field, if you could get into certain places, you'd find out what the Air Force and the government knows about UFOs...I called Curtis LeMay and I said, "General, I know we have a room at Wright-Patterson where you put all this secret stuff. Could I go in there?" I've never seen him get mad, but he got madder than hell at me, cussed me out, and said, "Don't ever ask me that question again!"[28]

One classic example of an alleged "cover-up" is represented in testimony by former Division Chief of the Accidents and Investigations Branch of the FAA , John Callahan, of a Federal Aviation Association's investigation following a Japanese airline-UFO incident in 1986. Callahan, who discussed the incident with President Reagan's Scientific Study Group, the FBI, and CIA said that a CIA agent told everybody they "were never there and this never happened," and admitted that they were "afraid of public panic." Upon retiring, Callahan discussed the incident,[29] which may be viewed at: www.ufoevidence.org/documents/doc1324.html.

Declassified documents clearly indicate that the UFO phenomenon was an issue of considerable concern to the U.S. government and military since the 1940s. They even considered the possibility that UFOs were physical craft from another planet. There is even some indication that an on-going secret UFO research agenda exists under the Unacknowledged Special Access Program, which is a designation for "security protocols that provides highly classified information with safeguards and access restrictions known only to authorized persons." These issues serve as a foundation for those involved in the UFO-exopolitical movement, many of whom believe in the cover-up by the government of their knowledge about UFOs and the existence of an active research program studying the phenomenon. For example, journalist Leslie Kean, in her book, *UFOs: Generals, Pilots, and Government Officials Go on the Record* (2010) wrote:

> A number of reliable sources have told me about their conversations with high-level military contacts who say they are aware of a deeply hidden program for UFO research, one of which is so closely guarded that even people at the highest levels of the military are denied access to it.[30]

Kane discussed this issue in 2009 with Commander Will Miller, U.S. Navy (Ret.) who held a Top Secret clearance with Sensitive Compartmented Information access (*i.e.*, "classified information concerning sensitive intelligence sources that is considered above Top Secret"). An excerpt from Miller's email response to Kane's request for an "overall assessment" follows:

> The "control group" cannot allow any information on their closely held UFO research to be accessed by anyone outside of those specially cleared for that USAP. Neither Joint Chiefs of Staff Intelligence nor the director of DIA himself could get ANY information on the subject; this is a fact. Yet I know that sources within multiple organizations maintain such information. Leadership remains "protected" from such knowledge. As far as I am concerned, the question is answered.[30a]

If Miller's position is valid, it would explain former President Bill Clinton's statement concerning his attempt to obtain information on UFOs in 2005:

> I did attempt to find out if there were any secret government documents that revealed things. If there were, they were concealed from me too. And if there were, well I wouldn't be the first American president that underlings have lied to, or that career bureaucrats have waited out. But there may be some career person sitting around somewhere, hiding these dark secrets, even from elected presidents. But if so, they successfully eluded me...and I'm almost embarrassed to tell you I did try to find out.[31]

Support for the possible existence of an organized clandestine effort to study UFOs was provided in a 1993 report titled, "Unidentified Aerial Phenomena Study," by UFO researcher Nick Pope:

> I am aware, from intelligence sources, that Russia believes that such a phenomena exist and has a small team studying it. I am also aware that an informal group exists in the U.S. intelligence community and it is possible that this reflects a more formal organization.[32]

Startling evidence of deliberate government action to "cover-up" or distort UFO incidents in the U.K. were also confirmed by Pope:

> I'm a little bit apologetic about this because obviously, when I was in MoD, I had to play this game myself. To really achieve our policy of downplaying the UFO phenomenon, we would use a combination of 'spin and dirty tricks.' We used terms like UFO buffs and UFO spotters—terms that mean these people are nut jobs. In other words, we were implying that this is just a very somewhat quaint hobby that people have as opposed to a serious research interest. Another trick would be deliberately using phrases like 'little green men.' We were trying to do two things: either to kill any media story on the subject, or if a media story ran, insure that it ran in such a way that it would make the subject seem ridiculous and that it would make people who were interested in this seem ridiculous.[33]

Admiral Lord Hill-Norton, Chief of Defense Staff, Ministry of Defense, Great Britain (1973), and Chairman, Military Committee of NATO (1974-77), also stated:

> I have frequently been asked why a person of my background—a former Chief of the Defense Staff, a former Chairman of the NATO Military Committee—why I think there is a cover-up of the facts about UFOs. I believe governments fear that if they did disclose those facts, people would panic. I don't believe that at all. There is a serious possibility that we are being visited by people from outer space. It behooves us to find out who they are, where they come from, and what they want.[34]

While such comments above are not an official declaration that any government has been engaged in a so-called "UFO cover-up," it does add a certain degree of credibility to the exopolitical agenda. A little known fact that also adds credibility to the "conspiracy theory" is the existence of Air force Regulation 200-2, written by U.S. Air Force, Chief of Staff, N.F. Twining, which states:

> For those objects which are not explainable, only the fact that Air Technical Intelligence Center will analyze the data is worthy of release, due to many unknowns involved.[35]

Additionally, considerable information relating to UFOs, which are "expected" to be "reported promptly," is provided for in the regulation, such as, shape, size, color, formation, number, flight path, manner of observation, velocity, weather conditions, etc. Another interesting provocative UFO "rule" is a 1994 Joint Army Navy Air Force Publication 146, that threatens to prosecute anyone who discloses reports of "sightings" which pertain to U.S. security.[36]

The Disclosure Project and The Citizens Hearing on Disclosure

Testimony presented to former members of the United States Congress of personal UFO experiences through the Disclosure Project, and The Citizens Hearing on Disclosure, has served to heighten awareness of the importance of the phenomenon and the attempt to reveal an alleged conspiracy of the UFO cover-up (See Chapter Four: UFO Evidence). The Disclosure Project, founded by Dr. Steven Greer, is a "research project working to fully disclose the facts about UFOs, extraterrestrial intelligence, and classified advanced energy and propulsion systems." "Disclosure" initiatives, predicated on the premise that governments know "the truth of UFOs," however, may continue to find limited, if any, success meeting their objectives if governments simply don't know more than what has already been disclosed through the FOIA, among other routes. The alternative notion is that the government will continue withholding UFO evidence (if it exists) despite persistent attempts to force "disclosure." Regardless of this well-intentioned initiative, different approaches, which have greater potential to develop organized governance and research initiatives to better understand the phenomenon, must compliment on-going exopolitical initiatives to help find the "truth behind UFOs" (See Chapter Nine: The UFO Phenomenon: A New Approach).

As a follow-up to Bassett's Citizen Hearing on Disclosure-led initiative, his Paradigm Research Group sent out a press release in May 2013 advocating for the United Nations to sponsor "a world conference addressing the possible evidence for an extraterrestrial presence engaging this planet."[37] The statement was signed by several former congress members who participated at the April-May 2013 Citizen Hearing on Disclosure at the National Press Club in Washington, D.C. A segment of this proposal states:

> And Whereas: given the enormous global implications if these craft are, indeed, of extraterrestrial origin, such an issue is a matter for the General Assembly of the United Nations; Therefore, we the undersigned request the Citizen Hearing Foundation use its offices

> to organize interested parties and raise the funds necessary to pursue a global campaign to convince one or more nations to propose a resolution within the General Assembly calling for United Nations sponsorship of a world conference addressing the possible evidence for an extraterrestrial presence engaging this planet.[38]

Commenting on the 2013 Citizen Hearing on Disclosure, held in Washington, D.C, leading UFO researcher Nick Pope wrote:

> In the final analysis, I doubt the event will lead to real Congressional hearings on UFOs just yet, let alone "Disclosure." But seeds have been planted, political contacts have been made and the Citizen Hearing on Disclosure has undoubtedly raised the profile of the UFO phenomenon with the media and the public.[39]

In an interview with Alfred Lambremont Webre, UFO researcher and historian Richard Dolan said that the "disclosure" of the truth behind the governments/military involvement with UFOs "will happen, but it will be forced."[40] He further contends: "the human controllers that possess the 'secret' of the ET presence have no real motivation to disclose it and may well decide to continue with their practice of continuing to conceal the ET presence."[40a] Official documents obtained under the FOIA clearly indicate government/military involvement and interest in UFOs. The paradox inherent in this position is whether to believe if there is an active campaign to withhold information of the UFO phenomenon, beyond what has already been disclosed. In other words, what do I want to believe about government/military involvement with UFOs and what do I actually know about their involvement? That is, sometimes we believe what we wish in the absence of sufficient evidence to support our position. Similar to other ufology-based topics is the question: How much of exopolitics is wishful speculation or fact-based conclusions? Based on existing evidence in the form of declassified documents that verify government/military knowledge of UFOs, it is understandable why many believe the government/military continue to withhold information of the "truth of UFOs." And if the government should happen to reveal that UFOs are extraterrestrial craft governed by NHI, this admission and its associated aura of suspicion and perceived threat would undoubtedly cause great concern among the people of the world. Assuming this as fact, the anticipated reaction would contradict the government's major directive to be in control of possible threats to our country and to protect its citizens. As a result, I do not think the government would "disclosure" this information since they would prefer to avoid a public confrontation, especially since they likely do not have all the answers to satisfactorily moderate people's concerns and feelings of insecurity regarding UFOs. What would be the compelling reason for the government to disclose the existence of UFOs to the public? I doubt they would think this revelation would benefit society. Thus, in my humble opinion, they will not disclose any time soon, if they have anything to disclose at all.

Extraterrestrial Contact

What would happen if extraterrestrial contact is verified? The outcomes will likely depend on the manner by which contact is made as in the form of a radio signal from another star system, government/military "disclosure" that unequivocally verifies extraterrestrial visitation of Earth, or a UFO landing on the White House lawn. Certainly, the admission of alien visitation will certainly be earth-shattering, having extensive, important, and unpredictable results. It is tempting to speculate upon the potential implications of such a revelation on our individual and collective psyche. In fact, protocols exist which outline a course of action in the event extraterrestrial contact is obtained by "signals" from another planet. A process developed by the SETI Permanent Committee of the International Academy of Astronautics, titled, "Declaration of Principles for Activities Following the Detection of Extraterrestrial Intelligence," deals with the nature of our response.[41] A few acknowledged issues are:

1. Whether or not to reply.
2. How to inform the public.
3. To determine the consequences of the message received.

According to Astrobiologist Paul Davies, chairperson of the SETI Post-Detection Taskgroup, responsible for advising world agencies on how to best react to the detection by SETI evidence of extraterrestrial intelligence, "the discovery of a signal from intelligent extraterrestrials could lead to "mayhem."[42] Additionally, a report titled, "Proposed Agreement on the Sending of Communications to Extraterrestrial Intelligence," recommends the formation of an international commission in response to the detection of extraterrestrial intelligence.[43] This commission would:

> determine to send a message to the extraterrestrial intelligence, and if so, would determine the contents of the message on the basis of principles such as justice, respect for cultural diversity, honesty, and respect for property and territory.

While protocol exists in response to a confirmed signal from another civilization, no guidelines exist, at least that have been made public, in response to direct "up front and personal" contact, as evidenced by UFO occupants landing and announcing their presence. If we assume "direct contact" is made and that our "visitors" announce their peaceful mission to understand our people, culture, and planet, the world will likely unite in unprecedented fashion as sociopolitical and perceived individual differences narrow among nations and people. Chaotic incidents and demonstrations by various personality disordered individuals will no doubt occur, and even the "well-balanced" among us will seek psychological, and/or religious/spiritual support and guidance to help adjust to the astonishing realization that "we are not alone." Some politicians will likely use the "alien card" to strengthen their platform, unprecedented media coverage will ensue, and a rush on banks for cash will result as stocks sink and gold soars, among many other consequences that are beyond the scope of this book to address in detail. Along the way, special U.N. meetings, with our "visitors" hopefully in attendance, will be held to discuss and develop plans to appropriately involve them (if willing) in various ways, with our global community. The primary goals will be to understand the reasons for their visit and to seek mutual agreement on ways to possibly benefit both worlds. And over time, society will adapt, and hopefully proceed in a better overall qualitative state, through the sharing of knowledge and associated interventions with our new "interstellar friends." Certainly, the significant implications for theology, science and technology, sociology, biology, among other disciplines, will depend on the nature and intent of the message received. Without question, our society's response to actual alien visitation would significantly surpass any reaction to an official acknowledgment that radio signals were received from beings living in another solar system. Reaction to communication from light years away is one thing, but alien beings on the White House lawn will present dramatically different reactions and outcomes. If this remarkable event actually occurs one day, would religions and economic and social institutions be dramatically altered, and possibly collapse into anarchy? I don't think so. However, government officials, who may be afraid of the possibility of such extreme outcomes, would likely elect to maintain secrecy of any possible knowledge of alien contact to preserve peace and order.

While the prior conjecture stretches the limit of imaginary thought, most of us, at least once, have likely considered the possibility of alien contact and the resulting outcomes on our personal and collective lives. Movies such as *Independence Day, Star Trek,* and *Close Encounters of the Third Kind* alone have probably facilitated such speculation. And with UFO "disclosure" projects underway, one can't help continue to consider the possible outcomes incurred by this revelation. If true, it will have pronounced, meaningful, and permanent consequences on an individual and societal level from that day forward, the nature of which will depend on our newly adopted "friends" intent (*i.e.,* peaceful or not), and how advanced they are intellectually, ethically, and technologically. Whether or not they land on our planet, as opposed to receiving radio signals from another solar system, presents a compounding variable with accompanying different circumstances. Several scenarios have been proposed to explain possible outcomes in response to extraterrestrial contact, one of which can be found in a comprehensive article titled, "Fear, pandemonium, equanimity and delight: human responses to extra-terrestrial life," by psychologist, Albert Harrison.[44]

In November 1959, the NASA contracted with the Brookings Institution to "undertake...the design of a comprehensive and long-term program of research and study regarding the social, economic, political, legal, and international implications of the use of space for peaceful and scientific purposes," which resulted in a report titled, "Proposed Studies on the Implications of Peaceful Space Activities for Human Affairs."[45] This report addressed the "Implications of a Discovery of Extraterrestrial Life," among other issues, which warned of "unpredictable" outcomes resulting from the realization that other intelligent life existed elsewhere. Regarding the awareness of extraterrestrial intelligent life, the report concluded:

> Anthropological files contain many examples of societies, sure of their place in the universe, which have disintegrated when they had to associate with previously unfamiliar societies espousing different ideas and different life ways; others that survived such an experience usually did so by paying the price of changes in values and attitudes and behavior. One can speculate, too, that the idea of intellectually superior creatures may be anxiety-provoking.[46]

Discussion

Collectively, evidence from the UFO-nuclear missile connection, pilot UFO sightings, compelling testimony from researchers, and key witnesses from military and government agencies, astronauts, air traffic controllers, and pilots, among others, have clearly documented that UFOs exist. To better understand what governs and regulates UFOs, scientists will need to consider appropriate research methods to study the various phenomena associated with alleged UFO encounters and related issues in ufology. This endeavor, while uniquely challenging, will likely contribute more towards our knowledge of the phenomenon than current qualitative, retrospective approaches used in exopolitical research, that primarily focus on disclosing and analyzing government UFO documents, studying what U.S. presidents know of UFOs, assessing the validity of alleged government disinformation and cover-up campaigns, and the authenticity of several UFO incidents like Roswell, New Mexico, 1947; the Phoenix Lights, 1997; Hudson Valley, New York, 1980s; and Rendlesham Forest, UK, 1980, etc. These approaches, while satisfying one's curiosity and advancing some informative and useful knowledge, have failed to provide sufficient information that contribute meaningfully towards the primary goal to define the phenomenon. Certainly, the same criticism can be made for many scientific-based investigations of the phenomenon. Accordingly, we should complement on-going qualitative investigations with multidisciplinary-based scientific research approaches, governed by an overarching administrative structure, in an attempt to better understand the nature and origin of the UFO phenomenon. (This issue is addressed in Chapter Nine: The UFO Phenomenon: A New Approach.)

A fundamental question related to the issue of "exopolitics" is "why government agencies have been engaged in alleged systematic cover-up and disinformation campaigns since the debated 'flying saucer' crash in Roswell, New Mexico in 1947?" Would the purpose be to prevent the possibility of panic and confrontations in a society thought to be unable to adequately cope and adjust to the knowledge of an extraterrestrial presence? If this rationale serves as the basis for the alleged cover-up, the government should be aware that general public reaction to the revelation of the alien presence, while initially astonished, will likely not result in uncontrolled panic, since millions of people are already convinced that beings have and continue to visit Earth. It is also important to keep in mind that no evidence provides irrefutable proof the conspiracy theory is valid. A government-led UFO conspiracy would also be an astounding achievement to pull off successfully, especially knowing that many people "in the know" would have been required to cover-up the alleged evidence for decades. Allegations of government "cover-up" campaigns, which are circumstantial and lack verification, tend to create disillusion in those whose support must be gained, and to also further alienate (no pun intended) the scientific community from engaging in UFO research.

CHAPTER NINE

The UFO Phenomenon: A New Approach

Rationale

A primary goal associated with "a new approach" to the UFO phenomenon is to establish a governance structure to provide the necessary leadership, direction, and related resource support, both human and fiscal, for a multidisciplinary team of leading scholars to study the phenomenon. The goals of this newly formed committee, which for purposes of discussion will be called the Committee to Study Unexplained Aerial Events (CSUAE), should include the application of prospectively based multidisciplinary scientific research to determine the extent to which the phenomenon is explicable within the framework of accepted scientific principles. The application of newly developed research models and techniques will also be required to facilitate the appropriate collection and analysis of acquired UFO evidence. Despite the many important contributions by several established UFO organizations (e.g., MUFON, NARCAP, NUFORC, J. Allen Hynek Center for UFO Studies, and CSETI, among others worldwide), without a purposeful new direction, the many controversial UFO theories and extraordinary claims will continue to serve as a source of debate, with little, if any, meaningful contributions made to better understand the phenomenon.

Ideally, all theories must be subjected to rigorous scientific study before it can be accepted or denied. This objective, however, has been compromised by several longstanding concerns associated with the study of the UFO phenomenon. Consequently, an essential goal must be for the CSUAE to address the following issues to help facilitate the need to better understand the phenomenon:

1. Scientific protocols for the collection and evaluation of UFO evidence should be standardized and consistently applied by research investigators worldwide.

2. There exists a lack of adequate resources to support research in the form of qualified and interested scientists, and reliable funding sources.
3. The lack of a centralized, internationally based governance structure to help lead, promote, and support scientific study of the phenomenon.
4. UFO investigations have been generally conducted by those with relatively little or no educational background or advanced degree in a scientific discipline.
5. Extraordinary claims by many leading UFO researchers have been made in the absence of compelling supportive evidence, *e.g.*, UFOs are extraterrestrial craft, aliens have abducted humans, and others.
6. The field of ufology lacks credibility as a legitimate area for scientific inquiry by the scientific and political communities.
7. Internationally, the ufology community is highly fragmented, lacks leadership, direction, research focus, and a widely approved theory of the phenomenon.

Collectively, these issues have contributed to the perception by the general scientific and political communities that ufology and UFO researchers lack a strong scientific foundation. Consequently, ufology has garnered an apathetic attitude from the scientific community to conduct UFO research and reluctance from political leaders to advocate for funding to support UFO investigations.

The incentive to establish the CSUAE is related to the need to complement and enhance existing programs dedicated to the study of the UFO phenomenon. Historically, there has been an inconsistent application of rigorous protocols that incorporate the scientific method by qualified scientists. A major contributing factor has been the general reluctance on the part of the general scientific community to conduct UFO research, due to the fear of ridicule, limited interest, and negative perspectives of ufology. They consider it an area of study filled will hoaxers, New Agers, and as a popular cultural movement and/or hobby. Thus scientists feel it may compromise their careers if they suddenly change course from their area of expertise to an area of study that lacks acceptance as a reputable research topic among their colleagues. As evidenced in the case of Harvard psychiatrist, Dr. John Mack, there is prejudice against those who engage in UFO research. Another related factor is that the past decades of study, which have not significantly advanced our understanding of the phenomenon, persuade scientists against conducting UFO research since it may result in a waste of time and effort uncovering inconclusive results. This is unfortunate since significantly more research is required instead of the current limited commitment of effort by qualified scientists resulting from prejudice and negative stigmas towards ufology. The UFO enigma, by virtue of its mystery and longstanding controversy (*e.g.*, alien visitation of our planet), also discourages those who may consider conducting research in this area. Importantly, the fact remains that leading UFO researchers have not convinced the scientific and political communities that even their best cases represent adequate evidence to stimulate sufficient interest for research and funding purposes.

In recent years, ufology has focused on issues that are not likely to significantly advance our understanding of the phenomenon. Research in areas that pertain to alien abductions, exopolitics/disclosure, and conspiracies have taken the place of rigorous scientific investigations of reported UFOs.

The following statements reflect similar perspectives:

In 1997, a group of scientists, known as the Sturrock Panel, noted some serious problems with the investigative process associated with the UFO cases that were presented. Astrophysicist, Dr. P. Sturrock concluded:

> It appears that most current UFO investigations are carried out at a level of rigor that is not consistent with prevailing standards of scientific research...It may therefore be valuable to carefully evaluate UFO reports to extract information about unusual phenomena currently unknown to science. However, to be credible to the scientific community, such evaluations must take place with a spirit of objectivity and a willingness to evaluate rival hypotheses.[1]

Tim Printy, a UFO researcher and amateur astronomer, in an article titled, "UFOs: What's 60 Years Accomplished," wrote:

> Unless we develop drastically new ideas and methodologies for the study of the baffling UFO cases and the human context in which they occur, we will watch the next thirty years of UFO report gathering simply mirror the futility and frustration of the last thirty years.[2]

Astronomer and main investigator for the Center for UFO Studies in the 1970s, Allan Hendry, in his book, *UFO Investigator's Handbook*, stated:

> No advancements have been made in ufology. Ufologists collect UFO reports and conclude that UFOs must be some form of craft under intelligent control. Although they never state "who" is controlling these "craft", there is always the implication that they are alien spaceships. What has Ufology done to demonstrate this is true?[3]

According to UFO blogger Michael Naisbitt:

> Until Ufology starts to police its own ranks it will be of no interest to the wider scientific community and, frankly, encouraging scientific/ academic involvement should be a priority. Unfortunately, the wider UFO community is so fractured and disjointed with nothing even remotely resembling a consensus on even the most basic assumptions,

> I fear there will never be a satisfactory resolution, and certainly not in the near future.[4]

Ufologist and Cryptozoologist, Nick Redfern, wrote:

> I guess my biggest concern is that nothing will have changed by then, aside from the field (ufology) having become even more dinosaur-like and stuck in its ways than it is today, still filled with influential souls who loudly demand we adhere to the Extra-Terrestrial Hypothesis and nothing else, still droning on about Roswell, still obsessed with what might be going on at Area 51, still debating on what Kenneth Arnold saw, and still pondering on what really happened at Rendlesham.[5]

Justification for an official organized study of the UFO phenomenon was provided by journalists Leslie Kane and Larry Landsman, co-founders of the Coalition for Freedom of Information (Cfi), who wrote:

> Amazingly enough, after over fifty years of documentation of UAP/ UFOs over nearly every region of the Earth, we are only in the first step of the logical progression towards knowledge. Data is still being gathered and very little analysis has been completed to date. International efforts are only beginning to compare data. There is no strong statistical information regarding frequency of occurrence, densities of observations by location, scope and variety of manifestations, etc. There are some convincing studies that demand careful consideration and certainly there have been incidents to cause concern for public safety. The documentation, debate, and peer review have not yet occurred and, to date, there has been no study of UAP that has been definitive in demonstrating the source or cause of at least one category of UAP known as UFOs. However, there is convincing, mature documentation of observations and incidents that involve UAP that do indeed seem to be objects, and these studies may demonstrate the existence of a phenomenon in need of further scientific examination and analysis.[6]

So, where do we go from here?

Future Directions in the Study of the UFO Phenomenon

Governance

Before developing a proposed "new approach" in the study of the UFO phenomenon, it is essential to first assess the current state of governance and research affairs within the UFO community. This evaluation reveals a discipline marred by a lack of leadership, a fragmented organizational structure lacking a defined mission and associated supporting goals, and limited application of rigorous, well-controlled scientific investigations of the UFO phenomenon. Accordingly, effective leadership must be provided, through a governance structure, provided by an over-arching committee (*e.g.*, Subcommittee of the United Nations, Senate, Congress, or public/private) composed of leaders from diverse backgrounds such as politics, business, military, academic, public/private agencies, among others, to provide the necessary direction, support, and related resources required for a multidisciplinary team (*e.g.*, psychology, biology, physics, sociology, optical physics, and astronomy, etc.) of leading scholars to study the phenomenon. Once a centralized governance structure (*e.g.*, CSUAE) is formed, it must be guided by an agreed-upon mission, facilitated by a strategic plan and supporting objectives and related action plans to realize its mission. The appointment of a qualified director, to lead committee members having extensive leadership experience in areas such as policy, strategic planning, ufology, research, communications, resource development, and grantsmanship, will be required to provide proper guidance and support for research teams to study the phenomenon. Additionally, policies must be established to:

1. Determine how resources will be utilized and aligned with the assessment of progress to inform future research and planning efforts.
2. Develop a plan for publishing and disseminating research results among governments, public and private agencies, and the media worldwide.
3. Develop a plan to secure funding to support continuous research efforts over time.

Central to this endeavour must be the full cooperation and transparency of all government/military knowledge on UFOs and past "black" box projects, such as advanced secret aircraft that may have contributed to UFO sightings (wishful thinking?).

Research Plan

The general findings and related conclusions from previous UFO based research, typically regarded as too unreliable by the scientific community, have not convinced cautious scientists and skeptics that the phenomenon is important and worthy of investigation. Consequently, a research plan should contain appropriate goals as part of a detailed protocol to help:

1. To attract and assemble an appropriate multidisciplinary team of renown scientists to develop methodological approaches to test agreed-upon hypotheses to study the phenomenon.

2. Develop collaborative arrangements with international research-based facilities and agencies (*i.e.*, government, public, and private).
3. Ensure representation on leading international scientific committees and agencies.
4. Centralize a newly developed UFO database to compile and analyze existing and future evidence obtained worldwide for research purposes.
5. Develop and implement educational training programs to help compliment and enhance one's preparation as a "UFO investigator (*i.e.*, integrate science and the everyday person). This will help ensure that standardized research protocols are applied in a consistent manner to properly collect, analyze, and document all known types of UFO evidence.
6. To publish research findings in established refereed scientific journals, and to present these results at appropriate international conferences.

Essential to this proposed research plan is the establishment of testable hypotheses to explain the phenomenon. Ideally, they should be "working hypotheses" that are widely accepted and which forms the basis of further experimentation. Several UFO hypotheses for research consideration may include:

1. Is the UFO phenomenon associated with non-human intelligence from another planet, dimension, and/or space-time?
2. Is the UFO phenomenon associated with psycho-cultural influences?
3. Is the UFO phenomenon associated with natural phenomenon, such as, atmospheric, geological, and/or meteorological?
4. Is the UFO phenomenon associated with man-made phenomenon?
5. Is the UFO phenomenon associated with the alien abduction phenomenon?

To help better understand the nature of this phenomenon, research of qualitative anecdotal evidence should define the characteristics of the phenomena as actually experienced and the impact such experiences have upon the individual. Using an inductive, descriptive approach, phenomenology research of the underlying process of each type of UFO experience encountered will help identify the essential characteristics and meaning of the phenomena. That is, the phenomenology of people's UFO experiences should be investigated more thoroughly to determine if the experiences have a "paranormal," "consciousness," or "personality," basis. The research analysis will explore the meaning of "what" and "how" the phenomenon was experienced through the examination of specific statements and themes, and a search for all possible significant meanings. Consequently, research should include observed correlations between reported UFO encounters and the person's personality and beliefs, and psychological and physiological effects, among other reported events associated with the experience.

The authenticity of the evidence and related conclusions should also inform the experimental protocol through the thorough analysis of any physical evidence such as photographic, radar, and trace elements at reported landing sites, by different independent researchers and laboratories to evaluate the repeatability and related validity of the investigative conclusions.

Critical to this research consideration is to stop studying the phenomenon as a separate science and, instead, to apply a multidisciplinary research-based approach (as mentioned previously). This is necessary since the UFO phenomenon represents many different scientific disciplines such as psychology, astronomy, astrophysics, physics, chemistry, biology, and optical physics, among others. That is, to better understand the UFO phenomenon and its impact on human behavior, society, technology, and possibly even our understanding of physical laws governing nature, UFO research must be conducted using different approaches unique to several fields of study. Related to this goal is the need to attract and assemble qualified scientists in each discipline.

As part of this comprehensive research effort, we must also determine if different approaches to studying the phenomenon, than are currently in use, are needed to more accurately measure and evaluate a pattern of behavior that appears to be inconsistent with accepted scientific principles of inertia and gravity. Admittedly, the nature of this bizarre phenomenon may impede our ability to adequately test hypotheses using established principles and methods. Accordingly, science may not be amenable to solving all the questions associated with the phenomenon, which means that different research paradigms and/or scientific principles may be needed to adequately evaluate the evidence to explain the UFO phenomenon. It is one thing to demonstrate that the UFO phenomenon exists, but it is another thing to determine its nature and origin.

It is also imperative that research investigations study anomalous atmospheric phenomenon like "plasma" to better understand the nature of its behavior and possible relationship to reported UFO encounters. This is necessary since:

1. Plasma physics is a poorly understood area of science, which can manifest as unusual appearing luminous behavior in the sky.
2. Atmospheric plasma and the kinematic behavior of UFOs exhibit similar characteristics, such as in its ability to split, rotate, disappear, and emit light. For these reasons, the source of many reported UFO sightings and close encounters may involve the interaction between humans and plasma energy (See Chapter Four: UFO Evidence, and Chapter Six: UFO Theories).

To help establish a solid scientific foundation, governed by agreed-upon principles that can be best applied towards the study of the phenomenon, investigations must be conducted in a consistent manner using the same research protocols and criteria to properly document and analyze UFO evidence. Such research endeavors must be conducted by those trained and tested through the same educational process to become a "certified UFO investigator." The nature and level of training must be thorough and scientific based, to include qualitative and quantitative research methods, statistics, biology, psychology, sociology, communication, physics, and optical physics. Research protocol should also incorporate prioritized criteria to inform investigators of UFO incidents most worthy of study. Some examples of high priority cases requiring a rapid response for subsequent investigation and analysis include UFO reports that involve multiple witnesses, simultaneous radar-visual sightings (from the ground and/or air), and witness claims of psychological and/or physiological effects from a UFO encounter, landing, and/or abduction.

It would be a mistake to rely upon any single research approach to study such a complex phenomenon. Thus one research objective must pertain to the replication of results in the study of UFOs. Replication is a fundamental check in scientific experiments and must be achieved to help shape our confidence in the study of all aspects of the phenomenon. For example, two different researchers studying the same UFO evidence in the same way should reach the same conclusion. Ultimately, conclusions made of the evidence must be verified by replicable results produced by independent scientists to help determine the nature and origin of this perplexing phenomenon. Unfortunately, the unique nature of the phenomenon does not easily lend itself to the replication of results and reproduction in a laboratory setting. In other words, since a UFO incident cannot be manufactured or repeated by the scientist, ensuring the validity of results and conclusions will present a major challenge to research scientists.

Other Proposed Research Strategies

Several research strategies have been proposed to better understand the phenomenon:

1. Journalist Leslie Kean, in her book,[7] *UFOs: Generals, Pilots, and Government Officials Go on the Record* (2010) discussed the need for a "workable model" to move the UFO issue "forward." This strategy incorporates the development of an:

   ...office or small agency within the U.S. government to handle appropriate UFO investigations, liaison with other countries, and need to demonstrate to the scientific community that this is indeed a subject worthy of study.

Based on her discussions with "serious" government and military officials, Kean contends there is agreement on "three basic points" to advance the UFO agenda:

1. That further scientific investigation is mandated, partly because of the impact of UFOs on aircraft and aviation safety.
2. That this investigation must be an international, cooperative venture involving many governments and transcending politics.
3. That such a global effort cannot be effective without the participation of the United States, the world's greatest technological power.

The above agenda may be facilitated, at some level, by the CFi which is dedicated towards:

A. Achieving scientific, congressional and media credibility for the study of unexplained aerial phenomena while working for the release of official information and physical evidence.
B. Developing a small government agency to investigate UFO incidents, and to act as a focal point for action at home and for research worldwide.
C. Stimulating scientific interest and to assist with the allocation of government and foundation grants for interested scientists in the academic, research, and aviation communities.[7a]

1. Dr. Peter Sturrock, professor emeritus of Space Science and Astrophysics at Stanford University and former president of the Society for Scientific Exploration, also offered a plan for UFO research:

A. Field investigations leading to case documentation and the measurement or retrieval of physical evidence.
B. Laboratory analysis of physical evidence.
C. The systematic compilation and analysis of data (descriptive and physical) to look for patterns and so extract significant facts.
D. The development of theories and the evaluation of those theories on the basis of facts.[8]

2. Another strategy was proposed by astrophysicist Dr. M. Teodorani, who wrote:

> The final step is entirely dedicated to the construction of quantitative physical models and numerical simulations. Once we have a self-consistent model in hand we might also predict the behavior of spherical UFOs, so that they would be really under a form of control from us. A further step might consist in trying to reproduce in a laboratory the observed phenomenon if it is really characterized by a plasma nature. Alternatively if the spherical object is of technological nature, we might try to build a similar one using a sort of reverse engineering, without any need of capturing one but only basing our deductions on the physical data that have been previously acquired in distance.[9]

The role of civilian and military pilots is understandably paramount to the study of UFOs. Since many remarkable UFO encounters by pilots have been reported since the 1940s, there is a need to better collect and analyze this type of essential evidence. With this goal in mind, Richard F. Haines, former NASA research scientist and Chief Scientist from the NARCAP, presented recommendations from "fourteen government officials, military leaders, pilots, academics, and others" in response to the following question: "What actions are needed today to improve the current climate of denial about unidentified aerial phenomena in aviation?" A summary of the findings is presented by Haines:

> A remarkable degree of consistency was found among these recommendations that may be summarized as (ranked in order of number of recommendations):
>
> 1) Exchange information broadly and openly;
> 2) Establish a central global organization to study and report its findings;
> 3) Carry out high quality research;
> 4) Develop new precautionary measures for pilots;
> 5) Strengthen and enforce existing aviation regulations regarding near-miss and related UAP events;
> 6) Work to change the present negative biases toward UAP; and
> 7) Improve UAP detection capabilities.[10]

Additionally, Deardorff, Haisch, Mcccabee, and Puthoff (2005) advised:

> Open scientific research on the subject is needed with special attention paid to high quality UFO reports exhibiting apparent indications that extraterrestrial intelligence and strategy are involved.[11]

Research physicist at the Institute for Advanced Studies in Austin, Eric Davis, emphasized, "they're wrong, naive, stubborn, narrow-minded, afraid, and fearful. It's a dirty word and a forbidden topic. Science is about open-minded inquiry. You shouldn't be laughing off people. You should show more deference and respect to them... Scientists need to get back to using the scientific method to study things that are unknown and unusual, and the UFO subject is one of them."[12]

Discussion

In light of the poorly understood and perplexing nature of the phenomenon, and the associated lack of research support from the government and scientific community, progress made to advance our understanding of the UFO phenomenon will likely continue to stagnate. Despite the important contributions of many established UFO organizations (e.g., MUFON, NICAP, NARCAP, CPTR, SERPA, NUFORC, etc,), until a newly established committee, guided by a shared governance structure and an agreed upon research plan, is formed to help define the nature and origin of this phenomenon, ufology will continue to be perceived as a pseudoscience, and a popular alternative cultural movement by the general scientific and political community. And while no guarantee can be made that a new scientific initiative will provide any meaningful answers to define the nature and origin of this phenomenon, it is imperative that we apply an appropriate level of commitment and resources to help initiate this proposed governance and research goal.

To help ensure the success of this proposed “new approach” to the UFO phenomenon, appropriate rationale must convince the scientific community and members of our political system of the need for collaborative research efforts and resources to more effectively study the phenomenon. As past well-intentioned congressional hearings, sponsored by the Disclosure Project, and the Citizens Hearing on Disclosure, have not been entirely successful in this regard, new approaches must be initiated to address this objective. And with proper leadership, provided within the context of an organized and shared governance structure, the chance of securing needed support and resources, while not guaranteed, should be enhanced.

Despite my wife’s encouragement for me to maintain a positive perspective, I am not optimistic that any level of support will be provided by the government and/or scientific community to help facilitate this proposed “new approach.” The ongoing costly Kepler and SETI initiatives, having achieved variable mission success, in combination with the political and scientific communities proven disinclination to support UFO-based initiatives, make it unlikely that resources will be granted for research purposes within the next few decades and beyond. Consequently, private funding will likely provide the only source of support for the “hypothetical” CSUAE to carry out its mission.

One potential ray of hope may emerge from the result of NASA’s on-going effort to search for extraterrestrial life. In July 2014, Dr. Matt Mountain, Director of the Space Telescope Science Institute and Professor at the Johns Hopkins University Department of Physics and Astronomy expressed his belief that over 100 million planets within our galaxy may be habitable and that evidence of extraterrestrial life may be discovered within 20 years. According to Dr. Mountain: “What we didn’t know five years ago is that perhaps 10 to 20 per cent of stars around us have Earth-size planets in the habitable zone. It’s within our grasp to pull off a discovery that will change the world forever.”[13]

A new scientific approach to the study of the UFO phenomenon must be developed and consistently applied in a timely manner by investigators worldwide in order to narrow the wide gap between science and UFO research. The CSUAE must serve to transform current practice into a more respectable and accepted scientific endeavor to adequately investigate future UFO evidence.

CHAPTER TEN

The UFO Phenomenon: Should I Believe?

Overview

One's answer to the question, "Should I believe in the UFO phenomenon?" results from what we wish to believe, the approach used to interpret the evidence, and possibly even a touch of one's "gut feeling." Achieving an appropriate balance is not an easy task, and adopting an agnostic approach may even present a greater challenge when trying to decide if you "should believe." Unfortunately, conclusions of the UFO evidence may reflect an error in inductive inference, evidenced by people who seek out and assign more weight to information or evidence that confirms their belief. Consequently, if we believe what we wish, we cannot objectively interpret evidence and may actually perceive opposing evidence to be weak in principle and resist revising our beliefs. In other words, if I hope or believe that some UFOs are extraterrestrial, I may lack objectivity when interpreting the evidence.

Driven by our instinctive sense of curiosity, we all like a good mystery to solve, and the UFO phenomenon is as mystifying as it gets. Ideally, a solution to a phenomenon should be derived from verifiable replicated results and associated conclusions from controlled independent scientific investigations. Unfortunately, the often controversial and predominate anecdotal nature of available evidence to study makes it difficult to apply this idealized approach for research purposes. Despite decades of official studies and individual research endeavors, we are far from solving this mystery.

So, "should I believe?" Or, maybe I should ask, "What should I believe?" Well, I believe strongly on the basis of existing empirical evidence, that something very unusual in our skies defies explanation. This extraordinary mystery, and its associated potential important implications, begs for a newly developed organized research initiative to effectively study the phenomenon. I say this because I do believe UFOs exist, as evidenced by apparent physical objects in the sky that cannot be logically explained. My position as a UFO agnostic does not apply to the existence of UFOs, but rather to its nature and origin. It is one thing to demonstrate that UFOs exist, but it is entirely another to determine the "who," "what," and "whys" associated with the phenomenon. And for that, I don't pretend to have a clue. Accordingly, after a methodical review and analysis of the existing evidence, I am not convinced one way or another as to whether UFOs are extraterrestrial, from another space-time, or a natural and/or man-made phenomenon.

If one conducts a thorough and objective review and analysis of the existing UFO evidence, it should be obvious that people from all over the world for several decades, and possibly centuries, have observed something very unusual in our skies. And given our limited understanding of this phenomenon, even just a small hint of what is going on would suffice for now until we initiate, if ever, a concerted, multidisciplinary scientific study to attempt to better understand, what leading UFO researcher and astronomer Dr. Hynek believes to be "a phenomenon so strange and foreign to our daily terrestrial mode of thought."[1] This statement would have likely applied to those who experienced a meteor shower centuries ago, which probably instilled the same level of curiosity and fear as that incurred during a current day UFO encounter.

The fundamental question regarding the UFO phenomenon is, how to determine if existing evidence "proves" that UFOs are intelligently controlled by alien beings from somewhere other than Earth. That is, what criteria should be used to verify, whether or not, non-human intelligence (NHI) has visited our planet? Since not everyone maintains the same definition and standards of such "criteria," there will be major differences of opinion as to what type(s) of evidence signify irrefutable "proof." Other than UFO occupants acknowledging their presence on CNN's "Breaking News," scientists will accept this conclusion only after applied research, using the scientific method, confirms this to be true. But "should I believe" that NHI governs UFOs if a pilot reports the sudden appearance and then disappearance of a silver object that accelerated at thousands of miles per hour out of sight, and confirmed by ground radar? Is a UFO extraterrestrial in origin since it appears to exhibit the application of physics and engineering principles clearly beyond our present-day capabilities? Such evidence does not provide irrefutable proof that alien beings are visiting Earth. Just because it defies logical explanation, similar to how the pyramids were built, introducing the "space alien" card as justification is a bold leap without additional supporting evidence. Admittedly, I cannot conclusively rule out the remote possibility that some unexplained UFOs may be physical craft from another solar system or space-time. I simply don't know.

Are the extraordinary claims of UFO encounters of various kinds symptomatic of mass hysteria brought on by cognitive hardwiring from countless hours spent with *Star Trek,* science fiction books and movies, and the *Twilight Zone*? Can there be a sociological or psychological explanation for the alleged UFO encounters, or is the documented testimony of UFO experiences by highly credible commercial and military pilots, military and government officials, and thousands of citizens worldwide sufficient to conclude that NHI has visited Earth? While many UFO researchers admit that conclusive proof of NHI visiting Earth exist, others remain skeptical enough to contend that the continued failure to provide undeniable, verifiable evidence means that other life forms have not visited our planet. Admittedly, it is hard to suppress the instinctual human trait to want to believe in something, and there is some degree of temptation to want to believe that the five to ten percent of unexplained UFOs are extraterrestrial in origin. But while "they" may in fact be from somewhere other than Earth, I need that elusive "smoking gun," or at least some highly potent gun powder, that provides undeniable proof for me to firmly "believe" that some UFOs are governed by NHI.

Collectively, the reported testimony of UFO experiences from credible witnesses, the diverse range of proposed theories to explain the many extraordinary UFO claims, combined with the government and NASA's official denial of extraterrestrial visitation of our planet, contribute to a confused public who yearn for answers. While there is no dispute that many people believe their UFO experiences of various types to be real events, the "high strangeness" or non-natural phenomena often associated with such encounters present a major obstacle for science to adequately address. Adding to this puzzle is the combination of sensible and nonsensical viewpoints on the nature and origin of the phenomenon from many UFO bloggers, authors, and even a few leading UFO researchers. Frustrated by our limited scientific understanding of the UFO phenomenon, and lack of reliable sources for UFO evidence and opinions to trust, we may attempt to obtain information to solve the mystery through alternative means and possibly become more confused in the process. Consequently, it is difficult to know who and what to believe and how best to filter the essential valid facts from fiction to better understand the phenomenon. Still, most people don't give the phenomenon much attention, believing that whatever it is has not had any impact on our planet and personal lives. Thus they adapt an apathetic attitude and either don't care to "believe" for this reason, or they may possess an unconscious fear of UFOs and deny its existence.

Many, if not most people who believe that UFOs represent an intelligent life form from somewhere other than our planet, do so without sufficient supporting evidence. The general public who are familiar, at varying levels, with issues related to the phenomenon, often form conclusions based on unsubstantiated and tenuous UFO evidence:

1. A "flying saucer" with dead aliens was recovered in Roswell, New Mexico in 1947.
2. The Phoenix Lights were UFOs from another planet.
3. We have reverse-engineered and applied advanced technology obtained from crashed UFOs.
4. The government is withholding knowledge of UFOs from the public.
5. Alien beings visiting Earth have abducted humans for DNA.

6. UFOs are from another solar system, dimension, and/or from our future, among others.

Despite such questionable viewpoints aligned with this mystery, it is important to maintain objectivity when evaluating the evidence. Consequently, when analyzing UFO evidence, ask yourself these questions: What do I want to believe about UFOs and what do I actually know about UFOs? That is, sometimes we believe what we wish. In other words, people tend to seek out and assign more weight to evidence that confirms their hypothesis. By nature, we tend to inherently seek information which support our opinions, and dispute evidence that does not. This psychological process is termed confirmation bias, which explains why people tend to generally recall only information that is consistent with their beliefs. Consequently, many who believe that UFOs are extraterrestrial craft visiting Earth avoid rejecting this belief when presented with contrary evidence. To elude this form of psychological deception, it may help to be aware that this error in judgment can adversely influence our decision-making process. Thus, if you continue to investigate the phenomenon, consider adopting an objective perspective until evidence-based conclusions are made by reputable scientists and replicated by independent scientific investigations (if ever, and if possible).

If I believe that the UFO phenomenon is governed by NHI from another solar system or space-time, am I using scientific or pseudo-scientific thinking? If I concur with this conclusion, in the absence of a scientific based analysis of the evidence, it would be inconsistent with the scientific method and reflect a pseudo-scientific interpretation. That is, a pseudo-scientific approach, characterized by the use of contradictory and uncorroborated beliefs and claims, may bias our interpretation of evidence which may lead to erroneous conclusions. To the skeptic exposed to only anecdotal UFO evidence, an informed conclusion cannot be reached with sufficient confidence without experimental analysis and verification of tangible evidence. So should we adopt a skeptical approach to the subject given the numerous compelling accounts of UFO sightings and incidents?

The UFO skeptics are firmly entrenched in the belief that the phenomenon can be explained in several ways:

1. Natural phenomena such as meteors, atmospheric, etc.
2. Psychological, as manifested by confirmation bias, confabulation, hoaxes, the psycho-cultural hypothesis, hallucinations, and mental disorders.
3. Physical objects in the form of satellites, advanced technology, weather balloons, and space debris.

Can these reasons account for all UFO sightings? Maybe they can, but part of me can't ignore the remote possibility that some UFOs are operated by an alien intelligence or represent an unknown phenomenon. But while this emotional based thought may lead to erroneous conclusions, critical thinking should prevail before one firmly believes that a reported UFO incident, such as Roswell, New Mexico (1947), the Phoenix Lights (1997), Rendlesham Forest, Suffolk, England (1980), Washington, D.C. (1952), among others, provides indisputable evidence that NHI has visited Earth. It is difficult to ignore these extraordinary albeit controversial incidents, and the authenticity of compelling accounts by experienced military pilots and personnel, and government officials, and astronauts, who have officially disclosed their UFO encounters through The Disclosure Project, and/or The Citizens Hearing for Disclosure to members of congress. Such testimony is hard to firmly discredit as examples of confabulation, confirmation bias, or just plain delusions. And while they help to support the notion that UFOs may be physical craft from another world, we cannot be certain that the strange moving object in the sky represents a visitation from another solar system, or a natural and/or man-made phenomenon, among other possible, yet to be discovered phenomena.

Why and How are "They" Here?

Let's assume, for argument sake, that the reported descriptions and behavior of UFOs represent intelligently controlled craft from somewhere other than Earth. Given this context, the next obvious question is: "What are their intentions?" "Should I believe their intention to be purely scientific-based to discover and analyze new life forms and their evolution and culture, or is it to simply satisfy a possible universal innate need, like us, to explore?

Curiously, their apparent "non-interference" directive and associated lack of formal contact implies the UFO occupants are not interested in engaging in a meaningful exchange of ideas, colonization, trade, hostile action, or teaching us new technological and medical approaches to benefit our quality of life. So, why are "they" here? My best guess is that an alien civilization's reason for visiting our pale, blue dot in space would most likely be that they're monitoring us, since we are reaching a point in our natural development that will allow us to access other solar systems. Other civilizations may be concerned that we've reached this technological level without ending hostilities and wars, which may be perceived as a potential threat for them in some way. Accordingly, they want to keep a close eye on things, just to make sure we don't get too big, too bad, too soon. Maybe they will eventually guide us into a federation of civilizations, if we someday behave ourselves and prove that we qualify.

The absence of formal contact by the UFO occupants, however, may provide an argument against the extraterrestrial theory. If we assume UFOs are intelligently controlled, you would at least consider they would announce their presence and possibly interact with purpose and meaningful intent. Alternatively, they may originate from another star system or space-time, but their level of intelligence, ethics, and/or mission dictates, for whatever reason, their apparent "non-interference" directive. There may be appropriate rationale for their hands-off approach, unless you accept alien abductions as real events. That remote possibility aside, it is tempting to speculate on such possible reasons:

1. Theoretically, if they are from our future, their influential outcomes may alter their reality.
2. Earth is their experiment and they do not want to influence the outcome, except to observe, record, and analyze.
3. They feel we are too intellectually inferior to engage in a meaningful exchange of ideas.
4. They may perceive our society as too unpredictable and aggressive to be trusted.
5. The only thing Earth can offer of potential value is DNA for genetic engineering.
6. They wish to only monitor our nuclear-related activities to prevent the possible launching of a nuclear weapon to protect Earth and its people.

They seem to interact with humans in unusual ways, as indicated from similar reports of alleged alien abduction experiences that involve biological procedures to retrieve eggs and sperm. If true, could DNA and genetic engineering be the reason? Other possibilities exist as to why "they" (if present) refuse to announce their presence, with the obvious one being that no intelligence is associated with the phenomenon. One possible rationale for this "non-interference" approach is provided by Robert Hastings, who wrote:

> The visitors may be adhere to a policy of very limited interaction with relatively primitive species such as ours—one which restricts direct communication, in one form or another, to situations in which a potentially disastrous, planetary-wide crisis is imminent—consequently requiring some type of interference in the affairs of those semi-savage societies. In short, if either of these scenarios has merit, there will be no dramatic UFO landing on the White House lawn, or in the Kremlin's courtyard, at least not anytime soon.[2]

If you believe NHI has visited Earth from another solar system, then you must explain how interstellar travel is possible. While some theories such as the faster-than-light, wormholes, multiverse, and superstring, offer potential solutions for overcoming incomprehensible distances and associated travel time, they exist only as concepts in quantum physics. Such theories serve as an initial required step in an evolving process to better understand the laws governing the universe, which if successfully applied, may eventually provide the means to easily travel between different parts of the universe in a blink of an eye. If such concepts are proven valid it may possibly explain the perplexing behavior of the phenomena's reported "high strangeness."

It is presumptuous to state that such theories are impossible, since history is filled with unrealistic ideas that eventually became fact. We should recognize that at this stage in our technological evolution and embryonic development, there is very likely a staggering amount we have yet to learn about scientific laws and principles, and the related technologies controlled by them. After all, it took only sixty-six years from the time Wilbur and Orville flew at Kitty Hawk to when Neil and Buzz walked on the moon. What will the next sixty-six years, and a few more decades, and generations reveal? Just wish I could be around to witness it all. Hopefully, some remnants of my DNA will!

My lack of conviction, that unequivocal evidence exists that proves that some unexplained UFOs are extraterrestrial or extra-dimension physical craft, causes me to wonder why many leading UFO researchers contend it does, despite the:

1. Limited tangible evidence to sufficiently analyze for study.
2. Lack of rigorous scientific investigations of the phenomenon.
3. Uncorroborated evidence to support extraordinary UFO claims.

Collectively, our limited understanding of the phenomenon makes it difficult to ascribe meaning to its origin and nature. Consequently, the evidence, which is not convincing enough to form a definitive conclusion of unexplained UFOs, is a paradox at many levels. And the subjective witness accounts serve to deepen the mystery by generating more layers of elusive questions, not easily explainable using current knowledge. But despite the unique and controversial nature of the phenomenon, and its potential important implications, the collective evidence suggests that our scientific communities and political systems worldwide should consider the phenomenon to be of paramount importance. Accordingly, a formal, officially appointed committee and associated scientific teams must develop appropriate plans, in an organized attempt to define the nature and origin of the UFO phenomenon. This is not a unique idea as it has been proposed over the past several decades by military officials, politicians, and UFO researchers, among others (see Chapter Nine: The UFO Phenomenon: A New Approach).

Discussion

Are intelligent beings visiting earth, or is an atmospheric or meteorological phenomena responsible for the small percentage of unexplained UFOs? Whether it is plasma or beings in physical craft from another planet or dimension, natural phenomena, or something yet to be discovered, the perplexing and compelling evidence clearly indicate that one or more phenomena exist in our skies, minds, or both.

There seems to be only two ways for the phenomenon to be realized. The easy route will be for the intelligence (if present and willing) governing the UFOs to announce their presence to the world. The more difficult, but likely required route (as previous mentioned) will be to establish a governance structure dedicated towards providing leadership to facilitate a multidisciplinary scientific research initiative, with sufficient support and resources, to study the phenomenon. Until either outcome is realized (if ever), the mystery will remain as a source of speculation, skepticism, and debate. We simply cannot continue to passively anticipate that the phenomenon will eventually announce its nature and origin to the world. We need to establish plans, set goals, and aggressively investigate this astonishing mystery in a proactive manner. After all, how much more do we know about the phenomenon today than we did decades ago? I think very little having any significance. Consequently, newly developed scientific based approaches, which offer the greatest potential to define the nature and origin of the phenomenon, must be applied to better understand a significant issue of our time.

Since our understanding of the universe is limited, many new scientific principles will eventually be discovered which will likely explain the perplexing nature of this phenomenon, among many other unsolved scientific theories. Consequently, the inherent paradox is that the UFO phenomenon may only be fully understood and explainable using scientific principles yet to be discovered. If true, we may be faced with a great challenge trying to test proposed hypotheses using established scientific methods and associated principles inconsistent with the force that governs this phenomenon. Accordingly, our attempt to study this phenomenon may be analogous to performing neurosurgery with stone knives.

Upon reviewing the evidence, it is difficult to not conclude that many people have and will likely continue to experience inexplicable UFO encounters. Many UFO researchers contend that the compelling witness testimony of observed UFOs by highly credible witnesses from different locations, and confirmed by radar, appear consistent in showing the phenomena under intelligent control and maneuverability that appear to counter laws of inertia and gravity. While there is no doubt that many witnesses to UFO events have seen something extraordinarily strange that defy logical explanation, there is no irrefutable evidence that what they have seen is, undeniably, a physical craft under intelligent control from another solar system and/or space-time.

In the final analysis, what can be said of ufology? While there are certainly incidents of deception, and confirmation bias and confabulation, there is still compelling anecdotal evidence by credible witnesses of an aerial anomaly that cannot be adequately explained. The scientific community must be convinced of the importance to investigate this phenomenon instead of ignoring it as if it was a matter of no significance. And if a thorough investigation proves it to be explainable within the context of a natural "earthly" phenomenon, that conclusion is important to know, especially with respect to aviation safety issues.

The UFO Phenomenon: Should I Believe?

Despite decades of investigative research, the UFO evidence fails to provide convincing rationale and justification, at least to the scientific community, to support the common belief that an alien intelligence is operating UFOs and interacting with humans. And while no guarantee can be made that a new scientific study will provide conclusive answers to the many questions associated with the UFO phenomenon, it is imperative that we apply the same level of commitment to achieve this objective as we did to step foot on the moon. If we can, at the very least, facilitate an organized multidisciplinary research initiative to investigate the phenomenon, then Neil Armstrong's statement upon first stepping foot on the moon that this is, "one giant leap for mankind," would also apply to this important concern. In fact, that first manned lunar landing may pale in comparison to the potential outcomes incurred by our greater understanding of the UFO phenomenon and contact with alien intelligence (if "they" exist).

So, should I believe? Before you answer this question, keep in mind that there exists a thin line between the existence of the phenomenon and one's belief or hope that unexplained UFOs are not from Earth.

After all, remember Carl Sagan's position that "somewhere something incredible is waiting to be known."

Endnotes

Chapter One: Introduction

1. David Clarke and Gary Anthony. "ufocasebook.com." Last modified 2006. Accessed August 19, 2013. www.ufocasebook.com/pdf/projectcondign.pdf.
2. "Project Blue Book Archive." Accessed August 19, 2013. www.bluebookarchive.org.

Chapter Two: The UFO Phenomenon, Ufology, and Science

1. "Seth Shostak on UFOs & SETI." Last modified July 10, 2000, http://rense.com/general2/seth.html., www.space.com:80/sciencefiction/phenomena/ufo_seti_000619.html.

2 Robert L. Hastings. *UFOs and Nukes: Extraordinary Encounters at Nuclear Weapons Sites.* Author House, 2008.

2a Ibid.

3. "Need to Know vs. Need to Believe in Ufology." Last modified 2009. Accessed July 19, 2013, http://fierycelt.tripod.com/xposeufotruth/needknow_vs_needbelieve.html.
4. "Neil deGrasse Tyson quotes." Last modified 2013. Accessed July 30, 2013, www.goodreads.com/author/quotes/12855.Neil_deGrasse_Tyson.
5. "UFOs: What's 60 Years Accomplished?" Last modified 2013. Accessed July 30, 2013, www.ourstrangeplanet.com/the-san-luis-valley/guest-editorials/ufos-whats-60-years-accomplished.
6. "The Tomb of Jesus Christ." Accessed July 30, 2013, www.tombofjesus.com/index.php/en/researchers-authors/dr-james-deardorff.
7. "Ufology and Science." Accessed April 13, 2013, www.nickpope.net/ufology-and-science.html.
8. "The Challenge of Unidentified Flying Objects." Accessed April 10, 2013, www.nicap.org/books/coufo/coufo_complete.html. Washington, D.C, 1961.
9. Peter A. Sturrock. *The UFO Enigma: A New Review of the Scientific Evidence.* New York: Aspect, 2000.
10. Michael Shermer. "Baloney Detection." Scientific American, November 2001, 36.
11. Robert L. Hastings. *UFOs and Nukes: Extraordinary Encounters at Nuclear Weapons Sites.* Author House, 2008.
12. "Statement on Unidentified Flying Objects, Prepared statement submitted to the House Committee on Science and Astronautics, July 29, 1968, by James E. McDonald," Accessed April 17, 2013, www.cufon.org/cufon/mcdon3.html.
13. Robert L. Hastings. *UFOs and Nukes: Extraordinary Encounters at Nuclear Weapons*

Sites. Author House, 2008.

14. "About UFOs and Nuclear Weapons." Accessed May 17, 2013, www.ufohastings.com.
15. "The failure of the 'science' of UFOlogy." Accessed May 19, 2013, http://debunker.com/texts/ObergCuttySark.html.
16. "The UFO Challenge." Accessed May 21, 2013, www.stantonfriedman.com/index.php?ptp=ufo_challenge.
17. "Pseudo-Science of Anti-Ufology." Accessed May 21, 2013, www.theufochronicles.com/2009/05/pseudo-science-of-anti-ufology.html., May 30, 2009.
18. Carl Sagan. *Cosmos*. New York: Random House. 1980.
19. "Ethical Implications of the UFO Abduction Phenomenon." Accessed May 23, 2013, www.anomalies.net/archive/investigation/ETHICS.EDI, 1987.
20. Carl Sagan. *Contact*. New York: Pocket Books, 1985.
21. "Prosaic Explanations: The Failure of UFO Skepticism." Accessed May 26, 2013, http://brumac.8k.com/prosaic6.html.
22. "Science and UFOs: Part 2—Occam's Rusty Razor." Accessed May 28, 2013, www.network54.com/Forum/594658/thread/1358750518/last-1358750518/Science+and+UFOs-+Part+2+-+Occam's+Rusty+Razor, March 2012.

22a Ibid.

23. "Dr. J. Allen Hynek Speaking at the United Nations, Nov. 27th 1978." Accessed May 28, 2013, www.ufoevidence.org/documents/doc757.html., UFO Evidence.com.

23a. Ibid.

24. "The UFO Challenge." Accessed May 21, 2013, www.stantonfriedman.com/index.php?ptp=ufo_challenge.
25. Stanton Friedman. *Flying Saucers and Science: A Scientist Investigates the Mysteries of UFOs: Interstellar Travel, Crashes, and Government Cover-Ups*. New Jersey: New Page Books, 2008.
26. "The Obama administration's startling UFO connections." Accessed May 29, 2013, www.openminds.tv/obama-administration-startling-ufo-connections/. Posted by Alejandro Rojas, October 28, 2009.
27. "Science in Default: Twenty-Two Years of Inadequate UFO Investigations." Accessed June 3, 2013, www.cufon.org/cufon/mcdon2.html. December 27, 1969.
28. "Yes, UFOs exist: Position statement by SEPRA head, Jean-Jacques Velasco." Accessed June 3, 2013, www.ufoevidence.org/documents/doc1627.html. April 2004.
29. "The UFO Challenge." Accessed May 21, 2013, www.stantonfriedman.com/index.php?ptp=ufo_challenge.
30. Edward J. Ruppelt, "The Report on Unidentified Flying Objects." BiblioBizarre, 2003.
31. Jacques Vallée and Janine Vallée. *Challenge to Science: The UFO Enigma*. New York: Ballantine Books, 1966.
32. "Statements About Flying Saucers And Extraterrestrial Life Made By Prof. Hermann Oberth, German Rocket Scientist." Accessed May 21, 2013, www.mufon.com/MUFONNews/znews_oberth.html. June 2002.
33. Timothy Good, Above Top Secret, Minneapolis, MN: Quill, 1988, 328-335.
34. "The High Strangeness of Dimensions, and the Process of Alien." Accessed May 18, 2013, Abductionwww.cassiopaea.org/cass/high_strangeness.html by Laura Knight-Jadczyk.
35. "General Lionel M. Chassin." Last modified June 14, 2012. Accessed May 18, 2013, www.zoominfo.com/p/Lionel-Chassin/45924532.
36. "UFOs in the United Kingdom: The Real X-Files." Accessed May 18, 2013, www.

theufotimes.com/contents/Articles_1%20.html.
37. Gillmor, Daniel. *Scientific Study of Unidentified Flying Objects*. September 28, 1965, letter to USAF Scientific Advisory Board requesting a review of the UFO project. New York: Times Books, 1969.
38. Victor Marchetti. "How the CIA Views the UFO Phenomenon." Second Look, Vol. 1, No.7, (1979).
39. W. De Brouwer. "Postface" in SOBEPS' Vague d'OVNI sur la Belgique-Un Dossier Exceptionnel, Brussels: SOBEPS, 1991.
40. "British Admiral was tireless UFO advocate at the House of Lords." Accessed May 19, 2013, www.openminds.tv/british-admiral-ufo-advocate-767. Posted by Antonio Huneeus, August 24, 2011.
41. Carl Sagan. *Other Worlds*. New York: Bantam, 1975. p.113.
42. "DOD Press release." Accessed May 22, 2013, www.ufoevidence.org/documents/doc1247.html.
43. Donald Menzel. *Physics Today*. June 1976.
44. Isaac Asimov. *Fantasy and Science Fiction*. Feb. 1975. p.132.
45. "99 Frequently Asked Questions {FAQs} about astronauts and UFOs." Accessed June 19, 2013, www.jamesoberg.com/99faq.html.
46. David Morrison. "Ask an Astrobiologist." October 2006.
47. "Conclusions and Recommendations." Accessed May 22, 2013, www.project1947.com/shg/condon/sec-i.html.
48. "The Skeptics Dictionary." Accessed May 22, 2013, www.skepdic.com/aliens.html.
48a. Ibid.
49. "UFOlogy: 50 Years of futility, frustration, and failure." Accessed May 23, 2013, http://home.comcast.net/~tprinty/UFO/50years.html.
49a. Ibid.
50. Stanton Friedman. *Flying Saucers and Science: A Scientist Investigates the Mysteries of UFOs: Interstellar Travel, Crashes, and Government Cover-Ups*. New Jersey: New Page Books, 2008.
51. Don Donderi. *UFOs, ETs and Alien Abductions: A Scientist Looks at the Evidence*. Virginia: Hampton Roads, 2013.

Chapter Three: UFO Behavior and Effects

1. "The Emerging Picture of the UFO Problem." Accessed June 23, 2013, www.nicap.org/emerge.html.
2. "National Aviation Reporting Center on Anomalous Phenomena." Accessed June 23, 2013, http://narcap.org/index.html. Updated May 16, 2013.
3. "Unexplained sightings met with denial." Accessed June 23, 2013, www.ufoevidence.org/documents/doc3.html.
4. "Aviation Safety in America: Under-Reporting Bias of Unidentified Aerial Phenomena and Recommended Solutions." Accessed June 23, 2013, www.narcap.org/reports/TR8Bias1.html. July 20, 2004.
5. "Physical Traces Associated with Unidentified Flying Objects: An Interim Report—Results of Processing Data—1490-2004." Accessed June 4, 2013, www.ufoevidence.org/documents/doc1172.html.
5a. Ibid.
5b. Ibid.
6. "Physical Evidence Related to UFO Reports—Sturrock Panel—Abstract, Summary

and Introduction." Accessed June 4, 2013, www.ufoevidence.org/documents/doc535.html.

6a. Ibid.

7 "Physical Evidence Related to UFO Reports: The Proceedings of a Workshop Held at the Pocantico Conference Center." Tarrytown, New York, September 29 to October 4, 1997.

8. Paul R. Hill. *Unconventional Flying Objects: A Scientific Analysis.* Newburyport, MA: Hampton Roads Pub Co, 1995.

8a. Ibid.

8b. Ibid.

8c. Ibid.

8d. Ibid.

9. "Hal Puthoff Reviews Paul Hill Book Synopsis of Unconventional Flying Objects." Accessed June 4, 2013, www.paranormalworld.com/blogs/item/1770-hal-puthoff-reviews-paul-hill-book-synopsis-of-unconventional-flying-objects.

10. "Aviation Safety in America—Spherical UAP." Accessed June 4, 2013, www.narcap.org/Projsphere/3.1.6_narcap_projSph.pdf.

10a. Ibid.

11. Richard Stothers, "Unidentified Flying Objects in Classical Antiquity." *The Classical Journal,* 103.1, 2007: 79-92.

12. "The UFO Evidence: NICAP's UFO Investigator and Selected UFO Documents." Accessed June 4, 2013, www.cufos.org/NICAP.html.

13. Dominique F. Weinstein. "Aviation Safety and Unidentified Aerial Phenomena: A Preliminary Study of 600 cases of Unidentified Aerial Phenomena (UAP) Reported by Military and Civilian pilots." NARCAP International Air Safety Report IR-4, 2012.

13a. "Physical Traces Associated with Unidentified Flying Objects: An Interim Report—Results of Processing Data—1490-2004." Accessed June 4, 2013, www.ufoevidence.org/documents/doc1172.html.

13b. Paul R. Hill. *Unconventional Flying Objects: A Scientific Analysis.* Newburyport, MA: Hampton Roads Publishing Company, 1995.

13c. Ibid.

13d. Ibid.

13e. "Physical Traces Associated with Unidentified Flying Objects: An Interim Report—Results of Processing Data—1490-2004." Accessed June 4, 2013, www.ufoevidence.org/documents/doc1172.html.

14. James McCampbell. *A Major Breakthrough in the Scientific Understanding of Unidentified Flying Objects.* Celestial Arts, 1976.

14a Paul R. Hill. *Unconventional Flying Objects: A Scientific Analysis.* Newburyport, MA: Hampton Roads Publishing Company, 1995.

14b. James McCampbell. *A Major Breakthrough in the Scientific Understanding of Unidentified Flying Objects.* Celestial Arts, 1976.

14c. Ibid.

15. Richard Hall. The UFO Evidence. Washington, D.C.: NICAP, 1964.

16. Dominique F. Weinstein. "Aviation Safety and Unidentified Aerial Phenomena: A Preliminary Study of 600 cases of Unidentified Aerial Phenomena (UAP) Reported by Military and Civilian pilots." NARCAP International Air Safety Report IR-4, 2012.

16a. Ibid.

17. "UFO-Related Human Physiological Effects." Accessed June 15, 2013, http://rr0.org/time/1/9/9/6/Schuessler_PhysiologicalEffects/index.html.
17a. James McCampbell. *A Major Breakthrough in the Scientific Understanding of Unidentified Flying Objects.* Celestial Arts, 1976.
17b "Physical Evidence Related to UFO Reports—Sturrock Panel—Abstract, Summary and Introduction." Accessed June 4, 2013, www.ufoevidence.org/documents/doc535.html.
17c. Paul R. Hill. *Unconventional Flying Objects: A Scientific Analysis*. Newburyport, MA: Hampton Roads Publishing Company, 1995.
17d. "The UFO Evidence: NICAP's UFO Investigator and Selected UFO Documents." Accessed June 4, 2013, www.cufos.org/NICAP.html.
17e. Ibid.
17f. Paul R. Hill. *Unconventional Flying Objects: A Scientific Analysis*. (Newburyport, MA: Hampton Roads Publishing Company. 1995).
17g. Ibid.
18. James McCampbell. *A Major Breakthrough in the Scientific Understanding of Unidentified Flying Objects*. Celestial Arts: 1976.
19. "The UFO Evidence: NICAP's UFO Investigator and Selected UFO Documents." Accessed Jun 4, 2013,www.cufos.org/NICAP.html.
20. "Physiological Effects of UFOs Upon People." Accessed Jun 15, 2013, www.ufocasebook.com/pdf/ufoeffects.pdf.
20a. Ibid.
20b. Ibid.
20c. Ibid.
21. Patrick Huyghe. *The Field Guide to Extraterrestrials*. London: Hodder and Stoughton, 1997, 6-7.
22. Richard Hall. *The UFO Evidence, Volume II: A Thirty-Year Report*. Oxford, UK: Scarecrow Press, 2001.
23. Jacques F. Vallée and Eric W. Davis. "Incommensurability, Orthodoxy and the Physics of High Strangeness: A 6-layer Model for Anomalous Phenomena." Physics of High Strangeness, (2003).

Chapter Four: UFO Evidence

1. "U.K. Condign Report (2000) Unidentified Aerial Phenomena in the U.K. Air Defense Region." Accessed July 22, 2013, www.uk-ufo.org/condign/condrep.html.
2. Z. Stichin, *The 12th Planet*. New York: Avon Books, 1976.
3. W. Bramley. *The Gods of Eden*. New York: Avon Books, 1989).
4. "Steven Greer and Disclosure." Accessed June 12, 2013, www.bibliotecapleyades.net/esp_autor_greer.html.
5. "The Robertson Panel." Accessed July 13, 2013, www.ufocasebook.com/robertsonpanel.html.
6. Leslie Kean. *UFOs: Generals, Pilots, and Government Officials Go on the Record.* New York: Three Rivers Press, 2011.
7. Peter A. Sturrock. *The UFO Enigma: A New Review of the Physical Evidence*. New York: Warner Books, 1999.
8. "PETITION, UFOS, WHITE HOUSE AND LIES." Accessed July 23, 2013, www.stantonfriedman.com/index.php?ptp=articles&fdt=2011.11.11.

8a. Ibid.
9. J. Hynek. *The Edge of Reality: A Progress Report on Unidentified Flying Objects.* New York: Quality Books, 1976.
9a. Leslie Kean. *UFOs: Generals, Pilots, and Government Officials Go on the Record.* New York: Three Rivers Press, 2011.
9b. Ibid.
10. "Conclusions and Recommendations Edward U. Condon." Accessed July 25, 2013, http://files.ncas.org/condon/text/sec-i.html.
11. "Symposium on Unidentified Flying Objects. Hearings before the Committee on Science and Astronautics. U.S. House of Representatives." Accessed August 10, 2013, www.project1947.com/shg/symposium/index.html.
12. "Project Blue Book Archive." Accessed July 25, 2013, www.bluebookarchive.org.
13. "Project Blue Book Special Report #14 (1954)." Accessed July 27, 2013, http://archive.org/details/ProjectBlueBookSpecialReport14.
14. Alan Hendry. *The UFO Handbook: A Guide to Investigating, Evaluating, and Reporting UFO Sightings*. New York: Doubleday, 1979.
15. J. Allen Hynek. *The UFO Experience – A Scientific Inquiry*. Jackson, TN: Da Capo Press, 1998.
15a. Ibid.
16. "Secret Twining Letter—"The reported phenomena are real." Accessed July 29, 2013, www.nicap.org/twining_letter.html.
16a. Ibid.
17. "Classified Documents Validate US Military/Presidential UFO Involvement." Accessed July 29, 2013, www.ufoevidence.org/documents/doc1746.html.
18. "U.S. Air Force Project Grudge and Blue Book Reports 1-12." Accessed August 1, 2013, www.nicap.org/docs/pbb/nicap_pbr1-12_srch.pdf.
19. Peter A. Sturrock. "An Analysis of the Condon Report on the Colorado UFO Project." J. Scientific Exploration, 1 (1987): 75.
20. "UFOs and Defense: What Should We Prepare For?" Accessed August 8, 2013, www.disclosureproject.org/docs/pdf/COMETA_part1.pdf.
20a. Ibid.
20b. Ibid.
20c. Ibid.
20d. Ibid.
21a. "U.K. Condign Report (2000) Unidentified Aerial Phenomena in the U.K. Air Defense Region." Accessed July 22, 2013, www.uk-ufo.org/condign/condrep.html.
21b. Ibid.
22. "Steven Greer and Disclosure." Accessed June 12, 2013, www.bibliotecapleyades.net/esp_autor_greer.html.
23. S. Greer. *Disclosure: Military and Government Witnesses Reveal the Greatest Secrets in Modern History*. Crozet, VA: Crossing Point, 2001.
23a. Ibid.
24. "National Press Club Witness Testimony." Accessed August 10, 2013, www.ufoinfo.com/news/npcwt.shtml.
25. "Parviz Jafari." Accessed August 11, 2013, http://uto.sigsno.org/freedomofinfo.org/national_press_07/jafari_statement.pdf.
25a. Ibid.
26a. Leslie Kean. *UFOs: Generals, Pilots, and Government Officials Go on the Record.*

New York: Three Rivers Press, 2011.
26b. Ibid.
26c. Ibid.
27. "National Press Club Conference: Pilots Speak Out About UFOs." Accessed August 10, 2013, www.mercuryrapids.co.uk/articles. ationalPressClubConferencePilotsSpeakOutAboutUFOs.html.
28. "Radar and Pilot Cases." Accessed August 11, 2013, www.disclosureproject.org/access/es-wit-test-radar-pilot.html.
28a. Ibid.
28b. Ibid.
28c. Ibid.
29. "Testimony of Dr. Richard Haines." Accessed August 10, 2013, www.bibliotecapleyades.net/disclosure/briefing/disclosure05.html.
29a. Ibid.
29b. Ibid.
30. "UFO Facts and a Solution to the Energy Crisis Testimony of 60 Government & Military Witnesses." Accessed August 12, 2013, www.wanttoknow.info/ufocover-up10pg.
30a. Ibid.
31. "Jean-Charles Duboc." Accessed August 10, 2013, http://uto.sigsno.org/freedomofinfo.org/national_press_07/duboc_statement.pdf.
32. "Peruvian Air Force pilot shoots at UFO." Accessed August 10, 2013, www.abovetopsecret.com/forum/thread573372/pg1.
32a. Ibid.
33. Leslie Kean. *UFOs: Generals, Pilots, and Government Officials Go on the Record*. New York: Three Rivers Press, 2011.
34. "Citizen's Hearing—Richard French, Ex-Air Force Lt. Colonel And Former UFO Debunker, Says He Saw A UFO And ... There Were ALIENS Aboard It?!" Accessed August 10, 2013, http://massufosightings.blogspot.com/2013/05/exopolitical-disclosure-citizens_14.html.
34a. Ibid.
35. "Nick Pope." Accessed August 11, 2013, www.ufodigest.com/article/disclosure-review-0601.
36. "Deathbed testimony about UFOs given by former CIA official." Accessed August 17, 2013, www.openminds.tv/deathbed-testimony-about-ufos-given-by-former-cia-official-video-1002.
37. "National UFO Reporting Center Case Briefs and Past Highlights." Accessed August 22, 2013, www.nuforc.org/CBIndex.html.
38. "The Disclosure Project Briefing Document." Accessed August 23, 2013, www.disclosureproject.org/access/docs/pdf/DisclosureProjectBriefingDocumentNoDocs.pdf.
39. C. Poher, and J. Vallée. "Basic Patterns in UFO Observations" (paper presented at the 13th Aerospace Sciences Meeting, Pasadena, California, January 20-22, 1975).
39a. Ibid.
40. "UFO Reports from China." Accessed August 24, 2013, www.paradigmresearchgroup.org/biblio/bib20.html.
41. UFO-Related Human Physiological Effects." Accessed August 25, 2013, http://rr0.org/time/1/9/9/6/Schuessler_PhysiologicalEffects/index.html.

41a. Ibid.
42. John F. Schuessler. *The Cash-Landrum UFO Incident.* Atlanta, GA: Geo Graphics, 1998.
43. Jacques Vallée. *Confrontations: A Scientist's Search for Alien Contact.* London: Souvenir Press, 1990, 112-39.
44. Paul R. Hill. *Unconventional Flying Objects: A Scientific Analysis.* Newburyport, MA Hampton Roads Pub Co, 1995.
45. Maurice Chatelain. *Our Ancestors Came From Outer Space.* London: Pan Books, 1980, 25.
46. "UFOs and astronauts: REPORTS AND STATEMENTS BY NASA ASTRONAUTS." Accessed August 27, 2013, http://ufologie.patrickgross.org/htm/astronauts.html.
46a. Ibid.
46b. Ibid.
47. "Russian Cosmonauts and Generals confirm: UFOs are real." Accessed August 27, 2013, www.ufoevidence.org/documents/doc437.html.
47a. Ibid.
48. Richard C. Hoagland. *Dark Mission: The Secret History of NASA.* Los Angeles, CA: Feral House, 2007.
49. "UFO—NASA Shuttle—Missed by Ground Based Energy Pulse Weapon." Accessed August 29, 2013, www.youtube.com/watch?v=ZN0XnDJKdWo.
50. "Shuttle Astronaut Musgrave Comes Clean: UFOs Exist." Accessed August 3, 2013, www.disclose.tv/forum/shuttle-astronaut-dr-story-musgrave-comes-clean-ufo-s-exist-t60326.html.
50a. Ibid.
51. Peter A. Sturrock. "An Analysis of the Condon Report on the Colorado UFO Project." J. Scientific Exploration, 1 (1987): 75.
51a. Ibid.
52. "Project 1947: Ted Phillips' Physical Trace Catalogue." Accessed August 3, 2013, www.project1947.com/47cats/phillips.html.
52a. Ibid.
52b. Ibid.
53. Timothy Good. *Above Top Secret.* New York: William M. Morrow & Co, 1988.
53a. Ibid.
54. Leslie Kean. *UFOs: Generals, Pilots, and Government Officials Go on the Record.* New York: Three Rivers Press, 2011.
55. Michel Bounias. "Biochemical Traumatology as a Potent Tool for Identifying Actual Stresses Elicited by Unidentified Sources: Evidence for Plant Metabolic Disorders in Correlation With a UFO Landing." Journal of Scientific Exploration 4 (1990): 1-18, 1990.
55a. Ibid.
56. J. Jacques Velasco. "Report on the Analysis of Anomalous Physical Traces: The 1981 Trans-en-Provence UFO Case," Journal of Scientific Exploration 4 (1990): 27-48, 1990.
57. J. Velasco. "Action Of Electromagnetic Fields In The Microwave Range On Vegetation." (Paper presented at a meeting of the Society for Scientific Exploration, Glasgow, Scotland, August 1994).
58. Leslie Kean. *UFOs: Generals, Pilots, and Government Officials Go on the Record.*

New York: Three Rivers Press, 2011.
59. "Valensole, France Landing (Maurice Masse Case)." Accessed August 18, 2013, http://ufoevidence.org/cases/case140.html.
60. "Socorro, New Mexico Landing (Lonnie Zamora) 1964." Accessed August 18, 2013, www.ufocasebook.com/Zamora.html.
60a. Ibid.
61. "CIA's Role in the Study of UFOs, 1947-90: A Die-Hard Issue." Accessed August 19, 2013, www.cia.gov/library/center-for-the-study-of-intelligence/csi-publications/csi-studies/studies/97unclass/ufo.html.
62. Carl Sagan. *The Demon Haunted World.* New York: Ballantine Books, 1996.
63. Arthur Shuttlewood. The Flying Saucer, New York: Sphere, 1978.
64. "Physical Evidence Related to UFO Reports (Sturrock Panel): Radar Evidence." Accessed August 18, 2013, www.ufoevidence.org/documents/doc492.html.
65. "The Condon Report, Scientific Study of Unidentified Flying Objects." Accessed July 2, 2013, www.ufoevidence.org/topics/condonreport.html.
65a. Ibid.
65b. Ibid.
66. "Harry A. Jordan: UFOs and USOs on the U.S.S. *Franklin D. Roosevelt* (1950s)." Accessed July 14, 2013, www.abovetopsecret.com/forum/thread481823/pg1.
66a. Ibid.
67. "Radar Visual Sightings." Accessed July 14, 2013, www.space-2001.net/html/radar.html.
67a. Ibid.
67b. Ibid.
67c. Ibid.
68. "A Preliminary Study of Sixty Four Pilot Sighting Reports Involving Alleged Electromagnetic Effects on Aircraft Systems." Accessed July 14, 2013, www.narcap.org/reports/emcarm.html.
68a. Ibid.
69. "Possible UAP-Related Accident Factors from the Modified ASAFE Taxonomy." Accessed July 17, 2013, http://narcap.org/reports/APPENDIX_2.html.
70. M. Teodorani. "A Comparative and Analytical Study of North American Databases on Unidentified Aerial Phenomena." Technical Report. NARCAP (2009).
71. R.F. Haines. "Aviation Safety in America – A Prĕviously Neglected Factor." Technical Report. NARCAP (2000): 1-88.
71a. Ibid.
72. "Brazilian Air Force Confirms UFO Reports and Regulates How To Handle Them." Accessed July 17, 2013, www.ufodigest.com/article/brazilian-air-force-confirms-ufo-reports-and-regulates-how-handle-them.
73. Dominique F. Weinstein. "Aviation Safety and Unidentified Aerial Phenomena: A Preliminary Study of 600 cases of Unidentified Aerial Phenomena (UAP) Reported by Military and Civilian pilots." Technical Report. NARCAP IR-4 (2012).
73a. Ibid.
74. "The Fantastic Flight Of JAL 1628." Accessed July 22, 2013, www.ufoevidence.org/documents/doc1316.html.
74a. Ibid.
75. "JAL Pilot's UFO Story Surfaces after 20 Years, Accessed July 29, 2013, www.ufocasebook.com/jal1628surfaces.html.
76. "The Fantastic Flight Of JAL 1628." Accessed July 2, 2013, www.ufoevidence.org/

documents/doc1316.html.
77. "Exclusive Mexican DoD Acknowledges UFOs In Mexico." Accessed July 13, 2013, http://rense.com/general52/deff.html.
77a. Ibid.
78. "The French SEPRA: An Interview with Director Jean-Jacques Velasco." Accessed July 2, 2013, www.ufoevidence.org/documents/doc1630.html.
79. "Operation Mainbrace." Accessed July 13, 2013, http://drdavidclarke.co.uk/secret-files/operation-mainbrace-ufos.
79a. Ibid.
80. R.F. Haines. "Aviation Safety in America—A Previously Neglected Factor." Technical Report. NARCAP (2000): 1-88.
81. Kevin D. Randle. I*nvasion Washington: UFOs Over the Capitol.* New York: HarperTorch, 2001.
81a. Ibid.
81b. Ibid.
82. Larry Warren and Peter Robbins. *Left at East Gate: A First-Hand Account of the Rendlesham Forest UFO Incident, Its Cover-up, and Investigation.* New York: Cosimo Books, 2005.
82a. Ibid.
83 Nick Pope, John Burroughs, and Jim Penniston. *Encounter in Rendlesham Forest: The Inside Story of the World's best-Documented UFO Incident.* New York: Thomas Dunne Books, 2014.
84. Don Ledger. Dark Object: The World's Only Government-Documented UFO Crash. New York: Dell, 2001.
84a. Ibid.
85. Kevin Randle. *A History of UFO Crashes.* New York: Avon, 1995.
85a. Ibid.
86. Richard L. Weaver and James McAndrew. "The Roswell Report, Fact Versus Fiction in the New Mexico Desert." U.S. Air Force, (1995).
87. Glen Schulze and Robert Powell. "Special Research Report Stephenville, Texas." Mutual UFO Network, (2008).
87a. Ibid.
88. "Best UFO Cases III: Belgium, 1989-1990." Accessed July 23, 2013, www.ufoevidence.org/documents/doc413.html.
88a. Ibid.
89. Don Berliner. "UFOs Briefing Document: The Best Available Evidence." CUFONS, FUFOR, MUFON, (1995).
89a. Ibid.
89b. Ibid.
89c. Ibid.
89d. Ibid.
90. Leslie Kean. *UFOs: Generals, Pilots, and Government Officials Go on the Record.* New York: Three Rivers Press, 2011.
91. Lynne D. Kitei. T*he Phoenix Lights: A Skeptics Discovery That We Are Not.* Charlottseville, VA: Hampton Roads, 2010.
91a. Ibid.
92. "New Yorkers stand by 1980s UFO sightings in Westchester, Putnam counties." Accessed August 23, 2013, http://onhudson.typepad.com/onhudsoncom/2008/11/25-years-removed-hudson-valley-ufo-phenomenon-lives-on.html.

92a. Ibid.
93. "Results of NARCAP Investigation concerning a UFO incident at O'Hare International Airport." Accessed August 23, 2013, www.cohenufo.org/ohare2006.html.
94. Leslie Kean. *UFOs: Generals, Pilots, and Government Officials Go on the Record.* New York: Three Rivers Press, 2011.
95. Robert L. Hastings. *UFOs and Nukes: Extraordinary Encounters at Nuclear Weapons Sites.* Author House, 2008.
95a. "Remarkable reports from the missile field." Accessed July 23, 2013, www.cufos.org/missiles.pdf
96. "New Revelations: Two Ex-U.S. Air Force Security Policemen Discuss UFO Activity at Nuclear Weapons Sites." Accessed August 30, 2013, www.ufohastings.com/articles/new-revelations.
96a. Ibid.
97. Robert L. Hastings. *UFOs and Nukes: Extraordinary Encounters at Nuclear Weapons Sites.* Author House, 2008.
97a. Ibid.
97b. Ibid.
97c. Ibid.
97d. Ibid.
98. "1989: Multiple Witness Case at Russian Missile Base." Accessed August 30, 2013, www.bibliotecapleyades.net/ciencia/ufo_briefingdocument/1989.html.
99. Robert L. Hastings. *UFOs and Nukes: Extraordinary Encounters at Nuclear Weapons Sites.* Author House, 2008.
100. Donald A Johnson. "Do Nuclear Facilities Attract UFOs?" Sun River Research, (2002).
101. "Testimony of Mr. Nick Pope, British Ministry Of Defense." Accessed August 30, 2013, www.bibliotecapleyades.net/disclosure/briefing/disclosure10.html.

Chapter Five: Theories and Cases of High Strangeness

1. Jacques F. Vallée and E. Davis. "Incommensurability, Orthodoxy and the Physics of High Strangeness: A 6-layer Model for Anomalous Phenomena." Physics of High Strangeness. (2003): 1-17.
2. J. Allen Hynek, Jacques F. Vallée. *The Edge of Reality: A Progress Report on Unidentified Flying Objects.* NTC/Contemporary Publishing: 1976.
3. Jacques F. Vallée. *Messengers of Deception: UFO Contacts and Cults.* UK: Daily Grail Publishing, 2008.
4. Stephen Hawking. *The Grand Design.* New York: Bantam Books, 2010.
5. "A Physicist Explains Why Parallel Universes May Exist." Accessed April 27, 2013, www.npr.org/2011/01/24/132932268/ a-physicist-explains-why-parallel-universes-may-exist.
6. "What Did Dr. J. Allen Hynek Believe About UFOs in 1967: And When Did He Say It?" Accessed April 30, 2013, www.ufodigest.com/article/what-did-dr-j-allen-hynek-believe-about-ufos-1967-and-when-did-he-say-it-part-ii.
7. Jacques F. Vallée. *Forbidden Science.* Berkeley, CA: North Atlantic Books, 1992.
8. "Shape-Shifting UFOs." Accessed May 3, 2013, www.ufodigest.com/news/1207/shapeshiftingufos.html.
8a. Ibid.
9. "UFOs: The Psychic Dimension." Accessed May 24, 2013, http://davidpratt.info/ufo2.html.

9a. Ibid.
9b. Ibid.
10. Roger K. Leir. *UFO Crash Over Brazil.* San Diego, CA: Book Tree, 2005.
10a. Ibid.
10b. Ibid.
11. "UFO CASE ARTICLE Voronezh, Russia—Report of sighting." Accessed May 12, 2013, www.ufoevidence.org/Cases/CaseSubarticle.asp?ID=122.
12. "Angels in space nothing but top secret hallucinations." Accessed June 13, 2013, Yokihttp://english.pravda.ru/society/anomal/14-06-2011/118195-angels-0.
12a. Ibid.
13. "UFOs: The Psychic Dimension." Accessed May 24, 2013, http://davidpratt.info/ufo2.html.
13a. Ibid.
13b. Ibid.
14. Frank Salisbury. *The Utah UFO Display: A Scientist's Report.* Springville, UT: Cedar Fort, Inc, 2010.
15. Colm Kelleher and George Knapp. "Hunt for the Skinwalker: Science Confronts the Unexplained at a Remote Ranch in Utah." New York: Paraview Pocket Books, 2005.
16. Frank Salisbury. *The Utah UFO Display: A Scientist's Report*. Springville, UT: Cedar Fort, Inc, 2010.
16a. Ibid.
16b. Ibid.
17. "H.E.R.O. Paranormal, Skinwalker Ranch." Accessed May 14, 2013, http://site.heroparanormal.com.
18. "Is A Utah Ranch The Strangest Place On Earth?" Accessed May 29, 2013, http://rense.com/general32/strange.html.

Chapter Six: UFO Theories

1. L. Kean, *UFOs: Generals, Pilots, and Government Officials Go on the Record.* New York: Three Rivers Press, 2011.
2. "Extraordinary Claims Require Extraordinary Evidence." Accessed June 14, 2013, http://skeptico.blogs.com/skeptico/2008/01/extraordinary-c.html.
3. J. Hynek. *The Edge of Reality: A Progress Report on Unidentified Flying Objects*. New York: Quality Books, 1976.
4. Jaques Vallée. *Messengers of Deception: UFO Contacts and Cults*. New York: Daily Grail Publishing, 2008
5. "Five Reasons Why UFOs Are Not Extraterrestrial Machines. Science Frontiers." Accessed June 23, 2013, www.science-frontiers.com/sf073/sf073g16.html.
6. Jaques Vallée. *Dimensions: A Casebook of Alien Contact.* Charlottesville, VA: Anomalist Books, 2008.
7. "Introduction to Wormholes." Accessed May 12, 2013, http://library.thinkquest.org/27930/wormhole.html.
8. Paul R. Hill. *Unconventional Flying Objects: A Scientific Analysis*. Newburyport, MA: Hampton Roads Publishing Company, 1995.
9. "Stephen Hawking's Time Machine." Accessed May 12, 2013, http://news.discovery.com/space/stephen-hawkings-time-machine.html.
10. "The J. Allen Hynek Center for UFO Studies." Accessed May 19, 2013, www.cufos.org/org.html.

10a. Ibid.
10b. Ibid.
11. J.A. Hynek. "The case against ET" in MUFON UFO Symposium, ed. Walter H. Andrus, Jr., and Dennis W. Stacy. (MUFON UFO Symposium, 1983).
12. N. Pope, *Open Skies, Closed Minds.* New York: Dell, 1998.
13. "The Release of the French UFO Files." Accessed August 2, 2013, *The UFO Digest.* www.bibliotecapleyades.net/ciencia/ciencia_flyingobjects29.html.
14. "The French Report on UFOs and Defense: A Summary." Accessed May 23, 2013, www.cufos.org/cometa.html.
15 "Statements About Flying Saucers And Extraterrestrial Life Made By Prof. Hermann Oberth, German Rocket Scientist." Accessed May 23, 2013, www.mufon.com/MUFONNews/znews_oberth.html.
16. "Reports of Suppression." Accessed August 22, 2013, www.perceptions.couk.com/reports.html.
17. "Whoa! Say what Carl Sagan? No UFOs would visit Earth?" Accessed June 12, 2013, www.abovetopsecret.com/forum/thread256949/pg1.
18. "Space and Time Warps." Accessed August 15, 2013, www.hawking.org.uk/space-and-time-warps.html.
19. "Ufology—A scientific introduction—Started in 2009." Accessed August 2, 2013, www.tarrdaniel.com/documents/Ufology/ufology.html.
20. "The Physics of Interstellar Travel—UFO Evidence." Accessed August 15, 2013,www.ufoevidence.org/documents/doc1060.html.
21. "White House: There's no sign of E.T. or UFO cover-up." Accessed August 12, 2013,www.nbcnews.com/id/45176460/ns/technology_and_science-space/t/white-house-theres-no-sign-et-or-ufo-cover-up/#.UbSM4_nVApA.
22. "UFO—An Appraisal of the Problem: A Statement by the UFO Subcommittee of the AIAA." Accessed August 20, 2013, www.ufoevidence.org/documents/doc594.html.
23. "Carl Jung and UFOs: A Debunker of Dubious Intellect." Accessed June 23, 2013, www.ufodigest.com/article/carl-jung-and-ufos-debunker-dubious-intellect.
24. "UFOs: The Psychocultural Hypothesis." Accessed May 14, 2013, The New England Skeptical Society, www.theness.com/index.php/ufos-the-psychocultural-hypothesis.
25. R. Bartholomew, Howard, George. *UFOs & Alien Contact.* Amherst, N.Y: Prometheus Books, 1998, p. 44.
25a. Ibid.
26. Marcia K. Johnson and Carol L. Raye False. "Memories and Confabulation." Trends in Cognitive Sciences 2 (1998).
27. "UFOs: Operation Trojan Horse: Some Gems." Accessed May 13, 2013, www.chodesh.info/ufos-operation-trojan-horse-gems.html.
27a. Ibid.
28. V. N. Tsytovich, G. E. Morfill, V. E. Fortov, N. G. Gusein-Zade, B. A. Klumov, and S. V. Vladimirov. From plasma crystals and helical structures towards inorganic living matter, New J. Phys. 9 (2007): 263.
28a. Ibid.
29. M. Teodorani. A Comparative Analytical and Observational Study of North American Databases on Unidentified Aerial Phenomena. NARCAP Technical Report. 2009:1-59.
30. "Are UFO Occupants Composed of Plasma, Their Life-Force Residing in Electric Energy?" Accessed June 8, 2013, www.ufodigest.com/article/are-ufo-occupants-composed-plasma-their-life-force-residing-electric-energy.
31. "Project Condign and UFOs." Accessed June 8, 2013, www.netplaces.com/guide-to-2012/atmospheric-plasma-and-ufos/project-condign-and-ufos.html.

31a. Ibid.
32. M. Teodorani. A Comparative Analytical and Observational Study of North American Databases on Unidentified Aerial Phenomena. NARCAP Technical Report. 2009:1-59.
32a. Ibid.
33. "Persinger's The Field Biology of Unexplained Events." Accessed June 10, 2013, www.ufoupdateslist.com/2000/dec/m14-002.shtml.
33a. Ibid.
34. "The Most Frequent Criticisms and Questions Concerning The Tectonic Strain Hypothesis." Accessed June 11, 2013, www.shaktitechnology.com/tectonic.html.
34a. Ibid.
35. "UFOS, Aliens, and the New Physics." Accessed June 14, 2013, www.stealthskater.com/Documents/Pitkanen_16.pdf.
35a. Ibid.
36. The Tectonic Strain Theory of Geophysical Luminosities." Accessed June 20, 2013, http://paul.rutgers.edu/~mcgrew/ufo/to-be-merged/tectonic-strain.
37. Paul Devereux. *Earth Lights Revelation—UFOs and Mystery Lightform Phenomena, the Earth's Secret Energy Force.* London, Blandford Press, 1990.
38. "Plasma Life Forms—Spheres, Blobs, Orbs and Subtle Bodies." Accessed May 26, 2013, www.dapla.org/plasma_orbs_bodies.html.
38a. Ibid.
38b. Ibid.
39. "BUFORA Review." Accessed June 24, 2013, http://uforesearchnetwork.proboards.com/user/200/recent?page=5.
40. "The Earthlight Hypothesis." Accessed May 26, 2013, www.davidicke.com/forum/archive/index.php/t-156030.html.
41. "UFOs: The Psychic Dimension." Accessed June 14, 2013, http://davidpratt.info/ufo2.html.
42. "A Sprightly Explanation for UFO Sightings?" Accessed June 14, 2013, www.aftau.org/site/News2?page=NewsArticle&id=8803.
42a IBid.
43. "The Grandfather Paradox." Accessed June 17, 2013, http://timetravelphilosophy.net/topics/grandfather.
44. "Stephen Hawking: The Official Website." Accessed June 17, 2013, www.hawking.org.uk.

Chapter Seven: The Alien Abduction Phenomenon

1. Bud Hopkins. *Intruders.* New York: Random House, 1987.
2. David Jacobs. *Secret Life: Firsthand Documented Accounts of UFO Abductions*. New York: Touchstone, 1992.
3. John E. Mack. *Abduction: Human Encounters with Aliens.* New York: Ballantine, 1995.
3a. Ibid.
4. "UFO Abductions: The Measure of a Mystery. Volume 1: Comparative Study of Abduction Reports." Accessed June 12, 2013, www.hyper.net/ufo/abductions.html.
5. C. Bryan. *Close Encounters of the Fourth Kind: A Reporter's Notebook on Alien Abduction, UFOs, and the Conference at M.I.T.* New York, Penguin Books, 1996.
6. David Jacobs. *Secret Life: Firsthand Documented Accounts of UFO Abductions*. New York: Touchstone, 1992.

7. M. Rodeghier. "A set of selection criteria for abductees." in Alien discussions: Proceedings of the Abduction Study Conference. ed. A. Pritchard, et al. Cambridge, MA: North Cambridge Press, 1994b, 22-23.
8. John E. Mack. Abduction: *Human encounters with Aliens*. New York: Ballantine, 1995.
9. Charles F. Emmons. *At the Threshold: UFOs, Science and the New Age*. Mill Spring, NC: Wild Flower Press, 1997, pp. 163-4.
10. Thomas Bullard. "The Variety of Abduction Beings." in Alien discussions: Proceedings of the Abduction Study Conference, ed. A. Pritchard, et al. Cambridge, MA: North Cambridge Press, 1989, 90-91.
11. David Jacobs. *Secret Life: Firsthand Documented Accounts of UFO Abductions*. New York: Touchstone, 1992.
11a. Ibid.
12. E. Loftus and S. Clark. "The Construction of Space Alien Abduction Memories." *International Journal of Peer Commentary and Review*. 2002.
13. David Jacobs. *Secret Life: Firsthand Documented Accounts of UFO Abductions*. New York: Touchstone, 1992.
14. P. Linse and D. Loxton. "Alien Abduction Part 2." Skeptic 12 (2006): 81–98.
15. I.I. Kirsch, II and S.J. Lynn SJ. "Alleged Alien Abductions: False Memories, Hypnosis and Fantasy Proneness." Psychological Inquiry 7 (1996): 151-155.
16. N.P. Spanos. "Multiple Identities & False Memories: A Sociocognitive Perspective. American Psychological Association." (1996): 122-3.
17 David Jacobs. *Secret Life: Firsthand Documented Accounts of UFO Abductions*. New York: Touchstone, 1992.
18. Thomas Bullard. "The Variety of Abduction Beings." in Alien discussions: Proceedings of the Abduction Study Conference, ed. A. Pritchard, et al. Cambridge, MA: North Cambridge Press, 1989, 90-91.
19. L. Newman and R. Baumeister. "Towards an Explanation of the UFO Abduction Phenomenon." Psychological Inquiry 7 (1996): 99-126.
20. John E. Mack. *Abduction: Human encounters with aliens*. New York: Ballantine, 1995.
21. R. F. Baumeister. Masochism and the self. Hillsdale, NJ: Lawrence Erlbaum Associates, Inc. 1989.
22. "Goodnight and Goodluck." Accessed June 12, 2013, http://fitdv.com/new/articles/article.php?artid=22.
23. S. Blackmore and S. Cox. "Alien Abductions, Sleep Paralysis and the Temporal Lobe." European Journal of UFO and Abduction Studies 1 (2000): 113-118.
24. N.P. Spanos. "Multiple Identities & False Memories: A Sociocognitive Perspective." American Psychological Association. (1996): 122-3.
25. Susan A. Clancy. *Abducted: How People Come to Believe They Were Kidnapped by Aliens*. First Harvard Press, 2005.
25a. Ibid.
26. Susan A. Clancy, R. McNally, R. Pitman, and D. Schacter. "Memory Distortion in People Reporting Abduction by Aliens," Journal of Abnormal Psychology 111. (2002): 455-461.
26a. Ibid.
27. D. Forrest. "Alien abduction: a medical hypothesis." Cortex 44 (2008): 1387-95.
28. C. French, J. Santomauro, V. Hamilton, R. Fox, and M. Thalbourne. "Psychological aspects of the alien contact experience." Transcultural Psychiatry 42 (2005): 113-22.

29. Charles F. Emmons. At the Threshold: UFOs, science and the new age. Mill Spring, NC: Wild Flower Press, 1997, 155-6.
30. S. Appelle. "The Abduction Experience: A Critical Evaluation of Theory and Evidence." Journal of UFO Studies (1995): 29.
31 John E. Mack. Abduction: Human encounters with aliens. New York: Ballantine, 1995.
32. C. McLeod, B. Corbisier, and J. Mack. "A More Parsimonious Explanation for UFO Abduction, Program for Extraordinary Experience Research." (1996): 156-168.
32a. Ibid.
33. "Clinical Discrepancies Between Expected and Observed Data in Patients Reporting UFO Abductions: Implications For Treatment Accessed." August 8, 2013, www.ufoevidence.org/documents/doc7.html.
34. J. Mack. "A Brief Review of Issues Relating to the Reality of the Abduction Phenomenon." Accessed August 3, 2013, www.ufoevidence.org/documents/doc11.html.
35. S. Appelle, "The Abduction Experience: A Critical Evaluation of Theory and Evidence." Journal of UFO Studies (1995): 29.
36. Nicholas Spanos. P. A. Cross, K. Dickson, and S. DuBreuil. "Close Encounters: An Examination of UFO Experiences." Journal of Abnormal Psychology 102, (1993): 624-32.
37. Mark Rodeghier, Jeff Goodpaster, and Sandra Blatterbauer. "Psychosocial Characteristics of Abductees: Results from the CUFOS Abduction Project." Journal of UFO Studies, 3, (1991): 59- 90.
38. Bud Hopkins. *Intruders*. New York: Random House, 1987.
38a. Ibid.
39. D. Jacobs. *The Threat: Secret Alien Agenda*. New York: Simon & Schuster, 1999.
40. J. Mack. Passport to the Cosmos: Human Transformation and Alien Encounters. New York: Three Rivers Press (1999).
41. J. Mack. "A Brief Review of Issues Relating to the Reality of the Abduction Phenomenon." Accessed August 3, 2013, www.ufoevidence.org/documents/doc11.html.
42. David Jacobs. *Secret Life: Firsthand Documented Accounts of UFO Abductions*. New York: Touchstone, 1992.
43. J. Randles. "Why are They Doing This?" in Alien discussions: Proceedings of the Abduction Study Conference. ed. A. Pritchard, et al. Cambridge, MA: North Cambridge Press, 1989, 69-70.
44. "Historian Richard Dolan—UFO and ET disclosure to occur in 5 years." Accessed August 23, 2013, http://youtube/4uARe8T9R7Q.
45. "A New World Order." Accessed July 29, 2013, http://projectavalon.net/forum4/archive/index.php/t-46028.html.?s=9dd228d5e7691390d4840f1c1dfb1826.
46. Karla Turner. "Taken: Inside the Alien-Human Agenda." Tallahassee, Florida: Rose Printing Company, Inc, 1994.
47. "The Marden-Stoner Study on Commonalities Among UFO Abduction Experiencers." Accessed July 11, 2013, www.kathleen-marden.com/commonalities-study-final-report.php.
47a. Ibid.
47b. Ibid.
48. Don Donderi. "UFOs, ETs and Alien Abductions: A Scientist Looks at the Evidence." San Francisco, CA: Hampton Roads Publishing, 2013.

48a. Ibid.
49. A.W. Scheflin and J.L. Shapiro. "Trance on Trial." New York: The Guilford Press, 1989.
50. J. Mack. Abduction: *Human Encounters With Aliens*. New York: Scribners, 1994.

Chapter Eight: Exopolitics

1. Richard Dolan. *A.D. After Disclosure: The People's Guide to Life After Contact*. Keyhole Publishing, 2010.
2. Michael E. Salla. "Exopolitics: Discipline of Choice for Public Policy Issues Concerning Extraterrestrial Life." World Affairs 12 (2008).
3. Clifford E. Stone. *Ufos Are Real: Extraterrestrial Encounters Documented by the U.S. Government*. Spi Books, 1997.
4. "CIA's Role in the Study of UFOs, 1947-90." Accessed July 12, 2013, www.cia.gov/search?q=ufo&x=-1008&y=53&site=CIA&output=xml_no_dtd&client=CIA&myAction=%2Fsearch&proxystylesheet=CIA&submitMethod=get.
5a. Michael E. Salla. "Exopolitics: Discipline of Choice for Public Policy Issues Concerning Extraterrestrial Life ." World Affairs 12 (2008).
6. "The Majestic 12 Papers—An Analysis." Accessed July 23, 2013, www.roswellfiles.com/FOIA/majestic12.html.
7. Stanton Friedman. *Top Secret/Majic: Operation Majestic-12 and the United States Government's UFO Cover-up*. New York: Marlowe & Co; 1996.
8. "CIA's Role in the Study of UFOs, 1947-90." Accessed July 12, 2013, www.cia.gov/search?q=ufo&x=-1008&y=53&site=CIA&output=xml_no_dtd&client=CIA&myAction=%2Fsearch&proxystylesheet=CIA&submitMethod=get.
9. "Citizen Hearing on Disclosure Remarkable Revelations Undercut By Distressing Disinformation." Accessed July 20, 2013, UFOs and Nukes, www.ufohastings.com/articles/citizen-hearing-on-disclosure.
10. "The 1947 Twining Memo: 63 Years Ago." Accessed July 20, 2013, www.afterdisclosure.com/2010/09/twining-memo-1.html.
11. "Twelve Government Documents That Take UFOs Seriously ." Accessed July 20, 2013, ttp://keyholepublishing.com/Leading-UFO-Documents.html.
11a. Ibid.
11b. Ibid.
11c. Ibid.
11d. Ibid.
12. "The Malmstrom AFB UFO/Missile Incident." Accessed July 25, 2013, www.cufon.org/cufon/malmstrom/malm1.html.
13. "The SAC Base UFO Flyovers." Accessed July 25, 2013, www.alien-ufos.com/ufo-alien-discussions/23228-sac-base-ufo-flyovers-oct-nov-1975-a.html.
14. "UFOs Intrude Into SAC Base Weapons Areas." Accessed July 25, 2013, www.ufocasebook.com/sacbaseweapons1975.html.
14a. Ibid.

15. "Citizen Hearing on Disclosure Remarkable Revelations Undercut By Distressing Disinformation." Accessed July 20, 2013, UFOs and Nukes, www.ufohastings.com/articles/citizen-hearing-on-disclosure.

15a. Ibid.
16. "The Rendlesham Forest Incident." Accessed July 29, 2013, www.ianridpath.com/ufo/appendix.html.
17. "Report on the Observation of UFOs During the Night of March 30-31." Accessed July 29, 2013, http://users.telenet.be/aura.oasis/BelgUFO.html.
18. "The Belgium Sightings (1989/90)." Accessed July 30, 2013, www.cohenufo.org/Belgium/unslvdmyst.html.
19. "The Smith Memo." Accessed July 30, 2013, www.roswellfiles.com/FOIA/smithmemo.html.
20. "UFOs or Not? The Guy Hottel Memo." Accessed July 22, 2013,www.fbi.gov/news/stories/2013/march/ufos-and-the-guy-hottel-memo.
20a. Ibid.
21. "U.K. Condign Report (2000) Unidentified Aerial Phenomena in the U.K. Air Defense Region." Accessed July 22, 2013, www.uk-ufo.org/condign/condrep.html.
22. "Newly released UFO files from the UK government." Accessed June 22, 2013, www.nationalarchives.gov.uk/ufos.
22a. Ibid.
22b. Ibid.
23. "Top-Secret 1949 Document." Accessed June 23, 2013, www.cufos.org/IUR_article1.html.
24. "Casual Articles—French Agency Releases UFO Files—Don't Start Serving The Crepes Just Yet." Accessed June 22, 2013, www.casualarticles.com. Article/187445/advice--French-Agency-Releases-UFO-Files--Don't-Start-Serving-The-Crepes-Just-Yet.html.
25. "The best of New Zealand's UFO files: Alien writing, masks and ships." Accessed June 23, 2013, http://io9.com/5719869/the-best-of-new-zealands-ufo-files-alien-writing-masks-and-ships.
26. Robert L. Hastings. *UFOs and Nukes: Extraordinary Encounters at Nuclear Weapons Sites*. Author House, 2008.
27. "NASA Statement: The US Government and Unidentified Flying Objects (UFOs)." Accessed June 25, 2013, www.ufoevidence.org/documents/doc846.html. NASA (National Aeronautics and Space Administration).
28 "Next frontier for Cheeks Kilpatrick: Panel exploring existence of alien life." Accessed June 26, 2013, www.turtleislandnews.info/2013_04_12_archive.html.
29. "Barry Goldwater and UFOs." Accessed June 26, 2013, http://groupbox.com/ViewTopic.aspx?&iTopicID=hZI77mvW8Zk-&iGroupID=XkGCL1x03Wc-.
30. "Disclosure Project: Testimony of John Callahan, Former FAA Division Chief." Accessed June 27, 2013, www.ufoevidence.org/documents/doc1324.html.
30a Ibid.
31. Leslie Kean. *UFOs: Generals, Pilots, and Government Officials Go on the Record.* New York: Three Rivers Press, 2011.
32. "Bill Clinton, September 2005 to CLSA (Credit Lyonnais Securities Asia) group." Accessed June 27, 2013, www.hillaryclintonufo.net/billclintonquotes.html.
33. "Ufology and Science." Accessed June 27, 2013, www.nickpope.net/ufology-and-science.html.
34. "As U.K. Releases UFO Files, Former UFO Project Chief Apologizes For 'Spin And Dirty Tricks." Accessed June 27, 2013, www.huffingtonpost.com/2011/08/17/uk-releases-ufo-files_n_927351.html.

35. "UFO Quotes." Accessed July 27, 2013, www.ufocasebook.com/ufoquotes1.html.
36. "Air Force Regulation 200-2." Accessed July 27, 2013, www.cufon.org/cufon/afr200-2.html.
37. "Ufology and Science." Accessed June 27, 2013, www.nickpope.net/ufology-and-science.html.
38. "Paradigm Research Group." Accessed July 29, 2013, www.paradigmresearchgroup.org/main.html.
39. "Citizen Hearing on Disclosure Washington Communiqué May 3, 2013." Accessed July 29, 2013, www.paradigmresearchgroup.org/Press_Releases/Press_releases.html.
40. "Nick Pope Citizen Hearing on Disclosure—Review." Accessed July 14, 2013, www.ufodigest.com/article/disclosure-review-0601.
40a. Ibid.
41. "Richard Dolan—UFO and ET disclosure to occur in 5 years from 2011." Accessed July 14, 2013, http://youtube/4uARe8T9R7Q.
42. "Declaration of Principles for Activities Following the Detection of Extraterrestrial Intelligence." Accessed July 14, 2013, www.setileague.org/general/protocol.html.
43. Sarah Zielinski. "Ready for Contact Humans have searched for extraterrestrial life for more than a century. What will we do when we find it?" Smithsonian (December 2010).
44. "Proposed Agreement on the Sending of Communications to Extraterrestrial Intelligence." Accessed July 3, 2013, www.setileague.org/iaaseti/position.html.
45. "JOINT ARMY-NAVY-AIR FORCE PUBLICATION 146(E)." Accessed June 12, 2013, www.cufon.org/cufon/janp1462.html.
46. "The Brookings Institution—Final Report Proposed Studies on the Implications of Peaceful Space Activities for Human Affairs." Accessed July 6, 2013, www.nicap.org/papers/brookings.pdf.

Chapter Nine: The UFO Phenomenon: A New Approach

1. "Sturrock UFO Panel's (Alleged) Findings Praised By CUFOS Official." Accessed May 25, 2013, www.csicop.org/specialarticles/show/klass_files_volume_54.
2. "UFOs: What's 60 Years Accomplished?" Last modified 2013. Accessed July 30, 2013, www.ourstrangeplanet.com/the-san-luis-valley/guest-editorials/ufos-whats-60-years-accomplished.
3. Hendry, Allan. The UFO Investigators Handbook. London: Sphere Books Ltd. 1980.
4. "The UFO Reality." Accessed May 25, 2013, http://ufor.blogspot.com/2008/05/drones-and-ufos-in-medieval-art.html.
5. "The Future of Ufology." Accessed May 25, 2013, http://mysteriousuniverse.org/2012/08/the-future-of-ufology/ by Nick Redfern.
6. Coalition for Freedom of Information." Accessed August 25, 2013, http://uto.sigsno.org/freedomofinfo.org/index.html.
7. Leslie Kean. UFOs: Generals, Pilots, and Government Officials Go on the Record. New York: Three Rivers Press, 2011.
7a. Ibid.
8. Peter Sturrock. The UFO Enigma. New York: Warner Books, 1999.
9. "A Comparative Analytical and Observational Study of North American Databases on Unidentified Aerial Phenomena." Accessed May 19, 2013, www.narcap.org/reports/ONNYCT_Paper_MT_2009_REVISED.pdf.

10. "Aviation Safety in America A Previously Neglected Factor." Accessed May 19, 2013, www.narcap.org/Technical_Reports.html.
11. J. Deardorf, B. Haisch, B. Maccabee, and H. E. Puthoff. "Implications for Extraterrestrial Visitation: Inflation-Theory Implications for Extraterrestrial Visitation." JBIS 58 (2005): 43-50.
12. "Why NASA Hesitates on UFO Research." Accessed July 7, 2014, http://guardianlv.com/2013/07/why-nasa-hesitates-on-ufo-research.
13. "NASA to find alien life 'within 20 years.'" Accessed July 18, 2014, www.unexplained-mysteries.com/news/269250/nasa-to-find-alien-life-within-20-years.

Chapter Ten: The UFO phenomenon: Should I Believe?

1. "Dr. J. Allen Hynek Speaking at the United Nations, Nov. 27th 1978." Accessed May 28, 2013, www.ufoevidence.org/documents/doc757.html. UFO Evidence.com.
2. Robert L. Hastings. *UFOs and Nukes: Extraordinary Encounters at Nuclear Weapons Sites*. Author House, 2008.

Bibliography

Appelle, S. "The Abduction Experience: A Critical Evaluation of Theory and Evidence." Journal of UFO Studies (1995): 29.

Asimov, Isaac. *Fantasy and Science Fiction*. Oklahoma City, OK: Mercury Press, 1975.

Bartholomew, Robert and George Howard. *UFOs & Alien Contact. (*Amherst, N.Y: Prometheus Books, 1998).

Baumeister, R. F. *Masochism and the Self.* (Hillsdale, NJ: Lawrence Erlbaum Associates, Inc. 1989).

Berliner, Don. "UFOs Briefing Document: The Best Available Evidence." CUFONS, FUFOR, MUFON, (1995).

Blackmore, S. and S. Cox. "Alien Abductions, Sleep Paralysis and the Temporal Lobe." European Journal of UFO and Abduction Studies 1. (2000): 113-118.

Bounias, Michel. "Biochemical Traumatology as a Potent Tool for Identifying Actual Stresses Elicited by Unidentified Sources: Evidence for Plant Metabolic Disorders in Correlation With a UFO Landing." Journal of Scientific Exploration 4 (1990): 1-1 8, 1990.

Bramley, William. *The Gods of Eden*. (New York: Avon Books, 1989).

Brouwer, W. De. "Postface" in SOBEPS' Vague d'OVNI sur la Belgique—Un Dossier Exceptionnel. (Brussels: SOBEPS, 1991).

Bryan, C. *Close Encounters of the Fourth Kind: A Reporter's Notebook on Alien Abduction, UFOs, and the Conference at M.I.T.* (New York, Penguin Books, 1996).

Bullard, Thomas. "The Variety of Abduction Beings." in Alien discussions: Proceedings of the Abduction Study Conference, ed. A. Pritchard, et al. (Cambridge, MA: North Cambridge Press, 1989.

Chatelain, Maurice. *Our Ancestors Came From Outer Space*. London: Pan Books, 1980.

Clancy, Susan. *Abducted: How People Come to Believe They Were Kidnapped by Aliens*. (Cambridge, MA: First Harvard Press, 2005).

Clancy, Susan. R. McNally, R. Pitman, and D. Schacter. "Memory Distortion in People Reporting Abduction by Aliens, Journal of Abnormal Psychology 111. (2002): 455-461.

Deardorf, J. B. Haisch, B. Maccabee, and H. E. Puthoff. "Implications for Extraerrestrial Visitation: Inflation-Theory Implications for Extraterrestrial Visitation." JBIS 58 (2005): 43-50.

Devereux, Paul. *Earth Lights Revelation—UFOs and Mystery Lightform Phenomena, the Earth's Secret Energy Force.* London, Blandford Press, 1990.

Dolan, Richard. *A.D. After Disclosure: The People's Guide to Life After Contact*. (Keyhole Publishing, 2010.)

Donderi, Don. *UFOs, ETs and Alien Abductions: A Scientist Looks at the Evidence*. (Virginia: Hampton Roads, 2013.)

Emmons, Charles. *At the Threshold: UFOs, Science and the New Age*. (Mill Spring, NC: Wild Flower Press, 1997.)

Fawcett, Lawrence and Barry Greenwood. *Clear Intent. (*New York: Prentice Hall Trade, 1984.)

Forrest, D. "Alien abduction: a medical hypothesis." Cortex 44 (2008).

French, C. J. Santomauro. V. Hamilton, R. Fox, and M.Thalbourne. "Psychological aspects of the alien contact experience." Transcultural Psychiatry 42 (2005): 113-22.

Friedman, S. *Flying Saucers and Science: A Scientist Investigates the Mysteries of UFOs: Interstellar Travel, Crashes, and Government Cover-Ups.* (New Jersey: New Page Books, 2008).

Friedman, Stanton. Top Secret/Majic: Operation Majestic-12 and the United States Government's UFO Cover-up. (New York: Marlowe & Co; 1996).

Gillmor, Daniel. Scientific Study of Unidentified Flying Objects. (September 28, 1965, letter to USAF Scientific Advisory Board requesting a review of the UFO project. (New York: Times Books, 1969).

Greer, Steven. Disclosure: Military and Government Witnesses Reveal the Greatest Secrets in Modern History. (Crozet, VA: Crossing Point, 2001).

Good, Timothy. *Need to Know: UFOs, the Military, and Intelligence.* (New York: Pegasus, 2007).

Good, Timothy. *Above Top Secret*. (New York: William M. Morrow & Co, 1988).

Hall, Richard. *The UFO Evidence*. (Washington, D.C.: NICAP, 1964).

Hall, Richard. *The UFO Evidence, Volume II: A Thirty-Year Report*. (Oxford, UK: Scarecrow Press, 2001).

Haines, Richard. "Aviation Safety in America—A Previously Neglected Factor," Technical Report. NARCAP (2000): 1-88.

Hastings, R.L. *UFOs and Nukes: Extraordinary Encounters at Nuclear Weapons Sites*. (Bloomington, IN: Author House, 2008).

Hawking, Stephen. *The Grand Design.* (New York: Bantam Books, 2010).

Hendry, Alan. *The UFO Handbook: A Guide to Investigating, Evaluating, and Reporting UFO Sightings.* (New York: Doubleday, 1979).

Hendry, Allan. *The UFO Investigators Handbook*. (London: Sphere Books Ltd. 1980).

Hill, Paul R. *Unconventional Flying Objects: A Scientific Analysis*. (Newburyport, MA Hampton Roads Publish Company, 1995).

Hoagland, Richard. *Dark Mission: The Secret History of NASA*. (Los Angeles, CA: Feral House, 2007).

Hopkins, Bud. *Intruders* (New York: Random House, 1987).

Huyghe, Patrick. *The Field Guide to Extraterrestrials.* (London: Hodder and Stoughton, 1997).

Hynek, J. Allen and Jacques F. Vallée. *The Edge of Reality: A Progress Report on Unidentified Flying Objects.* (NTC/Contemporary Publishing: 1976).

Hynek, J. Allen. *The UFO Experience—A Scientific Inquiry*. (Jackson, TN: Da Capo Press, 1998).

Hynek, J. Allen. "The case against ET." in MUFON UFO Symposium, ed. Walter H. Andrus, Jr., and Dennis W. Stacy. MUFON UFO Symposium, 1983.

Jacobs, David. *Secret Life: Firsthand Documented Accounts of UFO Abductions*. (New York, Touchstone, 1992).

Jacobs, David. *The Threat: Secret Alien Agenda.* (New York: Simon & Schuster, 1999).

Johnson, Donald. "Do Nuclear Facilities Attract UFOs?" Sun River Research, 2002.

Johnson Marcia and Carol L. Raye False. "Memories and Confabulation." Trends in Cognitive Sciences 2 1998.

Kelleher Colm and George Knapp. *Hunt for the Skinwalker: Science Confronts the Unexplained at a Remote Ranch in Utah.* (New York: Paraview Pocket Books, 2005).

Kirsch, I.I. and S.J. Lynn. "Alleged Alien Abductions: False Memories, Hypnosis and Fantasy Proneness." Psychological Inquiry 7 (1996).

Kitei, Lynne. *The Phoenix Lights: A Skeptics Discovery That We Are Not.* (Charlottseville, VA: Hampton Roads, 2010).

Ledger, Don. *Dark Object: The World's Only Government-Documented UFO Crash*. (New York: Dell, 2001).

Leir, Roger. *UFO Crash Over Brazil*. (San Diego, CA: Book Tree, 2005).

Linse P. and D. Loxton. "Alien Abduction Part 2." Skeptic 12 (2006): 81–98.

Loftus, E and S. Clark. "The Construction of Space Alien Abduction Memories." International Journal of Peer Commentary and Review, (2002).

Mack, John. *Abduction: Human Encounters with Aliens*. New York: Ballantine, 1995).

Mack, John. *Passport to the Cosmos: Human Transformation and Alien Encounters.* (New York: Three Rivers Press 1999).

Marchetti, Victor. "How the CIA Views the UFO Phenomenon." Second Look, Vol. 1, No.7, (1979).

McCampbell, James. *A Major Breakthrough in the Scientific Understanding of Unidentified Flying Objects*. (New York: Celestial Arts, 1976).
McLeod, C. B. Corbisier, and J. Mack. "A More Parsimonious Explanation for UFO Abduction." Psychological Inquiry 7 (1966):156-168.
Menzel, Donald. Physics Today, June 1976.
Newman L. and R. Baumeister. "Towards an Explanation of the UFO Abduction Phenomenon." Psychological Inquiry 7 (1996): 99-126.
Poher, C. and J. Vallée. "Basic Patterns in UFO Observations." (Paper presented at the 13th Aerospace Sciences Meeting, Pasadena, California, January 20-22, 1975).
Pope, Nick. *Open Skies, Closed Minds*. (New York: Dell, 1998).
Pope, Nick, John Burroughs, and Jim Penniston. *Encounter in Rendlesham Forest: The Inside Story of the World's best-Documented UFO Incident.* (New York: Thomas Dunne Books, 2014).
Randle, Kevin. *A History of UFO Crashes*. New York: Avon, 1995).
Randle, Kevin. *Invasion Washington: UFOs Over the Capitol*. (New York: HarperTorch, 2001).
Randles, J. "Why are They Doing This?" in Alien discussions: Proceedings of the Abduction Study Conference, ed. A. Pritchard, et al. Cambridge, MA: North Cambridge Press, 1989, 69-70.
Rodeghier, Mark. "A set of selection criteria for abductees," in Alien discussions: Proceedings of the Abduction Study Conference, ed. A. Pritchard, et al. (Cambridge, MA: North Cambridge Press, 1994b).
Rodeghier, Mark, Jeff Goodpaster, and Sandra Blatterbauer. "Psychosocial Characteristics of Abductees: Results from the CUFOS Abduction Project," Journal of UFO Studies. 3 (1991): 59-90.
Ruppelt, Edward J. *The Report on Unidentified Flying Objects*. (Charleston, SC: BiblioBizarre, 2003).
Sagan, Carl. *Other Worlds*. (New York:Bantam, 1975).
Sagan, Carl. *Cosmos*. (New York: Random House, 1980).
Sagan, Carl. *Contact*. (New York: Pocket Books, 1985).
Sagan, Carl. *The Demon Haunted World* (New York: Ballantine Books, 1996).
Salisbury, Frank. *The Utah UFO Display: A Scientist's Report.* (Springville, UT: Cedar Fort, Inc, 2010).
Salla, Michael. "Exopolitics: Discipline of Choice for Public Policy Issues Concerning Extraterrestrial Life ," World Affairs 12 (2008).
Scheflin A.W. and J.L. Shapiro. *Trance on Trial.* (New York: The Guilford Press, 1989).
Schuessler, John F. *The Cash-Landrum UFO Incident*. (Atlanta, GA: Geo Graphics, 1998).
Schulze, Glen and Robert Powell. "Special Research Report Stephenville, Texas." Mutual UFO Network, (2008).
Shermer, M. "Baloney Detection." *Scientific American*, (2001): 36.
Shuttlewood, Arthur. *The Flying Saucer*. (New York: Sphere, 1978).
Spanos, Nicholas. "Multiple Identities & False Memories: A Sociocognitive Perspective." American Psychological Association (1996): 122-3.
Spanos, Nicholas. A. Cross, K. Dickson, and S. DuBreuil."Close Encounters: An Examination of UFO Experiences." Journal of Abnormal Psychology 102 (1993): 624-32.
Stichin, Zecharia. *The 12th Planet.* (New York: Avon Books, 1976).
Stone, Clifford. *UFOs Are Real: Extraterrestrial Encounters Documented by the U.S. Government.* (New York: Spi Books, 1997).
Stothers, Richard. "Unidentified Flying Objects in Classical Antiquity." The Classical Journal 103.1, (2007): 79-92.
Sturrock, Peter A. "An Analysis of the Condon Report on the Colorado UFO Project." J. Scientific Exploration, 1 (1987): 75.
Sturrock, Peter. *The UFO Enigma*. (New York: Warner Books, 1999).
Sturrock, Peter. *The UFO Enigma: A New Review of the Scientific Evidence.* (New York: Aspect, 2000).
Teodorani, Massimo. "A Comparative and Analytical Study of North American Databases on Unidentified Aerial Phenomena." Technical Report. NARCA, (2009).
Tsytovich, V. N. G. E. Morfill, V. E. Fortov, N. G. Gusein-Zade, B. A. Klumov, and S. V. Vladimirov. "From plasma crystals and helical structures towards inorganic living matter." New J. Phys. 9 (2007): 263.

Turner, Karla. *Taken: Inside the Alien-Human Agenda.* (Tallahassee, FL: Rose Printing Company, Inc, 1994).

Vallée, Jacques and Janine Vallee. *Challenge to Science: The UFO Enigma.* (New York: Ballantine Books, 1966).

Vallée, Jacques. *Confrontations: A scientist's search for alien contact.* (London: Souvenir Press, 1990), 112-39.

Vallée, Jacques. *Forbidden Science.* (Berkeley, CA: North Atlantic Books, 1992).

Vallée, Jacques and E. Davis. "Incommensurability, Orthodoxy and the Physics of High Strangeness: A 6-layer Model for Anomalous Phenomena." Physics of High Strangeness. (2003): 1-17.

Vallée, Jacques. *Messengers of Deception: UFO Contacts and Cults.* (New York: Daily Grail Publishing, 2008).

Vallée, Jacques. *Dimensions: A Casebook of Alien Contact.* (Charlottesville, VA: Anomalist Books, 2008).

Velasco, J. "Action Of Electromagnetic Fields In The Microwave Range On Vegetation." Paper presented at a meeting of the Society for Scientific Exploration, Glasgow, Scotland, August 1994.

Warren, Larry and Peter Robbins. *Left at East Gate: A First-Hand Account of the Rendlesham Forest UFO Incident, Its Cover-up, and Investigation. (*New York: Cosimo Books, 2005).

Weaver, Richard and James McAndrew. "The Roswell Report, Fact Versus Fiction in the New Mexico Desert." U.S. Air Force, (1995).

Weinstein, Dominique. "Aviation Safety and Unidentified Aerial Phenomena: A Preliminary Study of 600 cases of Unidentified Aerial Phenomena (UAP) Reported by Military and Civilian pilots." NARCAP International Air Safety Report IR-4, (2012).

Zielinski, Sarah. "Ready for Contact Humans have searched for extraterrestrial life for more than a century. What will we do when we find it?" *Smithsonian* (December 2010).

Internet Resources

"1989: Multiple Witness Case at Russian Missle Base." Accessed August 30, 2013, www.bibliotecapleyades.net/ciencia/ufo_briefingdocument/1989.html.

"99 Frequently Asked Questions {FAQs} about astronauts and UFOs." Accessed June 19, 2013, www.jamesoberg.com/99faq.html.

"A Brief Review of Issues Relating to the Reality of the Abduction Phenomenon." Accessed August 3, 2013, www.ufoevidence.org/documents/doc11.html.

"A Comparative Analytical and Observational Study of North American Databases on Unidentified Aerial Phenomena." Accessed May 19, 2013, www.narcap.org/reports/ONNYCT_Paper_MT_2009_REVISED.pdf.

"A New World Order." Accessed July 29, 2013, http://projectavalon.net/forum4/archive/index.php/t-46028.html.?s=9dd228d5e7691390d4840f1c1dfb1826.

"A Physicist Explains Why Parallel Universes May Exist." Accessed April 27, 2013, www.npr.org/2011/01/24/132932268/a-physicist-explains-why-parallel-universes-may-exist.

"A Preliminary Study of Sixty Four Pilot Sighting Reports Involving Alleged Electromagnetic Effects on Aircraft Systems." Accessed Jun 17, 2013, www.narcap.org/reports/emcarm.html.

"A Sprightly Explanation for UFO Sightings?" Accessed June 14, 2013, www.aftau.org/site/News2?page=NewsArticle&id=8803.

"About UFOs and Nuclear Weapons." Accessed May 17, 2013, www.ufohastings.com.

"Air Force Regulation 200-2." Accessed July 27, 2013, www.cufon.org/cufon/afr200-2.html.

"Angels in space nothing but top secret hallucinations." Accessed June 13, 2013, http://english.pravda.ru/society/anomal/14-06-2011/118195-angels-0.

"Are UFO Occupants Composed of Plasma, Their Life-Force Residing in Electric Energy?" Accessed June 8, 2013, www.ufodigest.com/article/are-ufo-occupants-composed-plasma-their-life-force-residing-electric-energy from *UFO Digest*.

"As U.K. Releases UFO Files, Former UFO Project Chief Apologizes For 'Spin And Dirty Tricks." Accessed June 27, 2013, www.huffingtonpost.com/2011/08/17/uk-releases-ufo-files_n_927351.html.

Bibliography

"Ask an Astrobiologist." Accessed February 10, 2013, http://astrobiology2.arc.nasa.gov/ask-an-astrobiologist.

"Ask an Astrobiologist." Accessed May 22, 2013, http://ufoupdateslist.com/2006/oct/m05-022.shtml.

"Aviation Safety in America A Previously Neglected Factor." Accessed May 19, 2013, www.narcap.org/Technical_Reports.html.

"Aviation Safety in America:Under-Reporting Bias of Unidentified Aerial Phenomena and Recommended Solutions." Accessed Jun 23, 2013, www.narcap.org/reports/TR8Bias1.html. July 20, 2004.

"Aviation Safety in America—Spherical UAP." Accessed Jun 4, 2013, www.narcap.org/Projsphere/3.1.6_narcap_projSph.pdf.

"Barry Goldwater and UFOs." Accessed June 26, 2013, http://groupbox.com/ViewTopic.aspx?&iTopicID=hZI77mvW8Zk-&iGroupID=XkGCL1x03Wc-.

"Bill Clinton, September 2005 to CLSA (Credit Lyonnais Securities Asia) group." Accessed June 27, 2013, www.hillaryclintonufo.net/billclintonquotes.html.

"Brazilian Air Force Confirms UFO Reports and Regulates How To Handle Them." Accessed July 17, 2013, www.ufodigest.com/article/brazilian-air-force-confirms-ufo-reports-and-regulates-how-handle-them.

"British Admiral was tireless UFO advocate at the House of Lords." Accessed May 19, 2013, www.openminds.tv/british-admiral-ufo-advocate-767. Posted by Antonio Huneeus, August 24, 2011.

"BUFORA Review." Accessed June 24, 2013, http://uforesearchnetwork.proboards.com/user/200/recent?page=5.

"Carl Jung and UFOs: A Debunker of Dubious Intellect." Accessed June 23, 2013, www.ufodigest.com/article/carl-jung-and-ufos-debunker-dubious-intellect.

"Casual Articles—French Agency Releases UFO Files—Don't Start Serving The Crepes Just Yet." Accessed June 22, 2013, www.casualarticles.com/article/187445/advice--French-Agency-Releases-UFO-Files---Don't-Start-Serving-The-Crepes-Just-Yet.html.

"CIA's Role in the Study of UFOs, 1947-90." Accessed July 12, 2013, www.cia.gov/search?q=ufo&x=-1008&y=53&site=CIA&output=xml_no_dtd&client=CIA&myAction=%2Fsearch&proxystylesheet=CIA&submitMethod=get.

"CIA's Role in the Study of UFOs, 1947-90: A Die-Hard Issue." Accessed August 19, 2013, www.cia.gov/library/center-for-the-study-of-intelligence/csi-publications/csi-studies/studies/97unclass/ufo.html.

"Citizen Hearing on Disclosure Remarkable Revelations Undercut By Distressing Disinformation." Accessed July 20, 2013, UFOs and Nukes, www.ufohastings.com/articles/citizen-hearing-on-disclosure.

"Citizen Hearing on Disclosure Washington Communiqué May 3, 2013." Accessed July 29, 2013, www.paradigmresearchgroup.org/Press_Releases/Press_releases.html.

"Citizen's Hearing—Richard French, Ex-Air Force Lt. Colonel And Former UFO Debunker, Says He Saw A UFO And "... There Were ALIENS Aboard It?!" Accessed August 10, 2013, http://massufosightings.blogspot.com/2013/05/exopolitical-disclosure-citizens_14.html.

"Classified Documents Validate US Military/Presidential UFO Involvement." Accessed July 29, 2013, www.ufoevidence.org/documents/doc1746.html.

"Clinical Discrepancies Between Expected and Observed Data in Patients Reporting UFO Abductions: Implications For Treatment Accessed." August 8, 2013, www.ufoevidence.org/documents/doc7.html.

"Coalition for Freedom of Information." Accessed August 25, 2013, http://uto.sigsno.org/freedomofinfo.org/index.html.

"Conclusions and Recommendations Edward U. Condon." Accessed July 25, 2013, http://files.ncas.org/condon/text/sec-i.html.

"Conclusions and Recommendations." Accessed May 22, 2013, www.project1947.com/shg/condon/sec-i.html.

"Deathbed testimony about UFOs given by former CIA official." Accessed August 17, 2013, www.openminds.tv/deathbed-testimony-about-ufos-given-by-former-cia-official-video-1002.

The UFO Phenomenon: Should I Believe?

"Declaration of Principles for Activities Following the Detection of Extraterrestrial Intelligence." Accessed July 14, 2013, www.setileague.org/general/protocol.html.

"Disclosure Project: Testimony of John Callahan, Former FAA Division Chief." Accessed June 27, 2013, www.ufoevidence.org/documents/doc1324.html.

"DOD Press release." Accessed May 22, 2013, www.ufoevidence.org/documents/doc1247.html.

"Effects of UFOs Upon People." Accessed Jun 15, 2013, www.ufocasebook.com/pdf/ufoeffects.pdf.

"Ethical Implications of the UFO Abduction Phenomenon." Accessed May 23, 2013, www.anomalies.net/archive/investigation/ETHICS.EDI, 1987.

"Exclusive Mexican DoD Acknowledges UFOs In Mexico." Accessed July 13, 2013, http://rense.com/general52/deff.html.

"Extraordinary Claims Require Extraordinary Evidence." Accessed June 14, 2013, http://skeptico.blogs.com/skeptico/2008/01/extraordinary-c.html.

"Five Reasons Why UFOs Are Not Extraterrestrial Machines. Science Frontiers." Accessed June 23, 2013, www.science-frontiers.com/sf073/sf073g16.html.

"General Lionel M. Chassin." Last modified June 14, 2012, Accessed May 18, 2013, www.zoominfo.com/p/Lionel-Chassin/45924532.

"Goodnight and Goodluck." Accessed June 12, 2013, http://fitdv.com/new/articles/article.php?artid=22.

"H.E.R.O. Paranormal, Skinwalker Ranch." Accessed May 14, 2013, http://site.heroparanormal.com./

"Hal Puthoff Reviews Paul Hill Book Synopsis of Unconventional Flying Objects." Accessed Jun 4, 2013, www.paranormalworld.com/blogs/item/1770-hal-puthoff-reviews-paul-hill-book-synopsis-of-unconventional-flying-objects.

"Harry A. Jordan: UFOs and USOs on the U.S.S. *Franklin D. Roosevelt* (1950s)." Accessed July 14, 2013, www.abovetopsecret.com/forum/thread481823/pg1.

"Historian Richard Dolan—UFO and ET disclosure to occur in 5 years." Accessed August 23, 2013, http://youtu.be/4uARe8T9R7Q.

"Introduction to Wormholes." Accessed May 12, 2013, http://library.thinkquest.org/27930/wormhole.html.

"Is A Utah Ranch The Strangest Place On Earth?" Accessed May 29, 2013, http://rense.com/general32/strange.html.

"JAL Pilot's UFO Story Surfaces after 20 Years, Accessed July 29, 2013, www.ufocasebook.com/jal1628surfaces.html.

"Jean-Charles Duboc." Accessed August 10, 2013, http://uto.sigsno.org/freedomofinfo.org/national_press_07/duboc_statement.pdf

"JOINT ARMY-NAVY-AIR FORCE PUBLICATION 146(E)." Accessed June 12, 2013, www.cufon.org/cufon/janp1462.html.

"NASA Statement: The US Government and Unidentified Flying Objects (UFOs)." Accessed June 25, 2013, www.ufoevidence.org/documents/doc846.html. NASA (National Aeronautics and Space Administration).

"National Aviation Reporting Center on Anomalous Phenomena." Accessed Jun 23, 2013, http://narcap.org/index.html. Updated May 16, 2013.

"National Press Club Conference: Pilots Speak Out About UFOs." Accessed August 10, 2013, www.mercuryrapids.co.uk/articles.

"National Press Club Witness Testimony." Accessed August 10, 2013, www.ufoinfo.com/news/npcwt.html.

"National UFO Reporting Center Case Briefs and Past Highlights." Accessed August 22, 2013, www.nuforc.org/CBIndex.html.

"Need to Know vs. Need to Believe in Ufology." Last modified 2009, Accessed July 19, 2013, http://fierycelt.tripod.com/xposeufotruth/needknow_vs_needbelieve.html.

"Neil deGrasse Tyson quotes." Last modified 2013, Accessed July 30, 2013, www.goodreads.com/author/quotes/12855.Neil_deGrasse_Tyson.

"New Revelations: Two Ex-U.S. Air Force Security Policemen Discuss UFO Activity at Nuclear Weapons Sites." Accessed August 30, 2013, www.ufohastings.com/articles/new-revelations.

"New Yorkers stand by 1980s UFO sightings in Westchester, Putnam counties." Accessed August 23, 2013, http://onhudson.typepad.com/onhudsoncom/2008/11/25-years-removed-hudson-valley-ufo-phenomenon-lives-on.html.

"Newly released UFO files from the UK government." Accessed June 22, 2013, www.nationalarchives.gov.uk/ufos.
"Next frontier for Cheeks Kilpatrick: Panel exploring existence of alien life." Accessed June 26, 2013, www.turtleislandnews.info/2013_04_12_archive.html.
"Nick Pope Citizen Hearing on Disclosure—Review." Accessed July 14, 2013, www.ufodigest.com/article/disclosure-review-060142.
"Nick Pope." Accessed August 11, 2013, www.ufodigest.com/article/disclosure-review-0601.
"Operation Mainbrace." Accessed July 13, 2013, http://drdavidclarke.co.uk/secret-files/operation-mainbrace-ufos.
"Paradigm Research Group." Accessed July 29, 2013, www.paradigmresearchgroup.org/main.html.
"Parviz Jafari." Accessed August 11, 2013, http://uto.sigsno.org/freedomofinfo.org/national_press_07/jafari_statement.pdf.
"Persinger's The Field Biology of Unexplained Events." Accessed June 10, 2013, www.ufoupdateslist.com/2000/dec/m14-002.shtml.
"Peruvian Air Force pilot shoots at UFO." Accessed August 10, 2013, www.abovetopsecret.com/forum/thread573372/p.1.
"PETITION, UFOS, WHITE HOUSE AND LIES." Accessed July 23, 2013, www.stantonfriedman.com/index.php?ptp=articles&fdt=2011.11.11.
"Physical Evidence Related to UFO Reports (Sturrock Panel): Radar Evidence." Accessed August 18, 2013, www.ufoevidence.org/documents/doc492.html.
"Physical Evidence Related to UFO Reports: The Proceedings of a Workshop Held at the Pocantico Conference Center." Tarrytown, New York, September 29-October 4, 1997.
"Physical Evidence Related to UFO Reports—Sturrock Panel—Abstract, Summary and Introduction." Accessed Jun 4, 2013, www.ufoevidence.org/documents/doc535.html.
"Physical Traces Associated with Unidentified Flying Objects: An Interim Report—Results of Processing Data—1490-2004," Accessed Jun 4, 2013, www.ufoevidence.org/documents/doc1172.html.
"Plasma Life Forms—Spheres, Blobs, Orbs and Subtle Bodies." Accessed May 26, 2013, www.dapla.org/plasma_orbs_bodies.html.
"Possible UAP-Related Accident Factors from the Modified ASAFE Taxonomy." Accessed July 17, 2013, http://narcap.org/reports/APPENDIX_2.html.
"Project 1947: Ted Phillips' Physical Trace Catalogue." Accessed August 3, 2013, www.project1947.com/47cats/phillips.html.
"Project Blue Book Archive." Accessed August 19, 2013. www.bluebookarchive.org.
"Project Blue Book Special Report #14 (1954)." Accessed July 27, 2013, http://archive.org/details/ProjectBlueBookSpecialReport14.
"Project Condign and UFOs." Accessed June 8, 2013, www.netplaces.com/guide-to-2012/atmospheric-plasma-and-ufos/project-condign-and-ufos.html.
"Proposed Agreement on the Sending of Communications to Extraterrestrial Intelligence." Accessed July 3, 2013, www.setileague.org/iaaseti/position.html.
"Prosaic Explanations: The Failure Of UFO Skepticism." Accessed May 26, 2013, http://brumac.8k.com/prosaic6.html.
"Pseudo-Science of Anti-Ufology." Accessed May 21, 2013, www.theufochronicles.com/2009/05/pseudo-science-of-anti-ufology.html., May 30, 2009.
"Radar and Pilot Cases." Accessed August 11, 2013, www.disclosureproject.org/access/es-wit-test-radar-pilot.html.
"Radar Visual Sightings." Accessed July 14, 2013, www.space-2001.net/html/radar.html.
"Remarkable reports from the missile field." Accessed July 23, 2013, www.cufos.org/missiles.pdf.
"Report on the Observation of UFOs During the Night of March 30-31." Accessed July 29, 2013, http://users.telenet.be/aura.oasis/BelgUFO.html.
"Reports of Suppression." Accessed August 22, 2013, www.perceptions.couk.com/reports.html.
"Results of NARCAP Investigation concerning a UFO incident at O'Hare International Airport." Accessed August 23, 2013, www.cohenufo.org/ohare2006.html.
"Richard Dolan—UFO and ET disclosure to occur in 5 years from 2011." Accessed July 14, 2013, http://youtube/4uARe8T9R7Q.

"Russian Cosmonauts and Generals confirm: UFOs are real." Accessed August 27, 2013, www.ufoevidence.org/documents/doc437.html.
"Science and UFOs: Part 2—Occam's Rusty Razor." Accessed May 28, 2013, www.network54.com/Forum/594658/thread/1358750518/last-1358750518/Science+and+UFOs-+Part+2+-+Occam's+Rusty+Razor, March 2012.
"Science in Default: Twenty-Two Years of Inadequate UFO Investigations." Accessed June 3, 2013, www.cufon.org/cufon/mcdon2.html. December 27, 1969.
"Secret Twining Letter—'The reported phenomena are real.'" Accessed July 29, 2013, www.nicap.org/twining_letter.html.
"Seth Shostak On UFOs & SETI." Last modified July 10, 2000, http://rense.com/general2/seth.html., www.space.com:80/sciencefiction/phenomena/ufo_seti_000619.html.
"Shape-Shifting UFOs." Accessed May 3, 2013, www.ufodigest.com/news/1207/shapeshiftingufos.html.
"Shuttle Astronaut Musgrave Comes Clean: UFOs Exist." Accessed August 3, 2013, www.disclose.tv/forum/shuttle-astronaut-dr-story-musgrave-comes-clean-ufo-s-exist-t60326.html.
"Space and Time Warps." Accessed August 15, 2013, www.hawking.org.uk/space-and-time-warps.html.
"Statement on Unidentified Flying Objects. Prepared statement submitted to the House Committee on Science and Astronautics, July 29, 1968, by James E. McDonald." Accessed April 17, 2013, www.cufon.org/cufon/mcdon3.html.
"Statements About Flying Saucers And Extraterrestrial Life Made By Prof. Hermann Oberth, German Rocket Scientist." Accessed May 21, 2013, www.mufon.com/MUFONNews/znews_oberth.html. June 2002.
"Stephen Hawking: The Official Website." Accessed June 17, 2013, www.hawking.org.uk.
"Stephen Hawking's Time Machine." Accessed May 12, 2013, http://news.discovery.com/space/stephen-hawkings-time-machine.html.
"Steven Greer and Disclosure." Accessed June 12, 2013, www.bibliotecapleyades.net/esp_autor_greer.html.
"Straight Talk About UFO Abductions." Accessed June 15, 2013, www.ufoabduction.com/straighttalk.html.
"Sturrock UFO Panel's (Alleged) Findings Praised By CUFOS Official." Accessed May 25, 2013, www.csicop.org/specialarticles/show/klass_files_volume_54.
"Sturrock UFO Panel's (Alleged) Findings Praised By CUFOS Official." Accessed May 25, 2013, www.csicop.org/specialarticles/show/klass_files_volume_54.
"Symposium on Unidentified Flying Objects. Hearings before the Committee on Science and Astronautics. U.S. House of Representatives." Accessed August 10, 2013, www.project1947.com/shg/symposium/index.html.
"Testimony of Dr. Richard Haines." Accessed August 10, 2013, www.bibliotecapleyades.net/disclosure/briefing/disclosure05.html.
"Testimony of Mr. Nick Pope, British Ministry Of Defense." Accessed August 30, 2013, www.bibliotecapleyades.net/disclosure/briefing/disclosure10.html.
"The 1947 Twining Memo: 63 Years Ago." Accessed July 20, 2013, www.afterdisclosure.com/2010/09/twining-memo-1.html.
"The 1975 UFO Chronology." Accessed July 22, 2013, www.nicap.org/norad3b1.html.
"The Belgium Sightings (1989/90)." Accessed July 30, 2013, www.cohenufo.org/Belgium/unslvdmyst.html.
"The best of New Zealand's UFO files: Alien writing, masks and ships." Accessed June 23, 2013, http://io9.com/5719869/the-best-of-new-zealands-ufo-files-alien-writing-masks-and-ships.
"The Brookings Institution—Final Report Proposed Studies on the Implications of Peaceful Space Activities for Human Affairs." Accessed July 6, 2013, www.nicap.org/papers/brookings.pdf.
"The Challenge of Unidentified Flying Objects." Accessed April 10, 2013, www.nicap.org/books/coufo/coufo_complete.html. Washington, D.C., 1961.
"The Condon Report, Scientific Study of Unidentified Flying Objects." Accessed July 2, 2013, www.ufoevidence.org/topics/condonreport.html.

Bibliography

"The Disclosure Project Briefing Document." Accessed August 23, 2013, www.disclosureproject.org/access/docs/pdf/DisclosureProjectBriefingDocumentNoDocs.pdf.

"The Earthlight Hypothesis." Accessed May 26, 2013, www.davidicke.com/forum/archive/index.php/t-156030.html.

"The Emerging Picture of the UFO Problem." Accessed Jun 23, 2013, www.nicap.org/emerge.html.

"The failure of the 'science' of UFOlogy." Accessed May 26, 2013, http://debunker.com/texts/ObergCuttySark.html.

"The Fantastic Flight of JAL 1628." Accessed July 22, 2013, www.ufoevidence.org/documents/doc1316.html.

"The French Report on UFOs and Defense: A Summary." Accessed May 23, 2013, www.cufos.org/cometa.html.

"The French SEPRA: An Interview with Director Jean-Jacques Velasco." Accessed July 2, 2013, www.ufoevidence.org/documents/doc1630.html.

"The Future of Ufology." Accessed May 25, 2013, http://mysteriousuniverse.org/2012/08/the-future-of-ufology/

"The Grandfather Paradox." Accessed June 17, 2013, http://timetravelphilosophy.net/topics/grandfather.

"The High Strangeness of Dimensions, and the Process of Alien." Accessed May 18, 2013, Abductionwww.cassiopaea.org/cass/high_strangeness.html, by Laura Knight-Jadczyk.

"The J. Allen Hynek Center for UFO Studies." Accessed May 19, 2013, www.cufos.org/org.html.

"The Majestic 12 Papers—An Analysis." Accessed July 23, 2013, www.roswellfiles.com/FOIA/majestic12.html.

"The Malmstrom AFB UFO/Missile Incident." Accessed July 25, 2013, www.cufon.org/cufon/malmstrom/malm1.html.

"The Marden-Stoner Study on Commonalities Among UFO Abduction Experiencers." Accessed July 11, 2013, www.kathleen-marden.com/commonalities-study-final-report.php.

"The Most Frequent Criticisms and Questions Concerning The Tectonic Strain Hypothesis." Accessed June 11, 2013, www.shaktitechnology.com/tectonic.html.

"The Obama administration's startling UFO connections." Accessed May 29, 2013, www.openminds.tv/obama-administration-startling-ufo-connections/, Posted by Alejandro Rojas October 28, 2009.

"The Physics of Interstellar Travel—UFO Evidence." Accessed August 15, 2013,www.ufoevidence.org/documents/doc1060.html.

"The Release of the French UFO Files." Accessed August 2, 2013, The UFODigest www.bibliotecapleyades.net/ciencia/ciencia_flyingobjects29.html.

"The Rendlesham Forest Incident." Accessed July 29, 2013, www.ianridpath.com/ufo/appendix.html.

"The Robertson Panel." Accessed July 13, 2013, www.ufocasebook.com/robertsonpanel.html.

"The SAC Base UFO Flyovers." Accessed July 25, 2013, www.alien-ufos.com/ufo-alien-discussions/23228-sac-base-ufo-flyovers-oct-nov-1975-a.html.

"The Skeptics Dictionary." Accessed May 23, 2013, www.skepdic.com/aliens.html.

"The Smith Memo." Accessed July 30, 2013, www.roswellfiles.com/FOIA/smithmemo.html.

"The Tomb of Jesus Christ." Accessed July 30, 2013, www.tombofjesus.com/index.php/en/researchers-authors/dr-james-deardorff.

"The UFO Challenge." Accessed May 21, 2013, www.stantonfriedman.com/index.php?ptp=ufo_challenge.

"The UFO Evidence: NICAP's UFO Investigator and Selected UFO Documents." Accessed Jun 4, 2013, www.cufos.org/NICAP.html.

"The UFO Reality." Accessed May 25, 2013, http://ufor.blogspot.com/2008/05/drones-and-ufos-in-medieval-art.html.

"Top-Secret 1949 Document." Accessed June 23, 2013, www.cufos.org/IUR_article1.html.

"Twelve Government Documents That Take UFOs Seriously." Accessed July 20, 2013, http://keyholepublishing.com/Leading-UFO-Documents.html.

"Twelve Government Documents That Take UFOs Seriously." Accessed July 20, 2013, www.scribd.com/doc/24383799/4/The-Chadwell-Memo-of-December-2-1952.

"Twelve Government Documents That Take UFOs Seriously." Accessed July 20, 2013, www.scribd.com/doc/24383799/3/USAF-Intelligence-Report.
"U.K. Condign Report (2000) Unidentified Aerial Phenomena in the U.K. Air Defense Region." Accessed July 22, 2013, www.uk-ufo.org/condign/condrep.html.
"U.S. Air Force Project Grudge and Blue Book Reports 1-12." Accessed August 1, 2013, www.nicap.org/docs/pbb/nicap_pbr1-12_srch.pdf.
"UFO Abductions: The Measure of a Mystery. Volume 1: Comparative Study of Abduction Reports." Accessed June 12, 2013, www.hyper.net/ufo/abductions.html.
"UFO CASE ARTICLE Voronezh, Russia—Report of sighting." Accessed May 12, 2013, www.ufoevidence.org/Cases/CaseSubarticle.asp?ID=122.
"UFO Casebook—UFO Videos." Accessed July 21, 2013, www.ufocasebook.com/vid/vid10.html.
"UFO Evidence: UFOS: Are They for Real?" Accessed August 10, 2013, www.wanttoknow.info/ufos/ufos_evidence_larry_king.
"UFO Facts and a Solution to the Energy Crisis Testimony of 60 Government & Military Witnesses." Accessed August 12, 2013, www.wanttoknow.info/ufocover-up10pg.
"UFO Quotes." Accessed July 27, 2013, www.ufocasebook.com/ufoquotes1.html.
"UFO Reports from China." Accessed August 24, 2013, www.paradigmresearchgroup.org/biblio/bib20.html.
"UFO—An Appraisal of the Problem: A Statement by the UFO Subcommittee of the AIAA." Accessed August 20, 2013, www.ufoevidence.org/documents/doc594.html.
"Ufology and Science." Accessed June 27, 2013, www.nickpope.net/ufology-and-science.html.
"UFOlogy: 50 Years of futility, frustration, and failure." Accessed May 23, 2013, http://home.comcast.net/~tprinty/UFO/50years.html.
"Ufology—A scientific introduction—Started in 2009." Accessed August 2, 2013, www.tarrdaniel.com/documents/Ufology/ufology.html.
"UFO—NASA Shuttle—Missed by Ground Based Energy Pulse Weapon." Accessed August 29, 2013, www.youtube.com/watch?v=ZN0XnDJKdWo.
"UFO-Related Human Physiological Effects." Accessed Jun 15, 2013, http://rr0.org/time/1/9/9/6/Schuessler_PhysiologicalEffects/index.html.
"UFOs and astronauts: REPORTS AND STATEMENTS BY NASA ASTRONAUTS." Accessed August 27, 2013, http://ufologie.patrickgross.org/htm/astronauts.html.
"UFOs and Defense: What Should We Prepare For?" Accessed August 8, 2013, www.disclosureproject.org/docs/pdf/COMETA_part1.pdf.
"UFOs in the United Kingdom: The Real X-Files." Accessed May 18, 2013, www.theufotimes.com/contents/Articles_1%20.html.
"UFOs Intrude Into SAC Base Weapons Areas." Accessed July 25, 2013, www.ufocasebook.com/sacbaseweapons1975.html.
"UFOs or No? The Guy Hottel Memo." Accessed July 22, 2013, www.fbi.gov/news/stories/2013/march/ufos-and-the-guy-hottel-memo.
"UFOS, Aliens, and the New Physics." Accessed June 14, 2013, www.stealthskater.com/Documents/Pitkanen_16.pdf.
"UFOs: Operation Trojan Horse: Some Gems." Accessed May 13, 2013, www.chodesh.info/ufos-operation-trojan-horse-gems.html.
"UFOs: The Psychic Dimension." Accessed July 23, 2013, http://davidpratt.info/ufo2.html.
"UFOs: The Psychocultural Hypothesis." Accessed May 14, 2013, The New England Skeptical Society, www.theness.com/index.php/ufos-the-psychocultural-hypothesis.
"UFOs: What's 60 Years Accomplished?" Last modified 2013. Accessed July 30, 2013, www.ourstrangeplanet.com/the-san-luis-valley/guest-editorials/ufos-whats-60-years-accomplished.
"Unexplained sightings met with denial." Accessed Jun 23, 2013, www.ufoevidence.org/documents/doc3.html.
"Valensole, France Landing (Maurice Masse Case)." Accessed August 18, 2013, http://ufoevidence.org/cases/case140.html.

Bibliography

"What Did Dr. J. Allen Hynek Believe About UFOs in 1967: And When Did He Say It?" Accessed April 30, 2013, www.ufodigest.com/article/what-did-dr-j-allen-hynek-believe-about-ufos-1967-and-when-did-he-say-it-part-ii.

"White House: There's no sign of E.T. or UFO cover-up." Accessed August 12, 2013,www.nbcnews.com/id/45176460/ns/technology_and_science-space/t/white-house-theres-no-sign-et-or-ufo-cover-up/#.UbSM4_nVApA.

"Whoa! Say what Carl Sagan? No UFOs would visit Earth?" Accessed June 12, 2013, www.abovetopsecret.com/forum/thread256949/pg1.

"Yes, UFOs exist: Position statement by SEPRA head, Jean-Jacques Velasco." Accessed June 3, 2013, www.ufoevidence.org/documents/doc1627.html. April 2004.

"J. Allen Hynek: Speaking at the United Nations, Nov. 27th 1978." Accessed May 28, 2013, www.ufoevidence.org/documents/doc757.html., UFO Evidence.com.

"The Fantastic Flight of JAL 1628." Accessed July 2, 2013, www.ufoevidence.org/documents/doc1316.html.

Best UFO Cases III: Belgium, 1989-1990." Accessed July 23, 2013, www.ufoevidence.org/documents/doc413.html.

Clarke, D. and Gary Anthony. "ufocasebook.com." Last modified 2006. Accessed August 19, 2013. www.ufocasebook.com/pdf/projectcondign.pdf.

J. Allen Hynek: Speaking at the United Nations, Nov. 27th 1978." Accessed May 28, 2013, www.ufoevidence.org/documents/doc757.html. UFO Evidence.com.

Should I Believe?